*This volume is one of a series that explains and demonstrates
how to prepare various types of food, and that offers in each
book an international anthology of great recipes.*

Eggs & Cheese

BY
THE EDITORS OF TIME-LIFE BOOKS

TIME-LIFE BOOKS/ALEXANDRIA, VIRGINIA

Cover: Midway through the cooking process known as shirring *(page 21),* cream is poured over two eggs that have been lightly set in a little butter on the stove top. The upper layer of white is still semiliquid; to cook it through, the dish will go briefly into a hot oven.

Time-Life Books Inc.
is a wholly owned subsidiary of
TIME INCORPORATED

Founder: Henry R. Luce 1898-1967

Editor-in-Chief: Henry Anatole Grunwald
President: J. Richard Munro
Chairman of the Board: Ralph P. Davidson
Executive Vice President: Clifford J. Grum
Chairman, Executive Committee: James R. Shepley
Editorial Director: Ralph Graves
Group Vice President, Books: Joan D. Manley
Vice Chairman: Arthur Temple

TIME-LIFE BOOKS INC.

Managing Editor: Jerry Korn. *Board of Editors:* George Constable, George G. Daniels, Thomas H. Flaherty Jr., Martin Mann, Philip W. Payne, John Paul Porter, Gerry Schremp, Gerald Simons. *Planning Director:* Dale M. Brown. *Art Director:* Tom Suzuki; *Assistant:* Arnold C. Holeywell. *Director of Administration:* David L. Harrison. *Director of Operations:* Gennaro C. Esposito. *Director of Research:* Carolyn L. Sackett; *Assistant:* Phyllis K. Wise. *Director of Photography:* Robert G. Mason; *Assistant:* Dolores A. Littles. *Production Director:* Feliciano Madrid; *Assistants:* Peter A. Inchauteguiz, Karen A. Meyerson. *Copy Processing:* Gordon E. Buck. *Quality Control Director:* Robert L. Young; *Assistant:* James J. Cox; *Associates:* Daniel J. McSweeney, Michael G. Wight. *Art Coordinator:* Anne B. Landry. *Copy Room Director:* Susan B. Galloway; *Assistants:* Celia Beattie, Ricki Tarlow

Chairman: John D. McSweeney. *President:* Carl G. Jaeger. *Executive Vice Presidents:* John Steven Maxwell, David J. Walsh. *Vice Presidents:* George Artandi, Stephen L. Bair, Peter G. Barnes, Nicholas Benton, John L. Canova, Beatrice T. Dobie, Carol Flaumenhaft, James L. Mercer, Herbert Sorkin, Paul R. Stewart

THE GOOD COOK

The original version of this book was created in London for Time-Life International (Nederland) B.V.
European Editor: Kit van Tulleken; *Design Director:* Louis Klein; *Photography Director:* Pamela Marke; *Planning Director:* Alan Lothian; *Chief of Research:* Vanessa Kramer; *Chief Sub-Editor:* Ilse Gray; *Production Editor:* Ellen Brush; *Quality Control:* Douglas Whitworth

Staff for *Eggs & Cheese: Series Coordinator:* Liz Timothy; *Head Designer:* Rick Bowring; *Text Editor:* Tony Allan; *Anthology Editor:* Markie Benet; *Staff Writers:* Alexandria Carlier, Jay Ferguson, Ellen Galford, Thom Henvey; *Designer:* Mark Walton; *Researchers:* Sally Crawford, Deborah Litton; *Sub-Editors:* Katie Lloyd, Sally Rowland; *Design Assistants:* Sally Curnock, Ian Midson, Paul Reeves; *Editorial Department:* Pat Boag, Kate Cann, Debra Dick, Beverly Doe, Philip Garner, Aquila Kegan, Molly Sutherland, Julia West, Helen Whitehorn

U.S. Staff for *Eggs & Cheese: Series Editor:* Gerry Schremp; *Assistant Editor:* Ellen Phillips; *Designer:* Ellen Robling; *Chief Researcher:* Juanita Wilson; *Staff Writer:* Carol Dana; *Researchers:* Christine Bowie Dove (principal), Barbara Fleming, Ann Ready, Christine Schuyler; *Assistant Designer:* Peg Schreiber; *Copy Coordinators:* Nancy Berman, Allan Fallow, Tonna Gibert; *Art Assistant:* Robert Herndon; *Picture Coordinator:* Alvin Ferrell; *Editorial Assistants:* Brenda Harwell, Audrey Keir; *Special Contributor:* Susan Feller (text)

CHIEF SERIES CONSULTANT

Richard Olney, an American, has lived and worked for some three decades in France, where he is highly regarded as an authority on food and wine. Author of *The French Menu Cookbook* and of the award-winning *Simple French Food,* he has also contributed to numerous gastronomic magazines in France and the United States, including the influential journals *Cuisine et Vins de France* and *La Revue du Vin de France.* He is a member of several distinguished gastronomic societies, including L'Académie Internationale du Vin, La Confrérie des Chevaliers du Tastevin and La Commanderie du Bontemps de Médoc et des Graves. Working in London with the series editorial staff, he has been basically responsible for the planning of this volume, and has supervised the final selection of recipes submitted by other consultants. The United States edition of The Good Cook has been revised by the Editors of Time-Life Books to bring it into complete accord with American customs and usage.

CHIEF AMERICAN CONSULTANT

Carol Cutler is the author of a number of cookbooks, including the award-winning *The Six-Minute Soufflé and Other Culinary Delights.* During the 12 years she lived in France, she studied at the Cordon Bleu and the École des Trois Gourmandes, and with private chefs. She is a member of the Cercle des Gourmettes, a long-established French food society limited to just 50 members, and is also a charter member of Les Dames d'Escoffier, Washington Chapter.

PHOTOGRAPHERS

John Elliott, based in London, trained at the Regent Street Polytechnic. He has extensive experience in photographing a wide range of subjects for advertising and magazine assignments, but his special interest is food photography.
Bob Komar is a Londoner who trained at both the Hornsey and Manchester Schools of Art. He specializes in food photography and in portraiture.
Aldo Tutino, a native of Italy, has worked in Milan, New York City and Washington, D.C. He has won a number of awards for his photographs from the New York Advertising Club.

INTERNATIONAL CONSULTANTS

GREAT BRITAIN: *Jane Grigson* has written a number of books about food and has been a cookery correspondent for the London *Observer* since 1968. *Alan Davidson* is the author of several cookbooks and the founder of Prospect Books, which specializes in scholarly publications about food and cookery. *Jean Reynolds,* who prepared many of the dishes for the photographs in this volume, is from San Francisco. She trained as a cook in the kitchens of several of France's great restaurants. FRANCE: *Michel Lemonnier,* the cofounder and vice president of Les Amitiés Gastronomiques Internationales, is a frequent lecturer on wine. GERMANY: *Jochen Kuchenbecker* trained as a chef, but worked for 10 years as a food photographer in several European countries before opening his own restaurant in Hamburg. *Anne Brakemeier* is the co-author of three cookbooks. ITALY: *Massimo Alberini* is a well-known food writer and journalist, with a particular interest in culinary history. His many books include *Storia del Pranzo all'Italiana, 4000 Anni a Tavola* and *100 Ricette Storiche.* THE NETHERLANDS: *Hugh Jans* has published cookbooks and his recipes appear in a number of Dutch magazines. THE UNITED STATES: *Julie Dannenbaum,* the director of a cooking school in Philadelphia, Pennsylvania, also conducts cooking classes at the Gritti Palace in Venice, Italy, and at The Greenbrier in White Sulphur Springs, West Virginia. She is the author of several cookbooks and numerous magazine articles. *Judith Olney,* author of *Comforting Food* and *Summer Food,* received her culinary training in both England and France. In addition to conducting cooking classes, she regularly writes for gastronomic magazines. *Robert Shoffner,* wine and food editor of *The Washingtonian* magazine for five years, has written many articles on food and wine.

Correspondents: Elisabeth Kraemer (Bonn); Margot Hapgood, Dorothy Bacon, Lesley Coleman (London); Susan Jonas, Lucy T. Voulgaris (New York); Maria Vincenza Aloisi, Josephine du Brusle (Paris); Ann Natanson (Rome).
Valuable assistance was also provided by: Jeanne Buys (Amsterdam); Hans-Heinrich Wellmann, Gertraud Bellon (Hamburg); Judy Aspinall (London); Diane Asselin (Los Angeles); Bona Schmid, Maria Teresa Marenco (Milan); Carolyn T. Chubet, Miriam Hsia, Christina Lieberman (New York); Michèle le Baube (Paris); Mimi Murphy (Rome).

For information about any Time-Life book, please write:
Reader Information, Time-Life Books
541 North Fairbanks Court, Chicago, Illinois 60611

Library of Congress CIP data, page 176.

CONTENTS

A Protean Pair

No foods excite more lavish praise than eggs and cheese. "All cookery," effused the British author Henry Stacpoole, "rests on the egg. The egg is the Atlas that supports the world of gastronomy." Cheese, according to the American essayist Clifton Fadiman, "is milk's leap toward immortality."

In terms of nutrition alone, their qualities are remarkable: Both eggs and the milk from which all cheese is made are designed by nature to be complete foods—egg for the unborn chick, and milk for the infant mammal. And while each is held in high esteem in its own right, eggs and cheese also make a superb culinary pair. When used together they produce innumerable dishes indispensable to a cook's repertoire, from omelets to airy soufflés like the one shown in preparation at left.

This book explores the multitudinous opportunities for savory egg and cheese cookery. A guide on pages 8-9 explains how the size and freshness of eggs are gauged. Pages 10-11 show a step-by-step demonstration of the home manufacture of a simple fresh cheese, one that can be served on its own or incorporated in such dishes as gratins and pies. The introductory section of the book concludes with a primer for buying cheese and storing it, and describes 52 of the world's best-known cheeses.

Following the introductory section, three chapters deal with cooking eggs. Beginning with the basic methods of preparing whole eggs by frying, poaching, boiling, steaming and baking, these chapters go on to show how whole eggs may be used with other ingredients to create assembled dishes, and then illustrate the arts of scrambling eggs and omelet making. A final chapter features a range of dishes, from quiches to fondues, in which cheese is a principal element—often with eggs as its support. The second half of the book is an anthology of 220 egg and cheese recipes, chosen from the world's cookery literature.

The marvelous egg

Eggs have been part of man's diet from earliest times. Wild birds' eggs were no doubt a source of sustenance for primitive man, as they are today for the last remaining hunter-gatherers. As early as 2500 B.C., however, the domestication of fowl began to ensure a more predictable egg supply, and since that time the domestic hen has been carried to every corner of the globe.

Chickens are naturally prolific layers. Selective breeding has helped to increase their individual output to 200 or more eggs in a year (a goose, by contrast, lays only 15 to 30 eggs in the course of a year). Output has been boosted further by the battery—or mass-production—farming methods that were developed in the United States during the 1920s.

Traditionally, chickens were allowed to roam freely, existing on a haphazard barnyard diet of grass, grain and insects. In the modern battery system, however, large numbers of chickens—as many as a million in some operations—are kept in indoor cages so that all of the factors affecting egg production can be carefully regulated. Temperature and light are rigorously controlled, and the birds are fed a diet of commercially produced chicken feed, usually a blend of cereals and soy with added vitamins, proteins and minerals. Because battery birds have such a well-balanced diet, their eggs are generally higher in quality than those that are produced by free-ranging birds.

No matter how it is produced, a top-grade, newly laid egg will contain a firm, round yolk, surrounded by a viscous white—technically known as albumen. Close to 90 per cent of the egg white is water; the rest consists of proteins. The proteins trap air in a stable foam when the white is beaten—a quality exploited to the full in soufflés (pages 76-81).

Almost 20 per cent of the yolk is protein; the remainder is composed of water, a plentiful supply of fat, vitamins, minerals and a fatlike substance known as cholesterol. High levels of cholesterol in the blood are associated with an increased risk of heart disease, and many doctors caution against eating large quantities of eggs. However, the link between dietary intake of cholesterol and the amount in the bloodstream is still unclear, especially because the body itself manufactures the substance.

The proteins of both white and yolk thicken and solidify when heated—but each at a slightly different temperature. The white begins to coagulate at about 140° F. [60° C.], whereas the yolk remains liquid until about 150° F. [65° C.], and does not become firm until 160° F. [70° C.] is reached. This small difference chiefly accounts for the astonishing variety of textures that good cooks can obtain from eggs. The effects are most obvious in whole-egg cookery, where the aim usually is to produce a firm white surrounding a much softer yolk. But in beaten-egg cookery, too, texture can be all-important. The textural range of a single omelet, for example, might include a liquid center, a custardy mantle around this core, and a crisp exterior.

Milk transformed

Bel Paese is smooth and buttery while feta is crumbly and tangy; Cheshire is firm and piquant while Parmesan is granular and nutty flavored. But whatever its final texture or taste might be, all cheese is composed of coagulated milk solids. As is apparent by the rate at which fresh milk sours, coagulation can be rapid; cheese making is a method of controlling and modifying the coagulation process to yield a product capable of maturing instead of simply spoiling.

The nature of the milk begins the determination of a cheese's taste and texture. While cow's milk is the most common source of cheese, sheep's and goat's milk are also used. Sheep's milk lends pungency to French Roquefort, for example; goat's milk gives a tangy undercurrent to Greek feta and French bucheron. In making cheese, any milk may be used whole or skimmed. Whole milk produces cheeses with a creamy texture and a fat content, measured as a percentage of the cheese solids, of about 45 per cent. Skim-milk cheeses have a lower fat content, but a slightly rubbery texture. Other cheeses, such as the French double and triple cremes, are made with cream-enriched milk; they have a satiny texture and a fat content of 60 per cent or more.

All milk destined to become cheese must be curdled—broken down into solid curds and fluid whey. The curds are made up of coagulated casein, the principal milk protein, together with the fat that the casein enfolds. The whey includes proteins, sugar and minerals, but it is more than 90 per cent water. Although a few cheeses, such as Norwegian gjetost and some Italian ricottas, are made by heating whey until its solid matter coagulates, curds are the usual starting point.

Curdling occurs naturally if bacteria already present in raw milk are allowed to flourish. As they grow in numbers, the bacteria produce lactic acid, which coagulates casein. However, to kill potentially harmful organisms, much milk now used for cheese making is first pasteurized—held briefly at a high temperature. (A typical formula calls for the milk to be held at 161.6° F. [72° C.] for 16 seconds.) Since heating kills the useful lactic-acid-producing bacteria, too, these have to be reintroduced by adding a bacterial culture, or "starter." Even so, curdling can be a slow business, and another coagulating agent, such as rennet, is frequently added to accelerate the process. Rennet—an extract from the stomachs of unweaned calves—speeds the separation of the curds and whey, and also converts casein into an insoluble compound, thus yielding firmer curds. Because of this latter property, practically all cheeses destined for maturing are made with coagulating agents.

The traditional method of separating the curds from the whey—and the method commonly used to produce fresh, home-made cheese *(pages 10-11)*—is to allow the curds to rise naturally to the surface of the whey, then to hang the partially drained curds in a porous container so the remaining whey drains off. Although a cloth or perforated-metal container is normally used today, woven baskets were favored in classical times, and these gave cheese its name in many languages. In Greek, a basket is *formos,* which led to the French *fromage* and the Italian *formaggio.* The Latin word for basket, *cascus,* became the German *kase,* the Dutch *kaas,* the Spanish *queso* and the English "cheese."

Drained curds, perhaps embellished with cream or other flavorings, can be eaten immediately. Additional processing steps, however, are required for cheeses that are to be aged. Even before these cheeses are drained, the curds may be cut into even-sized pieces to help expel more whey. The finer the pieces, the more whey will be released. To produce a moist, soft cheese such

as Liederkranz, the curd is typically cut at half-inch [1-cm.] intervals. For a hard, granular cheese such as Parmesan, the curd is reduced to minuscule pieces and then further dried by heating and stirring it.

A number of cheeses—Cheddar, brick and Emmentaler, among them—are put in presses to expel still more whey. Pressing establishes the shape of a cheese and its moisture content. To develop its flavor and texture, a cheese then may be set aside to mature for periods ranging from a few weeks to several years. Under carefully controlled temperature and humidity levels, various microorganisms act on the curds, breaking down fat, proteins and other compounds to create a cheese's unique character. A blue cheese, for example, ripens from the inside out as mold spreads throughout the porous curds, producing distinctive greenish blue veins. Cheese such as Camembert and Brie are ripened from the surface inward by mold that forms an edible velvety rind. Appenzeller, Port-Salut, brick and Oka

represent another variation on surface-ripened cheese; during curing they are each washed at regular intervals with brine, brandy or some other solution specially formulated to encourage a particular type of mold, yeast or bacteria to grow on the exterior of the cheese.

An art becomes science

The great range of cheeses developed over the centuries is largely a result of customs and conditions prevailing at the local level—the availability of particular types of milk in a district or the presence of certain microorganisms. Roquefort cheese, for example, acquires its blue veins by being ripened in limestone caves harboring the mold that is now identified as *Penicillium Roqueforti*. English Cheddar cheese owes its flaky texture in part to a unique method—evolved in the village of Cheddar—for stacking and turning the blocks of curds. Eventually, the methods and microorganisms responsible for the differences in cheese were identified, and techniques were devised for applying molds and bacteria artificially to cheese. As a result, cheeses that were once made in only one locale can now be produced practically anywhere in the world.

Nonetheless, cheeses with the same name produced in different places—perhaps according to different standards—may vary widely in flavor and texture. To guard the reputation of some of the finest cheeses, the world's cheese-making nations signed an agreement in 1951 that allows certain names—including Roquefort and Parmigiano Reggiano—to be used only when the cheese is produced in the place where it originated. Still other cheeses—including France's Brie, Italy's Provolone, Holland's Edam and Gouda—may be replicated elsewhere, but the label must specify the country in which the cheese is made.

Along with the internationalization of many varieties of natural cheese, technology has brought about the development of processed cheeses. (These include the so-called American cheeses.) Typically, these begin with one or more natural cheeses that are pasteurized to lengthen their storage life, and then combined with emulsifiers to produce a uniformly smooth texture. Colorings and preservatives may be added, and the products that are labeled cheese spreads or cheese foods also may contain flavorings and liquid or dry milk products to increase volume and create a moister, more spreadable product. By United States government standards, only 51 per cent of the finished weight need be the cheese ingredient. Processing yields uniform cheeses that keep well, but they cannot duplicate the strength of flavor and distinctive texture of natural cheeses, which remain the best choice for cooking and eating.

Cooking with cheese

Delicious when eaten straight from the wheel or wrapper, natural cheeses develop a creamy texture and a more intense flavor as they are cooked. Cheddars liquefy to a golden mass as they melt to form a Welsh rabbit. Grating cheeses—Parmesan or Romano, for instance—disperse their pungence uniformly when they are stirred into casseroles, or create a rich brown gratin surface when sprinkled on top of foods and broiled or baked. The soft cheeses, from Brie to farmer, amalgamate with eggs and milk to produce the richest of custards.

The overriding rule when cooking cheeses is to heat them briefly and gently. Overly high heat or prolonged cooking will toughen proteins, making the cheese rubbery, and will also draw out the fats in the cheese, making the finished dish oily. Cheeses should be added to such dishes as omelets or sauces close to the end of the cooking period. Cheese dishes that are baked in the oven should be cooked at moderate temperatures—325° to 375° F. [160° to 190° C.]. When broiling cheeses, position the food about 3 inches [8 cm.] from the heat source, and be sure to watch it carefully to prevent excessive browning.

Serving wine with eggs and cheese

Although eggs are not normally regarded as suitable partners for wine, the two can, in fact, go together very well. A rosé or light, dry white can be a pleasant companion for many egg dishes—omelets or scrambled eggs among them. But the choice of wine should not be automatic. Because eggs are often used as a mild base to throw more assertive tastes into relief, the selection of wine may depend on the garnishes or flavorings used in the finished dish. The logical accompaniment to poached eggs in red wine sauce *(recipe, page 95),* for instance, is a red wine of similar depth. A rich, creamy sauce is nicely offset by a California Chardonnay or perhaps a French white Burgundy; both are

dry white wines, but they have enough body so that they will not seem thin when served with a thick sauce. In addition, these wines generally have sufficient distinction to accompany a more formal egg dish, such as eggs in aspic *(pages 46-47).*

By contrast, the gastronomic links between wine and cheese have been, if anything, overstressed. These are not always the best of companions: The bouquet of a subtle wine may be killed by a strong cheese, or the flavor of an indifferent wine may be masked—a fact not lost on wine merchants who occasionally offer such cheeses to prospective buyers before their less presentable vintages are tasted. For both wine and cheese to be shown off to best advantage, they must be matched with care.

The mildest of cheeses, such as Muenster, Monterey Jack and young brick, are best served with a correspondingly delicate wine—a rosé or a light red, such as Beaujolais—that will not overshadow the cheese's flavor. Cheeses with a little more assertiveness can stand up to wines of greater character. Port-Salut or Brie, for example, pair nicely with an elegant red such as a Bordeaux, as well as with a fruity white—including California Chenin Blanc and French Vouvray. The creamy texture of Brie is also nicely reinforced by the rich smoothness of one of the fine whites from the Côte de Beaune region of France—a Montrachet or Corton-Charlemagne, for example.

Strong-flavored cheeses need fairly robust wines. A zesty California Zinfandel or an Italian Chianti is a good companion for sharp Cheddar. The tanginess of Roquefort finds a nice contrast in the sweetness of white French dessert wines such as Sauternes and Barsac; Stilton, the English blue cheese, is tradi-

tionally served with vintage port. Extremely strong-smelling cheeses, such as Limburger and Liederkranz, are best with ale or beer, since their aromas would overpower a wine's bouquet.

When wine is to be served with more than one cheese at a time—with a cheese platter, for example—your own palate is the best guide, because the wine will take on a different character with each kind of cheese. The best strategy is to select the wine first, then sample a variety of cheeses until you find those most compatible with the wine. The process of discovery is likely to be a long and happy one.

Egg Classes and Grades

Mass production and distribution, along with uniform grading, take most of the guesswork out of buying eggs. Almost all of the eggs sold at retail are classed according to size, and graded for quality and freshness by virtually identical federal or state government standards.

Egg size, which increases with the age of the hen, is gauged by an egg's weight; the U.S. Department of Agriculture lists six size categories (below). In cooking whole eggs, the sizes can be used interchangeably. But with beaten eggs, the quantities specified in recipes may call for some adjustment, since most recipes are predicated on large-sized eggs.

Quality is determined by checking the shell for shape, cleanliness and smoothness, and then examining its contents through the shell with the aid of lighted, automated racks. The interior quality is judged by the thickness of the white, the compactness of the yolk and the amount of air in the egg. In a newly laid egg, the white is surrounded by a pair of membranes that cling to each other and the shell. As the egg ages, carbon dioxide and water evaporate through the shell pores; at the same time, air is absorbed, producing a visible pocket between the membranes at the egg's broad end.

The best, freshest eggs with the firmest yolks and smallest air pockets are

Buoyancy: A Measure of Freshness

A newly laid egg. To test the age of an egg, place it in water. A newly laid egg has only a tiny air pocket and is relatively heavy; it sinks and lies flat on the bottom.

A week-old egg. The air pocket, which forms in the broad, rounded end, expands and gives the egg buoyancy. The egg tilts in the water with its broad end uppermost.

A three-week-old egg. As the egg ages, the air pocket continues to expand until the egg becomes buoyant enough to stand upright in the water.

Egg sizes. The six official classifications for eggs, shown at right in actual average size, are determined by the minimum weight allowed per dozen. Jumbo eggs must weigh at least 30 ounces [850 g.] per dozen, extra-large eggs 27 ounces [765 g.], large eggs 24 ounces [680 g.], medium eggs 21 ounces [595 g.], small eggs 18 ounces [510 g.] and peewee eggs 15 ounces [425 g.]. The weights of the eggs within a dozen can vary by as much as 5 per cent, so that the smallest egg allowed in one classification may be the same size as the largest egg allowed in the classification below it.

Jumbo

Extra large

graded AA; slightly older eggs are graded A. Grade B eggs, only rarely available to the consumer, have thin whites and enlarged yolks and sometimes stained shells. Except for these, shell color is unrelated to quality; it is determined by the breed of hen that laid the egg. Brown or white specks on shells are the harmless result of uneven pigmentation or water molecules trapped in the pores.

Once sized, graded and packed, eggs generally reach the supermarket within four or five days. The grading date appears on the carton as a number: 048, for example, means they were graded on February 17, the 48th day of the year.

You also can judge an egg's freshness by the tests shown below. The buoyancy test measures the size of the egg's air pocket, hence its age. The dispersion test reflects chemical changes in the egg that govern its suitability for various cooking methods. The firm, round yolks and cohesive whites of newly laid eggs are important in poaching and frying. Older eggs are best for boiling and peeling; the contents of newly laid eggs cling so closely to the shell membranes that the eggs are hard to peel. Though eggs are edible until about five weeks of age, those more than two weeks old are best used where appearance is not a factor—for scrambling, omelet making, baking or in sauces.

Dispersion: A Manifestation of Age

  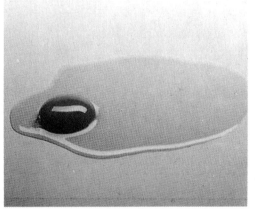

A newly laid egg. The yolk of the egg is compact and rounded. It is held near the egg's center by a dense, cohesive layer of white surrounded by a small, fluid outer layer.

A week-old egg. The dense layer of white becomes progressively more fluid, merging into the thinner white. The yolk moves away from the center of the white.

A three-week-old egg. The yolk spreads out and flattens. The egg's white thins to a uniform watery consistency.

Large   Medium   Small   Peewee

Making a Fresh Cheese at Home

The basic principles of cheese making apply alike to the simplest fresh cheeses—farmer, cottage, ricotta and cream cheese *(recipes, pages 162-164)*—and to the varied matured cheeses illustrated on pages 14-17. By producing the farmer cheese shown here, you will gain an understanding of the essential techniques.

The first step in making any cheese is to curdle milk—separate it into coagulated curds and liquid whey. Bacteria that produce lactic acid do this naturally with raw milk, but almost all milk sold in America is pasteurized—heated to kill bacteria, including those that manufacture lactic acid from the milk's sugar.

In order to make cheese from pasteurized milk—whether whole milk, skim milk or milk enriched with cream—you must add a so-called starter. Here the starter is buttermilk, which contains an active bacterial culture. When added to milk, the bacteria will multiply rapidly and within a day or less will produce enough lactic acid to coagulate the milk. An alternative way of coagulating milk is to use a food acid, such as lemon juice or vinegar, but this yields a blander cheese than one made with buttermilk.

To speed coagulation, the starter is often mixed with rennet, a substance taken from the stomachs of unweaned calves and sold in tablet form at supermarkets and pharmacies. Before the starter and rennet are added, the milk must be heated to 80° F. [27° C.], a temperature high enough to promote coagulation, but not so hot that it kills the bacteria. Use a dairy thermometer or a rapid-response type to test the temperature.

Once the milk coagulates, the mixture must be drained of whey. First, the curds are put in a piece of muslin or cheesecloth and left in a colander. After most of the whey has dripped through, the cloth is tied up into a bag and suspended, so that the curds drain under their own weight.

As soon as they acquire a firm consistency, the curds can be used in any recipe calling for farmer cheese. Or they may be served as a table cheese, either as is or with various enrichments and flavorings—cream, salt and pepper, a tangy blend of herbs such as chives, burnet and basil, or a sweetening of grated chocolate or chopped fruits and cinnamon.

1 **Heating the milk.** Set a wire rack in a pot half-filled with water and heat to 90° F.[32° C.] on a thermometer—a dairy thermometer is shown. Immediately remove the pot from the heat. Pour milk into a nonaluminum pan—aluminum may affect flavor—and set the pan on the rack in the water. When the milk reaches 80° F. [27° C.] stir in buttermilk.

2 **Testing the consistency.** Cover the pan of milk tightly. Leave the milk at room temperature—between 65° and 70° F. [18° to 21° C.]—for up to 24 hours, or until the curds form a solid layer above the whey. When a knife inserted into the curds comes out clean, the curds are firm enough.

6 **Completing the draining.** Tie the string to a support—a ceiling hook, for example—so that the bag hangs free above the bowl, which will collect the dripping whey. Allow the bag to drain for six to 10 hours. Take it down two or three times to check the cheese; if the texture seems uneven, scrape the outside cheese into the center.

7 **Unwrapping the cheese.** When the curds are firm, take down the bag, untie it and peel the cloth away from the mass of cheese *(above).* Invert the cheese onto a dish and refrigerate it, covered, unless it is to be served immediately. You can drink the whey either lightly salted or sweetened and mixed with fruit juice.

3 **Ladling out the curd.** Place muslin or cheesecloth in a colander set in a sink and pour boiling water over the cloth to sterilize it. With tongs, fold the cloth double and use it to line the colander. Place the lined colander over a deep bowl. Carefully ladle in the curds: Gentle treatment at this stage ensures that the cheese will drain evenly.

4 **Scraping the cloth.** Cover the curds with a pan lid or a piece of sterile cloth. Let the curds drain for about five hours, until the surface begins to dry out. With a spoon, scrape the dry curds at the sides of the liner onto the damper curds at the center of the mass.

5 **Tying up the cloth.** With the colander still set in the bowl, pull together the corners of the cloth to form a bag that encloses the curds completely. Tie the bag with string, leaving one end of string long enough to hang up the bag.

8 **Serving the cheese.** Serve the cheese unseasoned, or break it up with a fork (right) and incorporate salt and pepper and any additional flavorings. If unsalted, the cheese should be used on the day it is made. If it is salted, it can be refrigerated for two or three days.

A Cheese Buyer's Primer

Curdled milk drained of its liquid whey is the basis of almost all cheese. Served fresh, the curds become simple cottage cheese or farmer cheese *(pages 10-11)*. But the curds may also be heated or pressed to expel more whey, packed into molds and ripened in various ways to make any of 800 different cheeses. A representative sampling of them appears on the following pages. For convenience, this selection is divided between soft and firm cheeses, but each category includes a range of textures. Soft cheeses can be as creamy as Brie or as crumbly as feta; firm cheeses vary in texture from supple Gouda to granular sapsago.

The taste of a cheese varies according to the milk it is made from, the way it is made and the time it is aged. Goat's-milk cheeses have a strong, musky taste quite distinct from those made of cow's milk. Blue cheeses—those treated with molds that form blue or green veins throughout the cheese—also tend to be strong tasting. Aging intensifies a cheese's taste: A young Cheddar is mild; one aged for a year will be quite sharp.

All these cheeses and many more are described in detail in the glossary on the pages that follow. Remember, however, that the descriptions are general guidelines: The way to determine whether a cheese satisfies you is to taste it, and this is best done before you buy.

How to shop: Cheeses develop at different rates, but all are continuously ripening and changing in character, and all are perishable. Any cheese for sale should be kept under refrigeration; cold retards development. A supermarket is a reliable source for fresh cheeses such as cottage and cream cheese or its skim-milk counterpart Neufchatel, because the stock sells rapidly and a cheese is unlikely to linger too long on the shelf. However, for ripened cheese—particularly the rarer imported types and delicate soft cheeses enriched with cream—the best source is a cheese shop or specialty market whose staff is likely to be knowledgeable about selecting and caring for cheese.

The better shops stock their cheeses in large wheels, blocks or cylinders, cutting off portions to order. This storage method has several advantages over prepackaging. First, it helps preserve the cheese: A cut cheese dries out more quickly than one left whole. It allows you to buy the exact amount of cheese you need. Finally, when cheese is cut from a large block or wheel you have an opportunity to ex-amine and taste a sample before making your purchase.

When examining any cheese, begin by smelling it—any hint of ammonia means the cheese is overaged and will be unpleasant tasting. Look at the rind: On a cheese with a soft rind such as Pont l'Évêque, it should be evenly colored and somewhat moist. On a firm-rinded cheese such as Emmentaler, it should be free of cracks or bulges, which indicate improper ripening.

You cannot see the rind on wax-coated cheeses such as Gouda, of course, but you can press the cheese, as you should any other, to see how it responds. Good Gouda feels elastic, as do most firm cheeses, except lengthily aged ones such as Parmesan, which will feel quite hard. Do not buy a firm cheese in which you can feel any soft spots. Soft cheeses such as Brie or Camembert should feel supple and slightly soft, but not at all liquid.

When the cheese is sliced, you will be able to observe the interior. With the exception of blue cheeses, which should be well veined, the cheese should be even in color. White spots within a yellow cheese are a sign of inferior quality. A gray line under the rind of a Brie means

Tools for Handling Cheese

Shredding in a processor. Use the shredding disk of a processor, and put the semisoft or firm cheese chunks — Emmentaler, here — in the tube; press with the pusher as the machine runs. Hard cheese can be grated with the processor's steel blade.

Cutting with a wire. To cut wedges or slices, stretch a cheese wire taut and pass it through the cheese. The wire can cut all but the hardest cheeses, and is excellent for crumbly cheeses — blue, in this case — that tend to stick to a knife blade.

Slicing with a double wire. A fairly firm cheese, such as this Gouda, can be sliced with a double-wire cutter. The cutter rod runs along the cheese surface, acting as a guide. Taut wires on each side of the rod allow you to make slices of two different thicknesses.

that it is old, while a white line through the center of this type of cheese means that it has not yet fully ripened.

Brie, Camembert and certain other cheeses described in the glossary are sometimes made from raw rather than pasteurized milk. As a result, seasonality may be a factor in buying them. Cheeses made from pasteurized milk are fairly uniform in quality throughout the year, but raw-milk cheeses are best made from spring and summer or fall milk, taken when the cows graze in pastures rather than feeding on grain or hay, as they do in winter. The optimal time to purchase a raw-milk cheese depends on its ripening period. Reblochon, which is aged only briefly, is made in the summer and tastes best in late fall and winter; a Livarot made at the same time may not reach its peak until the following spring.

How to store: The prime rules for storing any cheese are that it should be well covered to prevent it from drying, and that it should be refrigerated to slow down its inevitable development.

Soft, fresh cheeses such as cottage or farmer's cheese are best kept in plastic or wax-coated containers. Protect the exposed surfaces of all other cheeses by sealing the cheeses in aluminum foil or plastic wrap. All strong-smelling cheeses such as Limburger should also be stored in tightly covered containers; otherwise, their odors may permeate other foods in the refrigerator.

No matter how carefully cheeses are treated, they will continue to ripen—to the point of overripeness or spoiling—in the refrigerator. As a general rule, uncured and soft cheeses are the most perishable: They usually should be eaten within a week of purchase. Firmer, drier cheeses—Cheddars and Swiss cheeses, for instance—may last several months. Very dry, aged cheeses such as Parmesan will keep almost indefinitely.

Even properly stored cheese may develop surface molds. These may simply be sliced off; cut ½ inch [1 cm.] below the mold to make sure you have removed it all. Dried-out bits of cheese may be salvaged too; shred or grate the cheese, store it in a tightly covered container, and use it in cooked dishes as soon as possible.

How to use: If the cheese will be eaten as is, bring it to room temperature so that its flavor—muted by refrigeration—can develop. Small cheeses need about an hour's warming; large wheels or blocks may require as much as two hours', depending on the temperature of the room.

Cheeses to be used in cooked dishes *(pages 70-90)* do not need to be warmed; when chilled, in fact, they are most easily sliced, shredded or grated for incorporation into other ingredients. Some of the implements suited to these tasks and the types of cheeses appropriate for each are described below.

Cheeses can enhance an immense variety of dishes. Soft cheeses, for example, lend body and delicate taste to assemblies such as tarts and cheese pancakes. The firmer cheeses are typically used in baked meat or vegetable dishes or to enliven soufflés, omelets or sauces. Hard cheeses provide flavorful toppings for soups or baked dishes.

As the descriptions on the following pages suggest, many cheeses are so similar in flavor and texture that they can be used interchangeably. A Colby or a Gouda can be substituted for Cheddar, for instance; Jarlsberg or Gruyère can replace Emmentaler; Romano or Asiago can substitute for Parmesan. In cooking with cheese—as in buying it—adventurous experimentation is the rule: The result can be the most delightful of surprises.

Shaving with a plane. This slicer — consisting of a sharp-edged slit set into a spatula-like blade — is pulled across the surface of cheese to make paper-thin slices. It can be used with semisoft or firm cheeses; a caraway-studded Danbo is shown.

Shredding with a flat grater. Use a grater with small or large holes, depending on the fineness needed. Brace it over a plate. Rub sections of cheese — Cheddar is shown — down against the holes. All but very soft or crumbly cheeses may be shredded this way.

Using a rotary grater. For hard cheese — Parmesan, in this demonstration — fit a rotary grater with a fine-holed drum; use a drum with larger holes for softer cheeses. Place cheese pieces in the receptacle, squeeze the pressure plate and turn the drum.

An Array of Soft and Semisoft Cheeses

Pyramide
Boursault
Livarot
Gorgonzola
Austrian Monastery
Bleu de Bresse
Bucheron
Cream havarti
Monterey Jack
Oka
Feta
Banon

As an aid to selecting natural cheeses, a sampling of 52 of the most common kinds is shown here and on the following pages. The cheeses are grouped by texture: Soft and semisoft cheeses appear above, hard and firm cheeses on pages 16-17.

Each entry in the glossary includes the cheese's country of origin, shape, texture and flavor. Unless otherwise noted, the cheese is made from pasteurized whole or partly skimmed cow's milk and has a butterfat content, measured as a percentage of cheese solids, of about 40 to 50 per cent. When the use of skim milk or cream alters the fat content—and therefore the richness—of a cheese, it is noted in the glossary entry.

Raw-milk cheeses, which can vary in quality through the year, are identified and their peak seasons listed. Entries also tell whether a cheese is made from sheep's or goat's milk, since these cheeses have flavors quite distinct from those

made of cow's milk. Finally, entries indicate cases in which different degrees of aging affect taste or texture.

Austrian Monastery: Austria. Wheel shaped. Buttery, semisoft; mild flavor.

Banon: France. Raw goat's milk; best from late spring to early fall. Disk shaped, sometimes wrapped in chestnut leaves. Soft texture; mild, lemony taste.

Bel Paese: Italy and elsewhere. Wheel shaped. Semisoft; mild, buttery flavor.

Bleu de Bresse: France. Whole cow's or goat's milk. Wheel shaped. Soft, creamy-textured, blue-veined cheese; milder flavor than most blues.

Boursault: France. Cream-enriched; 75 per cent fat. Wrapped in paper; boxed. Soft, smooth texture; buttery taste.

Brick: United States. Brick shaped. Semisoft, elastic texture; flavor is mildly sweet when aged two to three months, more pungent with longer aging.

Brie: France and elsewhere. Pasteur-

ized or raw, whole or skimmed cow's milk. (Raw-milk versions best in fall, winter and spring.) Disk shaped. Soft, creamy texture; buttery flavor.

Bucheron: France. Raw goat's milk; best in spring and summer. Log shaped. Soft, creamy; slightly tangy flavor.

Camembert: France and elsewhere. Raw or pasteurized whole cow's milk. (Raw-milk versions best from October to May.) Disk shaped. Soft, creamy texture; slightly tangy taste.

Cream havarti: Denmark and elsewhere. Cream-enriched; 60 per cent fat. Loaf or wheel shaped. Semisoft; buttery, often enlivened with caraway seeds.

Feta: Greece and elsewhere. Sheep's, goat's or cow's milk. Rectangular. Soft, crumbly; tangy, salty flavor.

Gorgonzola: Italy. Whole cow's and/or goat's milk. Wheel shaped. Semisoft blue

Mozzarella

Brick

Liederkranz

Pipo crem'

Bel Paese

Reblochon

Taleggio

Tomme de Savoie

Muenster

Camembert

Montrachet

Port-Salut

Limburger

Roquefort

Pont l'Évêque

Brie

cheese; a piquant flavor after aging for three months, more pungent when aged up to a year.

Liederkranz: United States. Rectangular; boxed. Soft, smooth texture, assertive flavor and strong aroma.

Limburger: Belgium and elsewhere. Rectangular. Soft texture; very strong taste and aroma.

Livarot: France. Raw, partly skimmed cow's milk; best in winter and spring. Disk shaped. Soft; similar to Camembert but spicier and stronger in aroma.

Monterey Jack: United States. Wheel shaped. Semisoft texture and mild flavor when aged three to six weeks; hard grating texture and zestier taste when aged up to six months.

Montrachet: France. Raw goat's milk; best in spring and early summer. Log shaped. Soft, creamy texture; relative-ly mild flavor for a goat's-milk cheese.

Mozzarella: Italy and elsewhere. Whole or skimmed cow's milk. Irregular spherical shape. Fresh varieties found in Italian markets have a tender, spongy texture and mild flavor; cheeses aged up to two months are drier and more elastic.

Muenster: Germany and elsewhere. Wheel or block shaped. Semisoft. American brands, aged from six to eight weeks, are mild and usually have light orange rinds; rindless European varieties, cured up to three months, are more pungent.

Oka: Canada. Wheel shaped. Semisoft texture; similar to French Port-Salut but with a more tangy, fruity flavor.

Pipo Crem': France. Cream-enriched; 60 per cent fat. Log shaped. Soft, smooth-textured blue cheese with a flavor similar to that of bleu de Bresse.

Pont l'Évêque: France. Raw milk; best in fall and winter. Boxed; square. Soft

and supple; piquant taste, strong aroma.

Port-Salut: France. Wheel shaped. Smooth texture and buttery flavor similar to Oka or Austrian Monastery.

Pyramide: France. Raw goat's milk; best in the spring and summer. Pyramidal. Soft texture; tangy taste. Sometimes called Valençay.

Reblochon: France. Raw whole cow's milk; best in late fall and early winter. Disk shaped. Soft texture; mild flavor.

Roquefort: France. Raw sheep's milk; best from June to October. Cylindrical. Semisoft blue-veined cheese with sharper flavor than most blues.

Taleggio: Italy. Raw milk; best in summer and fall. Squarish shape. Semisoft texture; creamy flavor.

Tomme de Savoie: France. Raw milk; best from late spring to fall; 20 to 40 per cent fat. Disk shaped. Semisoft, supple texture; nutty taste and earthy smell.

A Sampling of Firm and Hard Cheeses

Unlike the soft cheeses shown on the previous pages, the firm and hard natural cheeses presented here all have a fairly low moisture content. During processing, whey is expelled by such methods as close cutting of the curd, heating and pressing. Lengthy aging also increases a cheese's dryness and, therefore, its hardness.

Appenzeller: Switzerland. Raw milk; best in summer and fall. Wheel shaped. Firm texture; fruity taste from wine or cider wash during curing.

Asiago: Italy and elsewhere. Partly skimmed milk; 30 to 40 per cent fat. Cylindrical. Semisoft and mild when aged two months; firm texture, zesty flavor when aged a year and marked "old."

Caerphilly: Wales. Raw milk; best in late summer. Wheel shaped. Firm, flaky texture; slightly salty flavor.

Cantal: France. Raw milk; best in summer and fall. Cloth-covered; cylindrical. Firm supple texture; piquant nutty taste.

Cheddar: England and elsewhere. Wheel shaped. Firm; mild when aged two months, sharp when aged 12 months.

Cheshire: England. Cylindrical. Firm texture. Mellow, Cheddar taste if white or orange, piquant if blue-veined.

Danbo: Denmark and elsewhere. Wheel shaped. Firm; mild Emmentaler-like flavor enlivened with caraway seeds.

Edam: Holland and elsewhere. Whole or part-skim milk; minimum 40 per cent fat. Loaf or sphere shape; typically encased in red wax. Firm; mild when aged two months, tangy when aged longer.

Emmentaler: Switzerland. Part-skim raw or pasteurized milk. Wheel shaped. Firm texture; cherry-sized holes; mild, nutlike flavor. Similar so-called Swiss cheeses produced worldwide.

Fontina: Italy and elsewhere. Whole cow's or sheep's milk. Wheel shaped. Firm; nutty flavor, distinct odor.

Gjetost: Norway. Whey of cow's and goat's milk; 33 per cent fat. Loaf or small foil-wrapped cube shape. Firm texture; brown color and sweetish flavor from milk sugar caramelizing during boiling.

Gouda: Holland and elsewhere. Wheel

Gouda
Cheshire
Pecorino Romano
Sage Derby
Asiago
Mimolette
Jarlsberg
Fontina
Provolone
Sapsago
Noekkelost
Appenzeller

shaped, usually wax-coated. Firm; mild, nutty taste when aged two to six months and tangy when cured longer.

Gruyère: Switzerland and elsewhere. Large wheel shape. Firm texture; small, widely dispersed holes; nutty flavor.

Jarlsberg: Norway. Wheel shaped. Firm, buttery texture; tingly taste, similar to Emmentaler and Gruyère.

Mimolette: France. Flattened ball. Resilient, firm; mild Cheddar flavor.

Noekkelost: Norway and United States. Part-skim milk. Norwegian versions as low as 20 per cent fat; whole-milk domestic versions are 50 per cent fat. Loaf and cylindrical. Firm; spicy

from added cumin, cloves and caraway.

Parmesan: Italy and elsewhere. Those labeled Parmigiano Reggiano *(shown below)* are made only in Italy. Part-skim milk; 32 to 38 per cent fat. Cylindrical. Hard, dry, granular; sharp, nutty flavor.

Pecorino Romano: Italy. Sheep's milk; 38 per cent fat. Cylindrical. Hard; extremely sharp flavor. The goat's-milk version, caprino Romano, has a similar flavor; cow's-milk vacchino Romano is comparatively mild. Cow's-milk Romano made in the United States is even milder.

Provolone: Italy and elsewhere. Usually smoked. Pear, sausage and other shapes, often wax-coated and bound with cord. Firm, elastic; mild after six months'

aging, piquant if aged up to 14 months.

Raclette: Switzerland. Wheel shaped. Firm texture; mellow flavor.

Ricotta Salata: Italy. Sheep's milk. Wheel shaped. Semisoft when aged two months, hard if aged longer; pungent.

Sage Derby: England. Wheel shaped. Firm; Cheddar flavor enlivened by sage leaves. American version called sage.

Sapsago: Switzerland. A mixture of whey, skim milk and buttermilk; 5 to 9 per cent fat. Small cone shape. Hard, granular texture; piquant flavor enlivened by powdered clover leaves.

Stilton: England. Cylindrical. Firm, slightly crumbly-textured blue cheese; milder than Roquefort or Gorgonzola.

Swiss: See Emmentaler.

1
Whole-Egg Cookery
The Basic Methods

Perfect fried eggs

The double cooking of shirred eggs

The unique effects of deep frying

Soft-boiling to serve from the shell

A range of firmness for peeled eggs

Neat results from poaching

The benefits of baking

Tossed from its pan with a sweeping motion of the arm, a fried egg turns in mid-air to bring the top into contact with the hot pan. Once turned, the egg will need only a few seconds' additional frying to firm the white around the yolk.

Whether fried, boiled, poached, baked or steamed, eggs that are cooked whole, without stirring or beating, share a need for gentle heat to keep whites tender and yolks moist. Aside from this constraint, the methods have little in common; each makes different demands on the cook.

When eggs are fried in a shallow layer of butter or oil, for example, the temperature must be set low to prevent the undersides from burning while the tops cook. For eggs that are to be served sunny-side up, the tops can be firmed quickly by covering the pan with a lid that will reflect heat downward *(page 21)*. Alternatively, the eggs can be turned, either with a spatula or by tossing them *(opposite)*. A variation of shallow frying is to shirr eggs by setting the undersides in melted butter on the stove top, and finishing the eggs in the oven *(page 21)*.

Deep frying an egg helps to solve the problem of uneven cooking by applying all-around heat. However, to preserve the egg's tenderness, the temperature of the oil or fat must be markedly lower than is the case when deep frying most foods, and the white must be neatly and quickly folded around the yolk to protect it from overcooking.

Shells protect eggs cooked intact in water, a process called boiling, although, in fact, the water must be at a simmer to avoid toughening the whites. Because the cooking is concealed, accurate timing is essential: It may vary from three minutes for an egg to be eaten from the shell *(page 23)* to 10 minutes for an egg that is to be peeled *(page 25)*.

For poaching—immersing eggs in hot liquid without the protection of their shells—the temperature should be below a simmer: Bubbling liquid would break up the whites. The best way to control the temperature is to bring the liquid to a boil, then turn off the heat before adding the eggs. Covered with a lid, the pan and its contents stay warm enough to cook the eggs in a few minutes *(pages 26-27)*. Only the freshest eggs should be poached; their firm whites will cling to well-centered yolks.

Shaping is no problem when eggs are cooked in containers by baking or steaming. The use of containers also makes it possible for other ingredients, such as vegetable purées, to be cooked along with the eggs. Baking is most commonly done in an oven preheated to about 350° F. [180° C.]. Steaming is done in a covered water bath, placed either in the oven or on the stove top *(page 29)*.

Frying: Fast Cooking in Shallow Fat

When eggs are cooked in a thin layer of fat, heat is directed at them only from below. If the eggs are served sunny-side up, the cook's task is to ensure that the tops of the eggs cook at the same time the bottoms do, so that the thick rings of white surrounding the yolks set before the undersides burn. Basting the eggs by spooning fat over them will help cook the tops. In addition, you can cover the skillet with a lid to reflect heat downward, as shown in the top demonstration at right.

Alternatively, you can turn eggs over midway through frying, so that both the tops and the bottoms are brought into contact with the heated surface of the pan *(right, bottom)*. You will find it easiest to reverse eggs with the aid of a spatula *(Step 2, bottom)*, but some virtuosos prefer to flip eggs by tossing them, as shown on page 18. Because of the difficulty of flipping eggs simultaneously, or of turning several in one pan, both of these techniques work best with one or at most two eggs.

Whichever frying method you choose, you should add the eggs to the skillet as soon as the fat is hot to prevent it from burning and spoiling the taste of the finished dish. The fresh flavor of melted butter marries well with eggs; so does the fruity tang of olive oil.

Most cooks break the eggs directly into the fat, but some prefer to crack eggs onto a plate and then slide them into the pan so that if a shell accidentally crumbles, the fragments can be easily removed. After cooking the eggs, you can mix a little vinegar or lemon juice with additional melted butter in the pan to make a simple sauce *(Step 4, opposite page, bottom)*.

Shirring eggs is an extension of the pan-frying technique: The eggs start to cook on top of the stove, and are then placed in an oven or under a broiler to set the whites *(box, opposite)*. Gratin dishes just large enough for one or two eggs are traditionally used for this method. For the second stage of cooking, cream may be added to the eggs to enrich their flavor and give them a melting smoothness.

Reflecting Heat with a Pan Lid

1 **Breaking the eggs.** In a skillet over low to medium heat, warm sufficient butter to cover the bottom of the pan generously. As soon as the butter foams, break as many eggs into the skillet as it will hold easily — up to four eggs in a pan 12 inches [30 cm.] in diameter.

2 **Basting the eggs.** Once all of the eggs have been added, tilt the skillet and use a spoon to collect the butter on the lower side. Baste the eggs with the hot butter two or three times so that the tops start cooking. If the skillet is filled with eggs, it may be difficult to collect the fat; in that case, melt some butter in a separate pan and use it for basting.

Turned Eggs with a Simple Sauce

1 **Adding the egg to the pan.** Melt butter over low heat until it starts to foam. Break an egg into the hot butter *(Step 1, top)*. Alternatively, break the egg onto a small dish or saucer and slide it into the skillet *(above)*. Cook the egg until the underside sets — about one minute.

2 **Turning the egg over.** Slide a spatula far enough underneath the egg to support the yolk and as much of the white as possible. Raise the spatula a little, then turn it sideways so the egg slips back into the skillet, yolk side down.

3 **Covering the pan.** To set the thick layer of white surrounding each yolk, cover the skillet with a lid to reflect heat onto the tops of the eggs. After about one minute, remove the lid. The eggs are ready as soon as the whites set; the yolks should be soft and glistening.

4 **Serving the eggs.** Take the skillet off the heat. Gently shake the pan to free the eggs, then carefully tilt it to slide the eggs onto a warmed serving plate. Season to taste with salt and pepper, and serve the eggs at once.

1 **Adding cream.** Melt butter in a small gratin dish over medium heat, using a heat-diffusing pad if the dish is ceramic. Break in eggs, cook them about a minute, until the undersides set, then take the dish off the heat. Pour cream over the eggs *(above)*.

3 **Tipping out the egg.** Turn off the burner and allow the heat of the pan to cook the egg for a few seconds more to set the white surrounding the yolk. Then tilt the pan to slide the egg out onto a warmed plate.

4 **Making a pan-juice sauce.** Using the same skillet, melt a little more butter over medium heat; when it foams, add a dash of vinegar. Stir the butter-and-vinegar mixture for a few seconds, then pour it over the egg. Serve at once.

2 **Serving the eggs.** Place the dish in a preheated 350° F. [180° C.] oven and bake for four or five minutes, until the whites set uniformly. Serve the eggs in the gratin dish, set on a plate to protect the table from its heat.

Deep Frying: A Route to Crisped Whites

Deep frying is a cooking method not often associated with eggs—and in fact the usual deep-frying temperatures of 350° to 375° F. [180° to 190° C.] would burn eggs and make them rubbery. But if the oil or fat is kept at about 250° F. [120° C.], the eggs become crisp and brown outside while remaining soft and moist within.

The cooking process is rapid—it takes about a minute—and calls for some dexterity. To prevent overcooking, the white must be folded around the yolk as soon as the egg is immersed. Any white not submerged must be basted constantly to cook evenly. So delicate is this procedure that only one egg can be cooked at a time.

The choice of oil or fat is a matter of taste. Neutral-tasting peanut or corn oil will leave the eggs' flavor unchanged. Olive oil will impart a fruity savor, and lard will lend a faint sweetness.

Heat the oil or fat to the proper temperature before adding the egg. Test it with a rapid-response thermometer or drop in a stale bread cube—the oil or fat should sizzle but not brown the bread.

1 Setting the white. In a frying pan, heat ½ to 1 inch [1 to 2½ cm.] of oil until it is sizzling hot. Break an egg into the oil, then immediately tilt the pan to form a well of oil deep enough to immerse the egg. With a spoon, ease the exposed white away from the base of the pan *(above, left)*. Gently fold the white over the yolk to enclose it. The doubled layers of white *(right)* will protect the yolk from the heat and prevent it from overcooking.

2 Draining the egg. When the white appears firm and starts to brown, lift the egg out of the oil with a perforated spoon. Let excess oil drip back into the pan, then set the egg on paper towels to drain. Use more towels to blot any remaining oil from the top of the egg.

3 Serving the egg. Season the egg to taste and serve at once — in this case, on a slice of bread that has been buttered on one side and crisped for 5 minutes in a preheated 400° F. [200° C.] oven. If you like, garnish the egg with parsley, fried for a few seconds in the hot oil and drained on paper towels.

Soft-boiling: Two Approaches to Tender Whites

The simplest way to cook an egg is to immerse it, shell and all, in hot water. If the egg is intended to be eaten from its shell, its white must be kept tender. The quickest method for accomplishing this, as shown at right, is to bring a saucepan of water to a gentle bubble, plunge in the egg, and let it simmer uncovered over low heat. Vigorous boiling would overcook the outside of the white, making it tough and leathery.

The timing depends on the degree of doneness you want as well as on the size of the egg and its freshness. If the egg is medium-sized, allow three minutes for a barely congealed white *(Step 3, right)*, five minutes for a firm white. A large egg will be ready in four to six minutes. However, add another minute to times if the egg is newly laid; its compact white will take longer to set than the thinner, more alkaline white of an older egg.

An even gentler, if slower, method for soft-boiling an egg is coddling it. For this method, the water is brought to a boil, then removed from the heat before the egg is immersed. Covered with a lid, the water will cook a medium-sized egg in six to 10 minutes and a large egg in eight to 12 minutes—according to how firm you want the white.

With either method, the egg must be brought to room temperature before it can be immersed; otherwise, the sudden change in temperature is likely to crack the shell. To warm the egg quickly, let it stand in a bowl of tepid water until it no longer feels cool to the touch.

If you are soft-boiling or coddling several eggs at once, you can synchronize the moment at which they start cooking by lowering them into the water in a wire basket. Then, if you do not wish to cook all of the eggs for the same length of time, remove them individually with a slotted spoon as they become ready.

Soft-boiled or coddled eggs should be opened as soon as possible, lest the internal heat continue to cook them. They may be served just as they are in eggcups, or scooped from their shells into cups or bowls, to which butter and herbs may be added according to taste.

1 **Boiling the eggs.** Let the eggs warm to room temperature. Bring a saucepan of water to a simmer. Reduce the heat, if necessary, so that the water barely bubbles. Place the eggs in a wire basket and lower them into the water. Time the cooking from the moment the eggs enter the water.

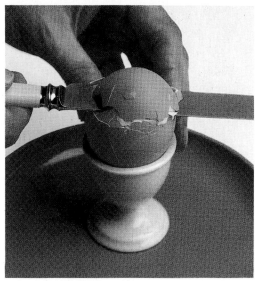

2 **Opening the eggs.** When they have cooked for the time required, remove the eggs from the water with a slotted spoon or in the basket. Set each one in an eggcup. Holding the egg, slice through the top by striking it with a knife at the point where it widens enough to admit a small spoon *(above)*. Or crack the top with a teaspoon, then use the spoon to open the egg.

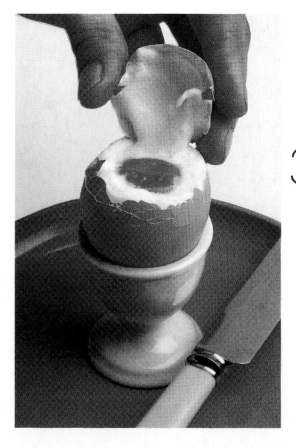

3 **Serving the eggs.** Lift the top off the egg and clear away any pieces of shell that may have fallen into it. Season with salt and pepper. If you like, add a dab of butter. The egg may now be eaten with a small spoon or by dipping strips of bread or toast into it.

Firming Whites for Easy Peeling

Eggs that are boiled and then peeled may serve as garnishes, as elements in assembled dishes, or they may be eaten as they are. Whether the eggs are cooked for four minutes or 10 (box, below), the whites must be firm enough to remain intact after the shells are pulled away. But the whites must also stay tender, even if the eggs are reheated (pages 40-45).

The best eggs for peeling after boiling are those about a week old—eggs that have developed the large air pockets that simplify the peeling process. To firm the whites during boiling, the eggs are started in cold water, which is then brought almost—but not quite—to a boil over moderately high heat and kept just below boiling temperature during cooking. High heat will toughen the whites and accelerate a chemical reaction between the iron of the yolk and the sulfur compounds of the white that results in green discoloration on the yolks.

Because the water in which they are immersed is cold, eggs can be used directly from the refrigerator without danger of cracking during boiling. However, the cooking period during which the water heats should not be counted as part of the boiling time: Timing begins when the water first starts to bubble. The heaviness of your pan, the amount of water you use and the number of eggs you cook will influence the time required. The times shown in the box at right are averages for eggs classed as "large." For bigger eggs, add a minute to each time; for smaller ones, subtract a minute.

After boiling the eggs, plunge them into cold water to arrest their cooking and to cool them for easy handling. Peeling, although not difficult, requires a light touch—particularly for a *mollet* egg (near right), a liquid-yolked, four-minute version that is easily damaged. It is best to peel eggs just before using them. The shells protect the whites from drying out and preserve flavor so effectively that whole boiled eggs can be kept in the refrigerator for up to a week.

Cooking the eggs. Arrange the eggs in one layer in a saucepan. Pour in enough cold water to cover the eggs by at least 1 inch [2½ cm.], and place the uncovered pan over medium-high heat (above, left). Time the eggs from the moment that a few large bubbles begin to rise from the bottom of the pan (right). Reduce the heat to keep the water below the boiling point. When the eggs have cooked for the time required, remove them from the pan individually with a perforated spoon and plunge them into cold water to stop further cooking.

From Soft-boiled to Overboiled

A four-minute egg. The white is only partly set and the yolk is still liquid. This is the *mollet* egg of French cooking. Because it stays soft inside but still holds its form, it is used whole in assembled dishes (pages 38-39).

A six-minute egg. The white is firmly set, as is most of the yolk, although the center is still soft and dark yellow. This egg is easier to handle and to shell than the *mollet* egg. It can be used whole or halved in assemblies calling for a hard-boiled egg; in fact, some cooks prefer its moister consistency.

2 **Cracking the eggs.** Crack the shell of each egg by grasping the egg in one hand and gently tapping it all over with the back of a spoon or the handle of a knife *(above)*. Alternatively, hold the egg under your palm and roll it back and forth on a smooth surface until the shell becomes marbled with cracks.

3 **Removing the shell.** Gently strip the shell away from the white of the egg, peeling clinging membrane at the same time. Rinse off any remaining shell fragments by dipping the egg in water. If the peeled eggs are not required immediately, store them in a bowl of cold water to keep them from drying. They can be safely kept in the water for two or three hours, if necessary.

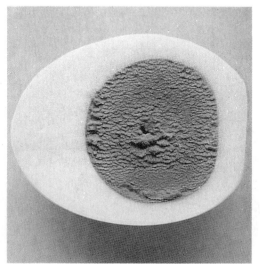

An eight-minute egg. Both the yolk and white are firmly set, although the center of the yolk remains tender. This egg can be cut into halves or quarters, sliced or chopped, but it keeps enough natural moisture so that it can be briefly reheated as part of an assembled dish.

A 10-minute egg. Yolk and white are firmly set and the yolk is pale yellow. This is the classic hard-boiled egg used for stuffing *(page 40)* and as a garnish in salads and other cold dishes. Halved or quartered, sliced or chopped, it can be reheated in sauce or turned into a gratin *(pages 42-43)*.

An overcooked egg. When cooked for much more than 10 minutes or boiled over high heat, the white of the egg turns rubbery and the yolk becomes dry and crumbly. Chemical reactions between the yolk and white may produce a green layer around the outer surface of the yolk and a strong, sulfurous smell.

Poaching: Gentle Heat for the Unprotected Egg

Freshness is a prerequisite in eggs for successful poaching. Immersed in hot liquid, the whites of newly laid eggs cling compactly to the yolks and poach neatly. The whites of eggs more than a week old, however, spread out and overcook.

No special equipment is needed for poaching other than a heavy sauté pan or skillet with a lid. Most so-called poaching pans, built with small cups to contain the eggs, do not actually poach: The eggs are cooked by steaming *(pages 28-29)* rather than by immersion.

The poaching liquid should be at least 2 inches [5 cm.] deep to immerse the eggs, and it should be preheated so that the eggs begin cooking as soon as they are added. Since the temperature of the liquid will drop when the eggs are broken into it, choose the most capacious pan you own to minimize heat loss—and never poach more than four eggs at a time.

The usual liquid is water. However, eggs can also be poached in milk, stock or wine, some of which may then be thickened with butter and flour and made into a sauce for the eggs. Whatever the liquid, it should be kept below a simmer while the eggs cook; stronger heat would turn the whites rubbery. An easy way to control temperature is to bring the liquid to a boil, turn off the heat, add the eggs, and cover the pan to keep the liquid warm.

Many cooks stir the liquid to create a miniature whirlpool before breaking an egg into the pan; the swirling water helps to compact the egg. Other cooks lift the white over the yolk as soon as the egg is immersed. Neither method should be necessary for fresh eggs, but both are useful to keep older eggs from spreading.

As soon as the eggs are done, dip them in cold water to prevent further cooking. Since even the freshest egg has a thin outer ring of white that may spread a little, the cooked egg will inevitably have a straggly outline: Trim off loose strands of white for a neat shape.

The eggs can be served at once—accompanied, if you wish, by an herb-and-butter sauce *(demonstration, bottom; recipe, page 95).* Otherwise, you can place the trimmed eggs in cold water to keep them moist; they can be refrigerated for up to 24 hours. Just before use, reheat the eggs by dipping them in hot water.

Ensuring a Compact Shape

1 **Breaking the eggs.** In a shallow sauté pan, bring 2 to 3 inches [5 to 8 cm.] of plain or lightly salted water to a boil. Turn off the heat and add the eggs at once. To minimize the spreading of the whites, break the eggs directly into the water: Open the shells carefully at the water's surface, so that the eggs slide into the water compactly.

2 **Poaching the eggs.** Cover the pan with a tight-fitting lid in order to retain the heat. Allow the eggs to cook undisturbed for about three minutes, then lift off the lid. When the whites are opaque and the yolks are covered with a thin, translucent layer of white, the eggs are ready.

An Herb and Butter Finish

1 **Reheating the eggs.** Melt some butter in a shallow skillet. When the butter begins to foam, turn down the heat and gently lower the poached eggs into the pan. It is best to use your hands to transfer the eggs to the pan: A spatula might break the fragile yolks.

2 **Adding herbs.** Sprinkle freshly chopped herbs — in this case, tarragon — over the eggs. Baste the eggs with the hot butter several times to warm their tops, then leave them for a few moments to heat through.

3 **Lifting out the eggs.** Remove the eggs from the pan with a perforated spatula and immediately place them in a shallow dish filled with cold water to arrest their cooking. Repeat Steps 1 and 2 as often as needed. The dish chosen for cooling the eggs should hold all of them without crowding.

4 **Draining and trimming.** Lift the eggs out of the water and drain them on a dampened kitchen towel. Using a small knife, trim the eggs by cutting away the thin outer ring of white around the edges. If you do not intend to use the trimmed eggs immediately, transfer them to a second dish of cold water to keep them moist.

3 **Serving the eggs.** When the eggs are hot, add a squeeze of lemon juice to accentuate the flavor of the sauce (above). Then lift the pan off the heat and tilt it over a warmed serving plate to pour out the sauce. Use a spoon to help slide the eggs onto the plate (right).

Steaming and Baking: A Reliance on Integral Garnishes

Though steaming cooks with moist heat and baking with dry heat, both methods envelop the foods in a constant, uniform warmth. Both are appropriate for whole eggs but, to keep their surfaces tender, the eggs must be swathed in protective coatings: cream, stock or sauce.

In the top demonstration at right, eggs are broken into small baking dishes, or ramekins, covered with a shielding layer of cream, and steamed in a water bath. The water is kept at a bare simmer to ensure gentle cooking, and the pan is kept covered to trap the steam and surround the eggs with heat. The water bath can be placed in the oven or, as here, kept on top of the stove.

Preheat the cream before you pour it into the dishes: The warmth will start cooking the eggs immediately, thus reducing the time required. You could add herbs or grated cheese to the ramekins, or replace the cream with butter, a spoonful of meat stock or tomato sauce.

In the bottom demonstration, eggs are baked, uncovered, on a bed of chopped spinach mixed with cream. The flavoring elements themselves provide protection against the oven's enveloping heat: The eggs are placed in depressions in the bed of spinach and are partly submerged by a sauce of heavy cream. Puréed peas, mushrooms or tomatoes would also make a suitable base for the eggs. In this demonstration, several eggs are baked together in one large dish; you could just as well bake the eggs on a vegetable base in individual serving dishes.

A Bath of Butter and Cream

1 **Preparing ramekins.** Lightly butter several ramekins. Warm some cream in a saucepan over medium heat. When the cream is hot but not boiling, spoon a little into each ramekin. Break an egg into the cream in each of the dishes *(above)*.

2 **Adding butter.** Place a small piece of butter on top of each yolk. Do not season the eggs at this stage; because salt on the yolks will mar their smooth finish and pepper may develop an acrid taste, the eggs should be seasoned just before serving.

A Creamy Bed of Spinach

1 **Preparing a spinach base.** Stem spinach leaves and wash them well in several changes of water to remove grit. Parboil the leaves for two minutes, then drain off the hot water. Run cold water over the leaves to cool them, squeeze out excess moisture, and chop the leaves. Melt butter in a pan and add the spinach *(above)*.

2 **Adding cream.** Toss the spinach in the butter over low heat, then pour cream over the spinach. Stir the spinach and cream together. Season to taste with salt, pepper and a pinch of nutmeg. Transfer the creamed spinach to a buttered gratin dish.

3 **Preparing the water bath.** Place the ramekins on a wire rack in a large, shallow pan. Pour enough boiling water into the pan to come two thirds of the way up the sides of the ramekins. Set the pan over low heat; the water should simmer gently. Cover the pan.

4 **Steaming the eggs.** The eggs will take about five minutes to cook. They are done when the whites have set but the yolks remain moist. Lift the ramekins out with a spatula and serve the eggs immediately, still in the ramekins.

3 **Adding the eggs.** With the back of a spoon, form shallow, evenly spaced pockets in the spinach. Break an egg into each depression.

4 **Topping with cream.** When all of the eggs are in place, spoon a tablespoon [15 ml.] of heavy cream over each of the tops. Set the dish in an oven preheated to 350° F. [180° C.].

5 **Serving.** After about eight minutes, check to see if the eggs have cooked; if the whites have not set, bake the eggs for a few minutes more. Serve the eggs on warm plates as soon as they are cooked, presenting each egg on a base of spinach (above). Season to taste.

2

Whole-Egg Presentations

The Art of Assembly

A *mollet* egg in a jacket of shimmering aspic is lifted from a serving dish. To produce the aspic, a clear, gelatinous meat stock was allowed to set in a mold around the eggs and watercress leaves. The jelly was then turned out and garnished with more watercress.

The basic methods of egg cookery are few in number, but egg dishes by the thousands are created by combining cooked eggs with garnishes, then swathing them in sauces. *Mollet* eggs—those boiled for only four minutes *(page 24)*—or poached eggs are most often the centers of such assemblies; their moistness guarantees dishes of surpassing luxury. But egg compositions may also be based on deep-fried eggs *(page 22)* or on hard-boiled eggs whose yolks have been scooped out, moistened with butter or sauce and returned to the whites *(pages 40-41)*. Among these choices, poached or boiled eggs may be prepared a day in advance; deep-fried eggs must be cooked just before a dish is arranged *(pages 24 and 26)*.

The list of possible garnishes and sauces *(pages 32-35)* is long indeed. Cured meats or fish such as Canadian bacon or smoked salmon will add body to an egg dish while providing an emphatic contrast to the eggs' bland taste. Chopped or puréed vegetables can offer subtler flavor contrasts and, if arranged as a bed for the eggs, will help anchor them in place; smooth and slippery poached or *mollet* eggs particularly need a steady foundation. Sauces serve double duty too: Besides adding richness and flavor, they prevent an egg from drying out if the dish is baked.

A solitary egg, garnished and sauced, becomes a beguiling individual package if it rests on an edible platform or is encased in an edible container. For instance, eggs Benedict is a marriage of poached eggs, ham or Canadian bacon, and hollandaise sauce *(recipe, page 166),* presented on an English muffin. More elaborate effects can be achieved by encasing an egg composition in pastry or in hollowed-out vegetables such as artichoke bottoms or baked potatoes *(page 36)*.

Egg assemblies need not always follow the traditional pattern of egg, garnish, sauce and case. For an equally attractive cold presentation, *mollet* eggs and their garnish frequently are suspended in a glistening mold of aspic *(opposite and pages 46-47)*. And hard-boiled eggs lend themselves to still other presentations. The firm yolks and whites may, for instance, be chopped, combined with flour, milk and butter, and formed into croquettes for frying *(pages 44-45)*. Or the chopped eggs may be coated with sauce and gratinéed *(pages 42-43)*. Such dishes, although perhaps less seductive in appearance than single-egg presentations, are no less a delight to a diner, and no less worthy of the cook's attention.

31

Garnishes That Furnish Body and Flavor

Whether the garnish for an egg dish serves as a bed or a covering, it should be prepared so that it will complement, not mask, the eggs' delicate texture and taste. Meats, and fish such as smoked salmon, should be sliced paper-thin or slivered; tiny fish such as salt anchovies may simply be split into fillets *(opposite, bottom right)*. Vegetables, the most commonly used garnishes, should be puréed or sliced thin.

Slicing is the best treatment for particularly fibrous vegetables—for example, green beans or asparagus *(opposite, center)*. The vegetable is usually cut up when it is raw; then the slices are briefly parboiled to tenderize them and quickly sautéed in butter to add flavor.

Dried morels *(opposite, bottom left)*, a delicious type of wild mushroom sold at specialty markets, also call for slicing—not because of fibrousness but to preserve their fine texture. The morels are first soaked in water to rehydrate them, then they are halved and thoroughly washed. The slices need no parboiling but should, like other sliced vegetables, be quickly heated in butter—or better still, in cream—to bring out their earthy taste.

Vegetables can be reduced to a purée in several ways, depending on their age and tenderness. In the case of young and tender leaves of spinach or sorrel *(opposite, top)*, you need only strip away the stems, shred the leaves and stew them in butter: The shreds will soften into a purée. Other vegetables must be puréed through a sieve or in a food mill or a food processor.

Mushrooms are tender enough to be puréed raw *(below, top)*, but almost all other vegetables must be softened beforehand by parboiling. Vegetables with skins, such as lima beans or peas, must be cooked, puréed, then forced through a fine-meshed sieve to remove any skins, ensuring a smooth purée *(below, bottom)*.

All vegetable purées benefit from an enrichment of cream or butter before they are paired with eggs.

A Butter-enriched Purée of Mushrooms

1 **Puréeing mushrooms.** Trim the earthy bases and wipe the mushrooms with a damp towel. Then force them through the medium disk of a food mill.

2 **Sautéing mushrooms.** Squeeze a little lemon juice over the puréed mushrooms to prevent darkening. Melt butter in a pan and stir in the purée.

3 **Finishing the purée.** Stirring continuously, cook the purée over fairly high heat for three or four minutes, or until most of the juices evaporate.

Peas Sieved Twice for Smoothness

1 **Preparing peas.** Cook fresh peas in salted, boiling water for five minutes, or until tender. Drain the peas and purée them through a strainer or a food mill.

2 **Removing skins.** Press the peas through a drum sieve by spoonfuls. Scrape the flesh from the underside into the bowl. Discard the skins.

3 **Binding the purée.** Stir the purée over high heat for two or three minutes. Remove from the heat and beat in a generous amount of butter or cream.

A Creamy Reduction of Sorrel

1 **Shredding sorrel.** Fold the leaves lengthwise and strip off the stems. Roll several leaves into a tight bundle. Slice the bundle into shreds with a knife.

2 **Stewing sorrel.** Melt butter over low heat in a heavy pot; do not use aluminum or cast iron, which would affect the sorrel's flavor. Stir in the sorrel.

3 **Thickening with cream.** Stirring occasionally, simmer for 10 minutes until a purée is formed. Stir in heavy cream, then reduce as desired.

Tender Pieces of Asparagus

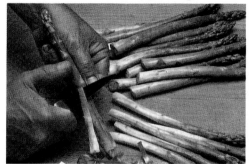  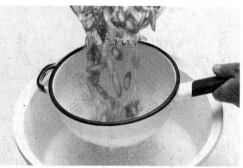

1 **Peeling stalks.** Trim off the woody base of each asparagus. Cutting toward the tip, pare the tough skin from the lower part of the stalk.

2 **Slicing stalks.** With a sharp knife, cut the stalks diagonally into thin slices. Plunge the slices into salted, boiling water for a few seconds to soften them.

3 **Finishing the cooking.** Drain the slices in a colander (above). Then sauté them in melted butter over high heat for a few seconds until glossy.

A Delicate Fusion of Morels and Cream

1 **Preparing morels.** Soak dried morels in cold water for at least an hour. Trim the stem ends, cut the morels in half and wash them under running water.

2 **Stewing.** Cook the morels in butter over low heat for three or four minutes. Stir in heavy cream. Simmer gently for two or three minutes more.

A Salty Savor of Anchovy

Boning anchovies. Soak salt anchovies in water to remove excess salt. With your fingers, pry the fillets away from the backbone of each anchovy.

A Trio of Basic Sauces

Eggs can be partnered by many diverse sauces, from creamy emulsions that accent the eggs' own flavor to spicy blends that provide a piquant contrast. Here, three classic preparations—white sauce, hollandaise and tomato sauce—represent the spectrum of possibilities. The white sauce (*right, top; recipe, page 165*) is based on a roux—a paste made by cooking flour with butter—thinned with milk. Hollandaise (*right, bottom; recipe, page 165*) is an emulsion made by beating butter into warmed egg yolks. The tomato sauce (*far right; recipe, page 166*) is a flavored purée that is prepared by cooking tomatoes until they turn soft, then sieving them.

All of these sauces benefit from gentle cooking. In the case of the white sauce, lengthy simmering removes the taste of raw flour. You can use the white sauce as is or enrich the completed mixture by stirring into it as much as half its volume of heavy cream. A white sauce may also act as a base for flavorings, stirred in just before serving. Add grated Parmesan or shredded Cheddar or Gruyère, for example, to make a cheese sauce.

Hollandaise cooks more quickly than white sauce, but requires more care: Too much heat will cause the emulsion to separate. Rather than risk problems by preparing the sauce over direct heat, cook the hollandaise in a pan set in a large pot of simmering water. As an additional precaution, mix a little water into the egg yolks before heating them to help keep them fluid.

Because tomatoes have a high water content, they need no additional liquid to form a sauce. After about 20 minutes of simmering—in a pan made of material other than aluminum, which would interact with the tomatoes to produce an off taste—their flesh will be soft enough for sieving. The sauce should then be returned to the heat and simmered, uncovered, for up to 15 minutes to reduce it to the consistency required. After only two or three minutes it will be thick enough to serve on its own. If reduced further, the purée can be added to other sauces to provide extra flavor and color; for example, 2 or 3 tablespoons [30 or 45 ml.] will give a white sauce a delicate tomato taste and a rose-pink hue.

White Sauce: Simmering for a Smooth Flavor

1 Making the roux. Heat the butter in a heavy saucepan set over low heat. As soon as the butter melts, add the flour, distributing it evenly in the pan.

2 Whisking the roux. Using a whisk or a wooden spoon, immediately stir the flour into the butter to form a smooth paste. Cook this roux gently for two or three minutes, stirring it constantly, until the mixture has a granular texture.

Hollandaise: An Emulsion of Egg Yolks and Butter

1 Preparing a water bath. Set a trivet or wire rack in a large pot. Half-fill the pot with hot water. Bring the water to a boil, then reduce the heat to keep it just below the simmering point. Put egg yolks into a pan small enough to fit inside the pot; add a tablespoonful [15 ml.] of cold water to the yolks.

2 Whisking the yolks. Stand the pan on the trivet; the water should reach two thirds of the way up the sides of the pan. With a whisk, beat the egg yolks to combine them with the water. Continue to whisk until the mixture becomes smooth and creamy.

3 **Adding milk.** Pour all of the milk into the roux at once, whisking the mixture to blend it smoothly. Increase the heat to medium. While the sauce is coming to a boil, continue whisking to prevent any lumps from forming.

4 **Simmering the sauce.** Turn the heat very low so that the sauce cooks at a bare simmer. Let it simmer uncovered for 30 to 40 minutes, stirring it occasionally, until the sauce clings to the whisk in a thick layer *(above)*. Before serving, season with salt, pepper and, if you like, grated nutmeg.

3 **Forming the sauce.** Add a handful of butter cubes to the pan, and whisk until the butter is absorbed into the egg mixture. Add the remaining cubes in batches, a few at a time; whisk in each batch before adding more butter.

4 **Finishing the sauce.** Continue whisking until the sauce is thick and creamy — about 10 minutes. Season to taste with white pepper, cayenne pepper and salt. Finish off the sauce by adding a few drops of lemon juice. If the sauce is too thick to pour easily, whisk in some lukewarm water to thin it.

A Fragrant Tomato Purée

1 **Starting the sauce.** Sauté chopped onion in olive oil until soft. Add garlic, herbs, seasonings, sugar and quartered tomatoes.

2 **Sieving the sauce.** Simmer for 20 to 30 minutes, until the tomatoes soften to a pulp. Then use a pestle to force the mixture through a sieve.

3 **Reducing the sauce.** Return the sauce to medium heat. Simmer it, stirring occasionally, until it reaches the desired consistency.

A Multiplicity of Edible Cases

Edible cases just the right size to hold an egg, its garnish and its sauce can be formed from bread, pastry or vegetables. The shape, texture and taste of each type of case play a large part in determining the nature of the assembled dish.

Hearty egg assemblies, for instance, might well begin with baked potatoes whose tops have been sliced off. The flesh can be scooped out, puréed and used to line the cases *(top)*. To prepare the potatoes for baking, simply scrub their skins and pierce them to allow steam to escape. Medium-sized potatoes will take about an hour to cook in a preheated 375° F. [190° C.] oven. The scooped-out flesh of the potato can be mashed with butter and seasonings, as shown here, or mixed with a puréed vegetable *(pages 32-33)*. Use the back of a spoon to pack the flesh back into the potatoes.

For a lighter dish, vegetable cases can be fashioned from hollowed-out tomato halves or from boiled artichoke bottoms *(right, bottom)*. Raw artichokes call for special measures to prevent discoloration. Use a stainless-steel knife for trimming and rub cut surfaces with lemon. As soon as you have trimmed the artichokes, put them into water mixed with lemon juice until you are ready to cook them— in an enameled, stainless-steel or tin-lined pan. After cooking, the inedible chokes—clusters of fine fibers in their centers—can be removed easily. For flavor and gloss, sauté the bottoms with the bases downward for two or three minutes, spooning melted butter into the hollow interiors; then turn them over to warm the tops.

To provide a contrast in texture to soft, cooked eggs, bread cases *(opposite page, top)* are made from firm, homemade-type bread that is slightly stale so that it can be shaped easily. Painted with melted butter, then baked, the bread crisps and turns deep gold.

By lining small tart pans with short-crust dough *(recipe, page 167)*, you can make shallow, individual pastry cases. Stack the lined pans to prevent the dough from bubbling *(opposite page, bottom)*, and bake them in a 425° F. [220° C.] oven. Separate the pans and spread them out for the last five minutes of cooking to crisp the pastry.

Hollowing Baked Potatoes

1 **Scooping out the flesh.** Bake potatoes in a hot oven until they are soft. Slice the top off each potato; scoop out the flesh and put it in a sieve.

2 **Lining the potato cases.** With a pestle, push the flesh through the sieve. Add butter and seasonings to taste. Line the cases with the purée.

Turning Artichoke Bottoms

1 **Removing outer leaves.** Break the stem off each artichoke. Snap off the tough outer leaves. Rub the cut surfaces with a lemon half.

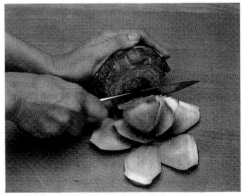

2 **Topping the artichoke.** Grasp the artichoke firmly. Using a stainless-steel knife, cut off the leafy tops at the point where the leaves are indented.

3 **Paring the bottom.** Starting at the stem, pare away the dark green exterior of the artichoke bottom. Put the bottom into acidulated water to await cooking.

4 **Removing the chokes.** Boil the bottoms until tender — about 20 minutes — then drain them on a towel. Scrape out the chokes *(above)*.

Sculpting Bread Rounds

1 **Shaping the cases.** Cut a round from a 1-inch [2½-cm.] slice of bread. Cut a circle ½ inch [1 cm.] inside the edge, down to ½ inch from the base.

2 **Hollowing the interior.** Insert a knife horizontally ½ inch [1 cm.] above the base of the bread round. Swivel the blade to free the central disk of bread.

3 **Baking the cases.** Lift out the centers and paint each case inside and out with melted butter. Bake at 325° F. [160° C.] for 25 minutes, until crisp.

Shaping Pastry Shells

1 **Combining butter and flour.** Put flour into a bowl with a little salt. Add cold butter, cut into cubes. Use two knives to cut the butter into the flour *(above)*.

2 **Adding water.** When the butter pieces are thoroughly coated with flour, pour in a little cold water and work it into the dough with a fork *(above)*.

3 **Gathering the dough.** Knead the dough briefly until you can gather it into a ball; then enclose it in plastic wrap and refrigerate it for at least one hour.

4 **Rolling out the dough.** Put the chilled dough on a cold, floured surface. Flatten the dough a little, then turn it to flour the other side. Roll it out thin.

5 **Lining tins.** Invert tart pans over the dough. Cut around each pan, allowing a 1-inch [2½-cm.] border. Line the pans; trim the edges with your thumb.

6 **Baking.** Stack the pans on a baking sheet; top with an empty pan. Bake for 15 minutes; unstack the pans *(above)* and bake for five minutes more.

Assemblies: Combinations without Limit

The choice of the garnishes, sauces and cases *(pages 32-37)* that are combined with cooked eggs naturally depends on personal taste and on what is available. But in selecting elements and in assembling them, it is important to consider how the eggs are cooked.

Poached, soft-boiled *mollet* and deep-fried eggs can all be used in such assemblages. Of these choices, a deep-fried egg blends particularly well with robust garnishes and sauces because of its own hearty flavor. The bread-case assembly shown on the opposite page *(far right, below)*, for example, combines a deep-fried egg with chopped spinach and salt anchovies. The golden tint of a deep-fried egg should not be masked by a sauce; instead, surround the assembly with a border of sauce—in this instance, a spicy tomato preparation.

Both the flavor and the appearance of poached or *mollet* eggs are enhanced by covering the eggs with mild-flavored sauces or purées. Then, if you like, the surface may be gratinéed to give the sauce or purée a brown top. For such a finish, sprinkle buttered bread crumbs over the assembly and bake it for a few minutes in a 425° F. [220° C.] oven, or run it under a broiler. The sauce will prevent the eggs from overcooking while the crumbs brown and crisp. Choose a white sauce—perhaps adding cheese, cream, or a spinach or tomato purée—for a gratin; a delicate sauce such as hollandaise would curdle in the high heat.

Alternatively, you can top the gratin with cheese instead of bread crumbs; the brief cooking process melts the cheese and gives the sauce a pale golden surface. The cheese should be a strongly flavored variety that is hard enough to grate—Parmesan or aged Cheddar, for example.

Whatever assembly you choose to prepare, plan the cooking of the different elements so that all are warm when the time comes to combine them. Make roux-based sauces first, so that they can simmer while you ready other ingredients. An emulsion type of sauce such as hollandaise is best made immediately before use but, if necessary, it will keep for up to half an hour if you stand the saucepan in hot water. Warm any precooked purée or garnish over low heat, stirring it frequently while it reheats to prevent it from sticking. Heat prepared pastry and vegetable cases in a slow oven.

Poached eggs should be trimmed after cooking and stored in cold water to keep them moist. Just before use, dip them briefly in hot water to warm them, then drain them on towels. *Mollet* eggs can be treated the same way. However, deep-fried eggs will not keep well and should be cooked immediately before composing any assemblage that includes them.

A pink-hued sauce. Make a white sauce *(page 34-35)*. Heat creamed morels *(page 33)* with slivers of ham. Fill prebaked pastry cases *(page 37)* with the morel mixture; top with poached eggs. Stir tomato purée into the sauce; pour it over the cases.

A hollandaise coating. Make a hollandaise sauce *(page 34-35)* and prepare bread cases *(page 37)*. Warm slivers of prosciutto in butter and pile them into the baked bread cases. Top with poached eggs. Pour the sauce over the cases and serve.

A prosciutto topping. Make a mushroom purée and a tomato sauce *(pages 32 and 35)*. Fill artichoke bottoms *(page 36)* with the mushroom purée and set them on a plate. Top the artichokes with *mollet* eggs, cover with the tomato sauce and garnish with slivers of prosciutto.

A cheese crust. Prepare a cream-enriched white sauce *(pages 34-35)*. Using a processor or food mill, purée well-squeezed parboiled spinach; mix it with puréed potato to fill potato cases *(page 36)*. Top with poached eggs. Set in gratin dishes. Cover with sauce, sprinkle with cheese, and gratiné.

An asparagus filling. Make a cream-enriched white sauce *(pages 34-35)*. Prepare an asparagus garnish *(page 33)*. Fill pastry cases *(page 37)* with the asparagus. Top with poached eggs. Place on ovenproof dishes. Cover with sauce, sprinkle with grated Parmesan and gratiné.

An anchovy garnish. Make a tomato sauce *(page 35)*. Prepare anchovy fillets *(page 33)*. Fill bread cases *(page 37)* with spinach that has been parboiled, squeezed dry, chopped and stewed in butter. Top with deep-fried eggs. Garnish with anchovies and surround with sauce.

Stuffing and Dressing Hard-boiled Eggs

Halved, hard-boiled eggs are prime candidates for assemblies if the yolks are first removed, mashed to a paste, and moistened with some creamy element that counteracts their relative dryness. Because the moistener binds the mashed yolks, the paste can be mounded up when it is stuffed into the whites, producing the shape of whole eggs. Since mashing and moistening add to the bulk of the yolks, some halved whites will normally be left over; chopped, they can be used to garnish other dishes.

In the demonstration here, the egg yolks are bound with butter and laced with mustard, salt and pepper. Cream or a vegetable purée could replace the butter. Instead of mustard, the yolks might be flavored with chopped fresh herbs or a *tapenade*—puréed ripe olives blended with anchovies, garlic, olive oil and capers *(recipe, page 166)*.

The stuffed eggs can be assembled with any one of the cases, purées and sauces shown on pages 32-37. In this demonstration, each egg is placed on an artichoke bottom that is first lined with a purée of peas; the eggs are then coated with a basic white sauce *(recipe, page 165)* that has been enriched with cream and lightly colored with tomato purée.

By the time the eggs have been stuffed, incorporated into the dish and covered with sauce, they will need reheating. You can place them in a 425° F. [220° C.] oven to warm them through simply as they are. Or the assemblies can be sprinkled with grated cheese, as here, and baked for a golden brown gratin topping.

1 **Preparing the stuffing.** Hard-boil eggs, then peel them *(page 25)*. Cut the eggs in half lengthwise. With the point of a small knife, remove the yolk halves from the whites *(above)*. Put the yolks in a bowl with softened butter, salt, freshly ground pepper and a little prepared mustard. Use a fork to mash the ingredients together thoroughly.

2 **Stuffing the eggs.** Fill the hollows in the neatest of the halved egg whites with the stuffing mixture. Then place more stuffing on top of each filled half. With a spoon, mold the stuffing to give the shape of a whole egg.

5 **Topping the eggs with cheese.** Grate some hard cheese *(page 11)*; Parmesan is used here, but aged Gruyère or Cheddar could be substituted. Sprinkle the cheese over the eggs and cases. Place the dish in a preheated 425° F. [220° C.] oven.

3 **Lining the cases.** Spoon a layer of warm pea purée *(page 32)* into artichoke bottoms that have been boiled and then sautéed in butter for extra flavor *(page 36)*. Use the back of a spoon to spread the purée smooth.

4 **Saucing the eggs.** Place the stuffed eggs on top of the beds of pea purée. Place the filled artichoke bottoms in a buttered ovenproof dish. Ladle a tomato-flavored white sauce over the eggs to coat them and their cases completely *(above)*.

6 **Serving the dish.** Bake the assembly for five to 10 minutes, until the eggs are heated through, the sauce is bubbling hot and the cheese is melted. If the cheese has not browned, place the dish under a hot broiler for a few seconds. Transfer the egg assemblies to plates and spoon sauce around them.

Coating to Counteract Dryness

In addition to being stuffed and presented in cases, hard-boiled eggs may simply be halved or quartered and reheated with a sauce. Besides contributing flavor, the sauce will counterbalance the relative dryness of the eggs.

Any thick, well-flavored sauce can be used to coat the eggs, including one made from a vegetable purée, such as tomato sauce *(page 166)*, or the creamed sorrel sauce featured in the top demonstration. Sorrel lends a refreshing hint of tartness to the dish; for a milder effect, you could substitute creamed spinach *(recipe, page 166)*. To add another textural dimension, a gratin of crisp bread crumbs can top the sauce. The crumbs will brown more evenly and have a finer flavor if they are first sautéed in butter *(Step 2, top)*.

A thickened, flavored white sauce also has sufficient body to complement hard-boiled eggs. In the bottom demonstration *(recipe, page 165)*, the sauce is prepared from a base of onions that have been softened in butter, then mixed with flour to form a sort of roux. Like any roux-based sauce, the mixture needs lengthy simmering to rid it of the taste of flour. Near the end of cooking, raw egg yolks and fresh herbs are stirred in for extra richness. The quartered eggs are added at the last minute to warm them through.

There are many possible variations on this simple sauce mixture. You can add extra ingredients—chopped chard leaves, green peppers or mushrooms, for example—to the onions midway through cooking, or else enrich the finished sauce with heavy cream. To further extend the range of flavors, you could replace the milk in the sauce with a meat stock to create a velouté.

A Creamed Sorrel Gratin

1 **Coating the eggs.** Prepare a creamed sorrel purée *(page 33)*. While the sorrel is stewing, peel hard-boiled eggs. Cut them in half lengthwise and place them in a buttered ovenproof dish with their cut sides up. Spoon the sorrel sauce over the eggs *(above)*.

2 **Preparing bread crumbs.** Remove the crusts from sliced bread; tear up the bread and grind the pieces in a blender or food processor to make crumbs. Melt butter in a skillet set over low heat. Stirring continuously, cook the bread crumbs for five or six minutes, until they turn a golden brown.

A Complementary Onion Sauce

1 **Starting the onions.** Melt butter in a heavy pan set over low heat. Cut the onions into thick slices and add them to the butter *(above)*. Stir until the onions are well coated with butter. If you like, season them with salt and pepper.

2 **Making the roux.** Cover the pan, set it over a heat-diffusing pad and let the onions cook at a gentle simmer. After eight to 10 minutes, when the onions have softened and become a pale golden color, sprinkle flour over them. Stir the onions until the flour and the butter form a smooth paste.

3 **Assembling the gratin.** Remove the bread crumbs from the heat. After about one minute, when the crumbs are cool enough to handle, use your fingers to sprinkle them liberally over the sorrel-coated eggs *(above)*.

4 **Serving the eggs.** Place the dish in an oven preheated to 400° F. [200° C.]. Bake for about 15 minutes, until the sauce and eggs are heated through and the surface is lightly browned. Remove the dish from the oven and serve the eggs on warmed plates, including some of the gratin topping in each portion.

3 **Making the sauce.** Pour milk into the onion roux *(above)*. Turn up the heat and stir continuously while the sauce comes to a boil. Reduce the heat to low and simmer the sauce for 25 to 30 minutes.

4 **Adding the eggs.** While the sauce is simmering, hard-boil and peel eggs. Cut the eggs into quarters. Stir in two or three raw egg yolks, beaten with a little cream, to enrich the sauce; for extra piquancy, sprinkle in some herbs — in this case, chopped parsley. Add the quartered hard-boiled eggs to the sauce *(above)*.

5 **Serving.** Leave the pan on low heat for two or three minutes to warm the eggs. Serve the eggs directly onto individual warmed plates. Alternatively, you could transfer the eggs to a shallow, buttered ovenproof dish, cover them with crumbs *(Steps 2 and 3, above)*, and gratiné the dish under a hot broiler for two or three minutes.

Soft-centered Packages with Crunchy Outer Crusts

Mixed with ingredients that bind and moisten them, chopped hard-boiled eggs can be shaped into patties, coated with a layer of bread crumbs, and fried to produce croquettes that are crisp on the outside and appetizingly tender within (recipe, page 106).

In this demonstration, the binder is made with the same ingredients as a white sauce, but the ratio of milk to roux is lower. The resulting mixture has a stiffer consistency than a white sauce, and it is cooked only long enough to thicken it to a paste. A raw egg yolk stirred into the paste adds extra richness. If you like, you can use stock instead of milk or flavor the binder with herbs, finely chopped mushrooms or ham.

After the egg pieces have been added, the mixture should be left to cool thoroughly: It will firm up and become easier to shape. While the mixture is cooling, you can prepare the bread crumbs; use bread at least two or three days old, which will crumble easily.

The croquettes can be cooked rapidly in deep oil. But you may find it more convenient to cook them, as here, in fairly shallow oil—just enough to half-cover them. Either way, the oil should be heated to about 375° F. [190° C.]. Check the temperature with a rapid-response thermometer or by dropping in a cube of stale bread: The bread will become golden brown in 60 seconds if the oil is hot enough. In shallow oil the croquettes must be turned over halfway through the cooking; depending on their thickness, they will take a total of five to 10 minutes to crisp on both sides.

1 **Preparing the eggs.** Peel hard-boiled eggs and cut each egg in half lengthwise. Lay the halves flat sides down and cut them into thick crosswise slices (above), then chop these slices into equal-sized pieces.

2 **Preparing the sauce.** Melt butter and stir in flour to make a thick roux. Then add milk and stir the mixture for four to five minutes, until it boils and thickens. Remove the pan from the heat and let the sauce cool slightly. Stir in a beaten egg yolk (above). Season the sauce to taste; if you like, add a little grated nutmeg or cayenne pepper.

5 **Frying the croquettes.** Pour oil — enough to reach about halfway up the sides of the croquettes — into a skillet. Set the pan over high heat. When the oil is hot but not smoking, adjust the heat to medium and lower the croquettes one by one into the oil. When the undersides have browned, after three to five minutes, turn the croquettes and brown the other sides. Drain the croquettes on paper towels; dry the tops with more towels.

3 **Adding the eggs.** Gently fold the chopped egg pieces into the hot sauce. Cool the mixture to room temperature — this takes about 30 minutes. You can place the mixture in the refrigerator to speed the cooling process.

4 **Shaping the egg croquettes.** Use a serving spoon to scoop up the cooled egg mixture, a heaped spoonful at a time. Set each spoonful in bread crumbs; sprinkle more bread crumbs over the top, then roll the croquette over until it is completely coated *(above, left).* Pat each croquette with the palm of your hand to flatten it slightly and to press the bread crumbs in place *(right).* Let the croquettes rest for a few minutes to set the coating.

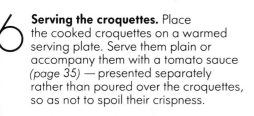

6 **Serving the croquettes.** Place the cooked croquettes on a warmed serving plate. Serve them plain or accompany them with a tomato sauce *(page 35)* — presented separately rather than poured over the croquettes, so as not to spoil their crispness.

A Gleaming Aspic Ring

A transparent amber jelly sets off the simple beauty of the egg's form, and the combination is as pleasing to the palate as it is to the eye. The softness of poached and *mollet* eggs, in particular, is enhanced by the jelly, itself moist enough to melt on the tongue.

Such a jelly, known as aspic, is essentially a veal stock made with some gelatinous meats—calf's or pig's feet, for example—so that the liquid will set firmly when it is chilled (*box, bottom; recipe, pages 164-165*).

Crystal clarity is the distinguishing feature of a good aspic. To achieve transparency, the stock must be scrupulously skimmed of impurities as it comes to a simmer, then strained through dampened muslin or cheesecloth at the end of cooking. Finally, when the jelly cools, every remaining trace of fat must be removed with a spoon or damp cloth.

If the jelly lacks the perfect transparency an aspic requires—perhaps because the stock accidentally reached a boil—you can clarify it. Melt the jelly by warming it over medium heat, then increase the heat to high and add one raw egg white and its crushed shell for each quart [1 liter] of liquid. Bring this mixture to a boil, then turn off the heat and let the stock rest without stirring for 10 minutes while the egg whites and shells bond with the impurities in the stock. Repeat the procedure twice, then strain the stock and chill it again.

Eggs are often set in aspic in individual molds. For a different presentation, you can set several eggs together in a ring mold, as shown in this demonstration. If you like, add garnishes to flavor and decorate the dish. Leaf garnishes—tarragon, for instance, or the watercress used here—should be dipped in hot water to wilt them so that they will lie flat. Other garnishes include slices of pitted ripe olives or strips of ham, prosciutto or roasted sweet peppers. Whatever your choice, set the garnish in the bottom of the mold between layers of aspic to keep it in place before adding the eggs.

1 **Setting the eggs.** Melt jellied stock *(box, below)* over low heat. Ladle a thin layer of the stock into a ring mold and refrigerate it for about 10 minutes, or until set. Dip sprigs of watercress in hot water, cut off the stems and dry the leaves. Dip them into the melted stock. Arrange the leaves around the mold, then refrigerate the mold again. Add another thin layer of stock, refrigerate, and when the second layer has set, position peeled *mollet* eggs between the leaves *(above)*. Add just enough stock to immerse the eggs, and cover the mold with foil or plastic wrap.

Making a Jellied Stock

1 **Assembling the meats.** Set a rack in a pot to prevent sticking. Put bones and meat—in this case, veal neck and shank and pig's feet—on the rack. Pour in cold water to cover the ingredients by 2 inches [5 cm.].

2 **Removing the scum.** Set the pot over low heat. As the water approaches a boil, skim off the froth that rises to the surface. Add cold water and skim again as the water returns to a boil. Repeat until no more scum rises. Do not stir.

2 **Unmolding.** Chill the mold for at least four hours to firm the jelly. Place a chilled serving plate face down over the mold and invert both plate and mold. Place a hot, damp cloth over the mold for a few seconds to loosen the jelly. Holding the mold tight against the plate, shake, then lift the mold *(above)*. The dish is now ready for serving *(right)*; divide it by cutting between the eggs.

3 **Flavoring.** Add salt and aromatics; carrots, onions (one stuck with cloves), garlic, and a bouquet of leek, celery, bay, parsley and thyme are used here. Partially cover the pot and barely simmer the stock for about five hours.

4 **Straining.** Drape a double layer of dampened muslin or cheesecloth inside a large colander set over a bowl. Empty the stockpot into the colander and let the liquid drain into the bowl. Do not press down on the ingredients.

5 **Setting the stock.** Refrigerate the stock for eight to 12 hours to set it. With a spoon or a hot, damp cloth, carefully remove the surface fat. The jelly should be perfectly clear *(above)*.

3
Beaten-Egg Cookery
The Many Guises of Scrambled Eggs and Omelets

The simple action of beating an egg makes a crucial difference in the way it cooks. Left whole, the white firms more rapidly than the yolk; blended, the white and yolk set simultaneously. If stirred constantly—scrambled—the beaten egg remains semiliquid. Unstirred, the egg thickens and coheres, a characteristic that is exploited to produce omelets.

Gentle cooking is essential for impeccable scrambled eggs: The lower the heat and the longer the cooking time, the creamier the finished dish will be. Standard additions are salt, pepper and butter, which is used to coat the pan and to enrich the eggs. However, all sorts of new flavors and textures can be created by including other ingredients. For instance, sliced precooked asparagus *(page 52)* can be added midway through scrambling to warm with the eggs, or the eggs can be stirred into semiliquid vegetable mixtures while these are cooking gently *(pages 54-55)*.

Omelets are usually cooked over high heat to create firm outer casings with soft interiors. They, too, can be varied in a multitude of ways. Rolled *(opposite)* or folded, they may be served as they are or else used to enclose a filling—either wrapped inside or inserted into a slit cut in the omelet's upper surface *(pages 56-59)*. Left unrolled, a pair of omelets may sandwich a filling *(pages 60-61)*. Combining eggs with a generous quantity of other ingredients *(pages 62-63)* produces pancake omelets, to be served on their own or as a multilayered loaf *(pages 65-67)*. For an unusually fluffy omelet that will puff up in the pan, the whites and yolks may be beaten separately before they are folded together *(pages 68-69)*.

Eggs can be scrambled in any heavy-bottomed pan that will conduct heat well, but for the most delicate versions of this dish the pan is set in a water bath or over a heat-diffusing pad. An omelet, however, should be prepared in a special heavy omelet or crepe pan with sloped sides that will allow it to slip out easily. Omelet and crepe pans are traditionally made of heavy carbon steel and, when new, require seasoning with flavorless vegetable oil to ensure a slick surface. First wash and dry the pan, then brush the inside surfaces generously with oil and pour in more oil to a depth of ¼ inch [6 mm.]. Set the pan over very low heat. When the oil starts to smoke, pour it off and wipe the pan dry.

Once you season the pan, never wash it, or you will have to season it again; simply wipe the pan after use with a dry cloth or a paper towel.

A classic rolled omelet, its center still slightly liquid, slips from the pan onto a warmed serving plate. The golden product of nothing more than eggs beaten with cubed butter and seasonings, the omelet has cooked in melted butter over high heat for less than a minute—just long enough to color its underside lightly.

An American Approach to Scrambling

Scrambled eggs is a favorite American dish, and one that lends itself to a number of subtle variations. The cook is presented with choices at the very first step of the operation—beating the eggs. You can beat them only until the yolks break, so that the final dish will be streaked with white; or you can blend yolks and whites to a uniform golden color, as in this demonstration.

Seasonings such as salt, pepper and herbs will permeate the dish best if incorporated when the eggs are beaten. Some cooks also add up to a teaspoon [5 ml.] of water for each egg to make the end product lighter and more delicate in flavor. Adding milk, cream or sour cream instead yields richer eggs.

After beating, the eggs are cooked very gently to keep them tender: High heat would drive off moisture and toughen eggs. Constantly stirring the eggs trans-

forms them into soft curds, leaving no trace of hard lumps.

How long the scrambled eggs cook depends on whether the diners want them firm or creamily moist. In any case, the pan should be removed from the stove while the eggs are still slightly underdone; they will continue cooking for a minute or more. To arrest their cooking at the precise degree of doneness desired and to add a sheen to the eggs, some cooks will stir in bits of butter, a splash of cream or a beaten raw egg.

The traditional garnishes for scrambled eggs range from bacon, ham and scrapple to sausages such as the plump homemade-style links shown here. For perfect links, pierce the sausages before starting to cook them in cold water *(box, below)*. By the time the water evaporates, the sausages will have released enough fat for frying.

1 **Beating the eggs.** Break eggs into a bowl; in this example 10 eggs are used to provide four servings. Mix the eggs with a whisk or fork until the whites and yolks are blended but not foamy. Season the eggs with salt and pepper.

Sausages Browned in Their Own Juices

1 **Piercing the sausages.** Cut the sausages into individual links. In a quick, jabbing motion, pierce each link in several places with a fork or skewer. Place the sausages in a heavy skillet.

2 **Starting in water.** Add enough cold water to cover the bottom of the skillet, and bring the water to a boil over medium heat. Cook the sausages until the water evaporates, rolling them from time to time with a spatula in order to cook them evenly.

3 **Frying the sausages.** Reduce the heat to low. Fry the sausages in their exuded fat for 15 to 20 minutes, turning them occasionally to keep them from sticking. When the sausages are browned, lift them out of the skillet with the spatula and drain them on paper towels before serving.

2 **Beginning the cooking.** In a heavy skillet over medium heat, melt 1 or 2 teaspoons [5 or 10 ml.] of butter for each egg. When the butter foams, but before it browns, pour in the eggs and tip the skillet to spread them evenly. Immediately turn the heat to low.

3 **Stirring the eggs.** With a wooden spoon, stir the eggs in a continuous figure-8 motion, moving the spoon across the bottom of the skillet and around its sides to scrape the cooked portions of the eggs into the uncooked portions. Stir until the eggs are uniformly thick and no longer runny, yet still soft and moist.

4 **Serving the eggs.** Tip the scrambled eggs onto a warmed platter. Dot the top with butter to make them glossy. Surround the eggs with a ring of link sausages and garnish them with freshly chopped parsley.

Gentle Cooking for a Custardy Result

Not all scrambled eggs develop into soft curds. In fact, the most refined version of the dish has an extraordinarily smooth, custard-like consistency, the result of slow, gentle cooking and a generous investment of butter.

A heavy pan that will conduct heat uniformly is essential to success. It is possible to achieve the desired creaminess by setting the pan on a heat-diffusing pad over low heat. But that method may need 20 minutes or more of almost constant stirring, whereas the eggs can be scrambled in 15 minutes or less if the pan is first placed on a wire rack set in a large casserole of hot water, as demonstrated here. The water surrounds the eggs to warm them evenly, thereby minimizing the risk of overcooking, yet speeding the thickening process.

Scrambled in this fashion, the eggs are delicious on their own. However, you can add extra flavors by sprinkling herbs — marjoram or chervil, for example — into the eggs before scrambling them. Or, for the epitome of luxury, you can include

truffle, available fresh during the winter months at some specialty food markets. To obtain the full benefit of its pervasive aroma, add slices or parings of the truffle to the unbeaten eggs about an hour ahead of time and allow them to steep at room temperature.

A more substantial garnish, such as the asparagus slices shown here, should be fully cooked and added while still hot toward the end of the cooking, just as the eggs begin to thicken. Other suitable vegetable garnishes are sautéed celery slices, parboiled peas or green beans, or sliced artichoke bottoms that have been stewed in butter. Or you could add sautéed chicken livers, ham julienne, and either fresh or smoked fish.

Whether the eggs are served on their own or with a garnish, it is vital to prevent them from drying into lumps after the right consistency is reached. Extra butter or a little cream stirred into the eggs as soon as they are removed from the heat will arrest the cooking while providing further enrichment.

1 **Preparing the eggs.** Coat a heavy saucepan generously with softened butter. Break eggs into a bowl; season with salt and pepper, and add 1 tablespoon [15 ml.] of cubed butter for every two eggs. Beat the eggs with a fork to blend the yolks and whites, and tip them into the pan (above).

3 **Adding a garnish.** When the eggs thicken lightly, you can add any hot, precooked garnish — in this demonstration, sliced asparagus that have been parboiled for a few seconds, drained and then briefly sautéed in butter (page 33). Stir the garnish into the scrambled eggs (above).

4 **Checking consistency.** Remove the pan from the water. Continue to stir: The heat from the pan and its contents will keep the mixture cooking. Should the eggs fail to reach the consistency you require, replace the pan briefly in the hot water to further thicken the mixture.

5 **Serving the eggs.** When the mixture has reached the desired creamy consistency, add a handful of cold butter cubes to arrest the cooking and to provide extra richness. Stir until the butter is thoroughly incorporated, then serve the scrambled eggs straight from the pan onto warmed plates.

2 **Scrambling the eggs.** Place a wire rack inside a large casserole set on the stove. Stand the pan of eggs on the rack and pour enough boiling water into the casserole to come two thirds of the way up the sides of the pan. Turn on the heat and adjust it to keep the water just below the boiling point. With a wooden spoon, stir the eggs as the butter melts *(above, left)*. Continue stirring — scraping the bottom and sides of the pan, where the mixture cooks first — as the eggs thicken and turn opaque *(right)*.

6 **Garnishing with croutons.** If you like, garnish each serving of scrambled eggs with a scattering of croutons *(right)*, made by sautéeing small cubes of slightly stale bread in butter for two to three minutes until golden *(recipe, page 166)*. Drain the croutons on paper towels before serving.

Scrambling Eggs in Aromatic Blends

The technique of scrambling eggs *(pages 50-53)* can be adapted to a range of dishes that share a smooth creaminess yet vary widely in flavor. Combined with a liquid and grated cheese, for instance, scrambled eggs yield a pungent, flowing mixture reminiscent of a Swiss fondue *(pages 86-87)*. In the demonstration at right, the liquid is white wine, reduced to concentrate its flavor *(recipe, page 116)*; you could substitute a well-reduced meat stock *(recipe, pages 164-165)* or the roasting juices of meat or poultry.

To make a more aromatic dish, you can soften vegetables in butter or oil and then add the eggs halfway through cooking, as demonstrated below. Stirred constantly as they thicken, the eggs will bind the mixture and give it a luxurious texture. Tomatoes and fresh basil are used here to add a Provençal flavor *(recipe, page 117)*. Other appealing bases are diced eggplants *(recipe, page 116)* or a Spanish mixture of tomatoes, zucchini, onions and peppers *(recipe, page 118)*.

A Smooth Mélange of Wine and Cheese

1 **Reducing wine.** Pour white wine into a saucepan; add peeled, chopped garlic. Set the pan over medium heat. Bring the wine to a boil and let it bubble until it is reduced to half of its original volume. Strain the wine through a fine-meshed sieve into a bowl to remove the garlic. Let the wine cool.

2 **Mixing the ingredients.** Butter the bottom and sides of an earthenware casserole and break eggs into it. Add more butter — cubed for rapid melting — and the cooled wine, pepper and salt. Beat the mixture lightly until the yolks and whites blend. Then add the cheese — here, shredded Gruyère.

A Chunky Base of Tomatoes and Herbs

1 **Preparing the tomatoes.** Core tomatoes, then dip them into boiling water for a few seconds to loosen their skins. Cool, then peel them. Cut each tomato in half horizontally, and squeeze the halves gently to force out the seeds and some of the juice. Chop the halves into small chunks.

2 **Cooking the tomatoes.** Heat olive oil in a skillet. Add the chopped tomatoes, lightly crushed whole garlic cloves, salt, a little sugar and a bouquet of herbs. Cook the mixture over low heat, stirring occasionally, until most of the juices evaporate. Remove the garlic and the bouquet *(above)*.

3 **Adding the eggs.** Break eggs into a bowl, and add butter cubes and salt and pepper to taste. Beat the eggs lightly to blend yolks and whites. Add the mixture to the simmering tomatoes.

3 **Cooking the mixture.** To protect the casserole, place it on a heat-diffusing pad set over low heat. With a whisk or fork, stir the egg-and-cheese mixture slowly while the butter and cheese melt *(above, left)*. Then stir more briskly until the mixture thickens *(right)*, constantly using the whisk or fork to scrape the sides and bottom of the casserole, where the eggs cook most rapidly.

4 **Serving.** Take the casserole off the heat, but stir for another minute or so while the casserole's heat cooks the eggs further. When the fondue reaches the consistency of thick cream, spoon it onto warmed plates. Garnish with croutons *(recipe, page 166)* or serve accompanied by crusty bread.

4 **Scrambling the eggs.** With a wooden spoon, stir the eggs to distribute them evenly through the tomatoes. Continue to stir constantly as the eggs cook, carefully scraping the bottom and sides of the pan to prevent bits of egg from hardening there.

5 **Flavoring with basil.** When the eggs begin to thicken, add a handful of fresh chopped basil leaves *(above)*. Stir the leaves into the mixture.

6 **Serving the dish.** Remove the pan from the heat. Continue to stir for a few more seconds while the heat of the pan continues to thicken the mixture. When the eggs have reached the desired consistency, serve them at once on warmed plates *(above)*.

The Classic Omelet: A Masterpiece in a Moment

A classic omelet—rolled on itself or folded in half—is an object lesson in culinary economy. It is quickly made and requires no special equipment other than a heavy, carefully seasoned pan. The only indispensable ingredients are fresh eggs, butter, salt and pepper.

The eggs should be beaten lightly, just enough to combine yolks and whites well without incorporating air bubbles that might make the omelet dry out. Butter—diced for fast, even melting—is beaten in as an enrichment (more butter will be used during cooking), and seasonings, herbs, or any of a variety of other non-bulky flavorings are added at the same time. Fresh marjoram, parsley or a fines herbes mixture—parsley, chervil, chives and tarragon—bring a breath of fragrance to an omelet. If fresh herbs are unavailable, dried marjoram or oregano are good aromatic substitutes.

Other ingredients that can be added—with discretion—include chopped anchovy fillets, sautéed diced mushrooms or finely shredded sorrel leaves.

More substantial garnishes (sliced lettuce leaves, sautéed and moistened with a cream sauce, for example, or strips of smoked salmon blended with sour cream) can be prepared ahead and rolled or folded inside the omelet as soon as it is cooked (box, right). This is also the time to incorporate grated or shredded cheese; if added at the start of cooking, cheese melts, causing the omelet to stick.

Whatever flavorings or fillings are selected, cooking must be brisk. Heat the pan thoroughly before adding the eggs. The pan itself should be broad enough so that the omelet forms a layer about ¼ inch [6 mm.] deep and sets within 60 seconds or so; the bottom will be firm, the top still creamy. If the omelet is cooked slowly, either because of insufficient heat or too small a pan, it will lose its moistness.

For a two-egg omelet, a small omelet or crepe pan—one that measures 6 or 7 inches [15 or 18 cm.] across the top—is suitable. A three- to five-egg omelet requires an 8- to 9-inch [20- to 23-cm.] pan, a six- to eight-egg omelet, a 10- to 12-inch [25- to 30-cm.] pan.

1 Assembling ingredients. Break eggs into a dish. Season with salt and freshly ground black pepper and add diced cold butter, allowing about 1 tablespoon [15 ml.] of butter for every two or three eggs. If you like, add flavorings — in this instance, salmon moistened with sour cream (box, below).

2 Beating the eggs. Warm a seasoned pan for a few seconds over high heat. Add butter — 1 tablespoon [15 ml.] is enough to coat an 8-inch [20-cm.] pan. While the butter melts, beat the eggs and diced butter lightly with a fork (above).

Folding In Flavor

Adding a filling. When the edges are firm but the top of the omelet is still moist (Step 7, right), quickly spoon a garnish — in this case, smoked salmon moistened with sour cream — onto one side of the omelet to form a strip parallel to the handle of the pan. With a fork or spatula, lift the other side of the omelet over the filled side. Slide the omelet onto a warmed plate at once.

6 Rolling the omelet. With the fork, fold the near edge of the omelet into the omelet's center. Tilt the pan away from you, then slide the tines of the fork under the fold and roll the omelet over toward the far side of the pan.

3 **Adding the eggs.** Tilt the pan from side to side to coat the bottom with the melted butter. When the butter begins to foam, but before it starts to brown, pour in the beaten eggs *(above)*.

4 **Stirring the mixture.** Pass the flat of the fork through the eggs two or three times to expose as much of the mixture as possible to the heat of the pan. Never stir with the tips of the fork tines; they would scratch the seasoned surface of the pan, making the omelet stick.

5 **Lifting the omelet's edge.** When the underside of the omelet begins to set, use the fork to lift the edge of the omelet *(above)*. Tilt the pan at the same time, so that any uncooked egg from the top will run under the cooked egg and set. Repeat the lifting and tilting process around the pan to let as much liquid egg as possible run underneath.

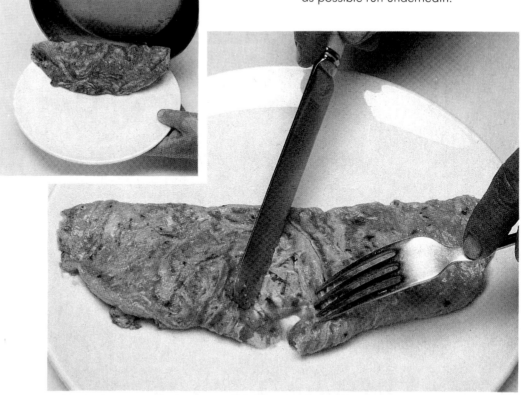

7 **Sealing the roll.** With the tines of the fork, pull the far edge of the omelet back from the side of the pan over the rolled section. Seal this flap by gently pressing down on the top of the omelet with the flat of the fork for a second or two. Keep the tilted pan over the heat for three or four seconds so that the bottom of the omelet browns slightly. Remove the pan from the heat.

8 **Serving.** Tip the pan up against the edge of a warmed plate so that the omelet rolls out browned side uppermost *(inset)*. To give the omelet a sheen, impale a piece of butter on a fork and draw it across the surface. Serve immediately while the omelet is still hot and moist, and soft inside *(above)*.

A Packet for Enrichments

The usual way to fill an omelet is to fold it around its garnish *(page 56)*, but for a more dramatic effect, you can slit open the top of a large rolled omelet to form a pouch for a filling. In turn, the filling may serve as a foundation in which to embed additional garnishes, and you can transform the omelet into a full-scale assembly by coating it with a sauce, sprinkling it with bread crumbs or grated cheese, and putting it under a broiler for a gratin finish *(recipe, page 124)*.

To keep the omelet moist and succulent, the garnishes and sauce, which may be the same ones used for whole-egg assemblies *(pages 32-35)*, must be prepared ahead of time: If the prepared omelet has to wait, it will dry out.

In this demonstration, a mushroom purée provides a bed for poached eggs *(page 27)*, which are then masked with a white sauce. You could substitute puréed peas or morels stewed in butter for the mushrooms. *Mollet* eggs, sautéed chicken livers or stewed oysters might replace the poached egg. And cheese or puréed tomatoes could be added to the white sauce.

1 **Opening the omelet.** Prepare the garnishes — in this case, mushroom purée and trimmed poached eggs — and make a white sauce *(pages 34-35)*. Keep the garnishes and the sauce hot while you make a large rolled omelet *(pages 56-57)* — here a seven-egg omelet, cooked in a 12-inch [30-cm.] pan. Tip the omelet, with the folded side underneath, onto a warmed ovenproof dish. Cut a fairly long slit along the top of the omelet *(above)*, leaving about 1½ inches [4 cm.] of omelet intact at each end. Take care not to cut through the underside of the omelet.

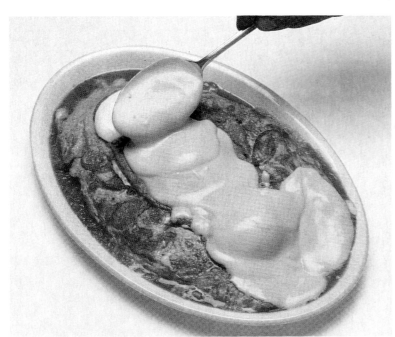

4 **Coating the omelet.** Remove the white sauce from the heat, then stir into it enough heavy cream to increase its volume by half. If you like, you also can add grated Parmesan or aged Gruyère cheese. Taste the sauce for seasoning. Spoon the sauce over the omelet to coat its top surface generously *(above)*.

5 **Topping with grated cheese.** Sprinkle grated cheese — Parmesan is used in this demonstration — evenly over the sauce. Position the omelet under a preheated broiler so that its top surface is about 2 inches [5 cm.] from the heat source. Broil it for two to three minutes, or until the sauce is lightly browned.

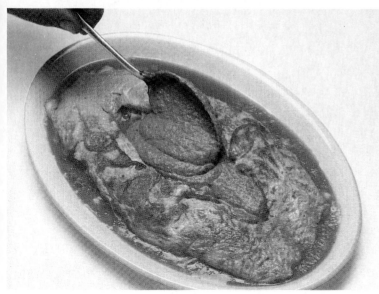

2 **Filling the omelet.** With a knife blade, ease open the slit in the omelet to make a shallow pouch. Spoon in enough of the mushroom purée to fill the pouch completely; an omelet the size of this one will take about 3 tablespoonfuls [45 ml.] of purée. Smooth down the purée with the back of the spoon.

3 **Adding poached eggs.** Lift the poached eggs from the cold water in which they have been placed after cooking. Dip them into hot water for a few seconds to warm them. Using your hands to lessen the risk of breaking the fragile yolks, arrange the eggs, side by side, in a neat row along the top of the purée.

6 **Serving the omelet.** Remove the dish from the broiler *(left)*, and divide the omelet into individual portions, making sure that each diner has a poached egg. Spoon any sauce remaining in the dish over the servings. The yolks of the poached eggs should still be liquid when the omelet is served *(above)*.

An Omelet Sandwich Finished in the Oven

Even without rolling or folding, omelets may be used to enclose fillings. Kept flat, a pair of omelets can be layered with a creamy filling—held in check by strips of fried bread or sausage links—to create a hearty omelet sandwich such as the one demonstrated here *(recipe, page 126)*. A brief baking allows the omelets to absorb the flavors of the filling while a gratin coating forms on top of the sandwich.

Freshly cooked vegetables make ideal fillings for such a sandwich; their clean taste and moist texture complement the eggs. Here, shredded sorrel, wilted almost to a purée, adds a pleasantly acid note. Among the alternatives to the sorrel are sliced asparagus that has been parboiled and lightly sautéed *(page 33)*, sliced artichoke bottoms stewed in butter, or tomatoes, onions and peppers simmered with oil to evaporate excess juices.

To give them body, vegetable fillings must be bound with egg and thickened with some sort of starchy ingredient. In the demonstration shown here, egg yolks and cream give the sorrel filling a sauce-like smoothness; bread crumbs and grated cheese contribute bulk and flavor. Juicier vegetables, such as the tomato, onion and pepper mixture, could be combined with cooked rice for body, and bound with beaten egg.

For an entirely different effect, you could use a seafood filling—for instance, shrimp parboiled for three minutes until pink, then peeled and bound with a white sauce *(pages 34-35)* and bread crumbs.

In order to set off the filling, the omelets themselves should be flavored only with a little butter, salt and pepper. They need not be turned: Any liquid egg on the lower omelet's surface will blend into the filling, while the top omelet, positioned with its moist side uppermost, will brown delicately as the sandwich is gratinéed. To ensure that the omelets stay creamy enough to be reheated without drying, both the filling and its bread or sausage border should be prepared ahead of time.

1 **Preparing the filling.** Cook finely shredded sorrel leaves in butter over low heat for five minutes until the sorrel has cooked down to a purée-like consistency. In a small bowl, beat egg yolks with heavy cream; reserve the whites. Stir the yolk-and-cream mixture into the sorrel with a wooden spoon *(above, left)*. Then stir in equal amounts of bread crumbs and grated Parmesan *(right)*. As soon as the mixture thickens, remove the pan from the heat.

4 **Adding the filling.** Spoon the sorrel mixture onto the omelet *(above)*. Use the back of the spoon to smooth the filling so that it is level with the top of the bread strips. Make a second flat omelet *(Step 2)*. Slide it out of the pan, moist side up, onto the sorrel filling, aligning the edges of the omelet with the border of bread strips.

2 **Preparing the omelet base.** Mix the eggs with butter cubes and seasonings. Prepare a classic omelet (*pages 56-57*), but do not roll or fold it. Instead, slip it — still flat — onto a warmed, ovenproof serving dish as soon as the underside has cooked enough for the omelet to slide easily in the pan.

3 **Making a border.** Drain the fried bread strips on paper towels, roll the strips in the reserved egg whites, and arrange them around the edge of the omelet to form a border. To make the strips, cut stale white bread into finger shapes about ¾ inch [2 cm.] wide and 3 inches [8 cm.] long. Over low heat, melt butter with oil in a skillet. Fry the bread strips for about 10 minutes, turning frequently with a spatula, until they crisp on all sides. Remove the skillet from the heat and cover it to keep the strips warm.

5 **Creating a gratin.** Spoon melted butter over the upper omelet. Sprinkle with bread crumbs and grated Parmesan. Place in a preheated 450° F. [230° C.] oven for five minutes.

6 **Serving the sandwich.** Remove the omelet sandwich from the oven; if the surface has not colored, set the dish under a hot broiler for a few seconds to brown the top lightly. With a knife or a cake server, cut between the bread strips to divide the omelet into wedges *(above)*. Place the wedges on plates and serve.

Flat Omelets, Thick and Thin

The heartiest of omelets are pancake omelets—called *crespeus* in Provence, *frittatas* in Italy and *tortillas* in Spain—which contain more flavoring than they do eggs. Indeed, in these omelets the flavoring often amounts to as much as a cupful [¼ liter] to each egg. The result is too bulky to roll or fold, so pancake omelets are always served flat and cut into slices or wedges at the table.

Depending on the volume of ingredients and the breadth of the pan in which they cook, pancake omelets may be made thin or thick, as in the two demonstrations shown here. When the mixture is spread to a depth of no more than half an inch [1 cm.], the omelet will be thin enough to cook over high heat like a classic omelet *(pages 56-57)*. Because this version cannot be rolled or folded onto itself, however, the upper surface will remain moist. The simplest way to firm it is to flip over the omelet by tossing it *(Step 3, top)*. Or the top may be set by sliding the pan under a hot broiler.

A thick pancake omelet starts over high heat to set the underside, but—in order to cook the eggs gently—the temperature then must be reduced and the pan covered *(Step 2, bottom)*. Too cumbersome to toss, such an omelet may be reversed onto an inverted plate, then slid back into the pan to set the top. Or, like a thin pancake omelet, it can be finished under a broiler—perhaps sprinkled with cheese or crumbs for a gratin top.

The possibilities for flavoring pancake omelets are virtually infinite. Vegetables of every sort can serve—singly, in combinations, or mixed with fish, shellfish or meats such as ham or sausage *(recipes, pages 128-132)*.

Because even thick pancake omelets cook quickly, the flavorings must be fully prepared before being mixed with eggs. So that they do not release liquid that would make the omelets runny, moist vegetables such as cucumbers or zucchini need to be shredded, salted, squeezed and sautéed *(box, opposite)*. Mushrooms, onions or peppers should be sautéed, tomatoes stewed to a purée *(page 35)*. Leafy vegetables such as the spinach shown at right must be parboiled, squeezed, chopped and then tossed in butter.

A Marbling of Shredded Zucchini

1 **Starting the omelet.** Prepare zucchini *(box, opposite)*. In a large bowl, lightly beat eggs with cubes of butter and a little pepper. Stir in the sautéed zucchini; in this case, two eggs are combined with 1 pound [½ kg.] of prepared zucchini. Over high heat, warm butter or oil in a seasoned pan. Pour in the egg-and-zucchini mixture.

2 **Cooking the omelet.** With a fork, spread the mixture evenly in the pan. Allow the pancake omelet to cook undisturbed for about one minute, until the underside becomes firm enough so that the omelet slides easily in the pan.

Spinach: An Assertive Partner

1 **Starting the omelet.** Parboil spinach; squeeze it dry, chop it and cook it briefly in butter. Beat eggs with butter cubes, salt and pepper. Stir in the spinach; here, six eggs are combined with 2 pounds [1 kg.] of spinach. Over high heat, warm butter or oil in a seasoned pan. Then add the egg-and-spinach mixture *(above)*.

2 **Cooking the omelet.** Smooth the surface of the mixture with the flat of a fork. Reduce the heat, and cover the pan with a lid *(above)*. Continue to cook gently for about five minutes, or until the top of the pancake omelet begins to set. Take the pan off the heat.

3 **Tossing.** Lift the pan a little off the heat and tilt it so that the omelet slides to the far edge of the pan. Then, with a rapid scooping movement of your whole arm, lift the pan upward and toward yourself in an arc, so that the omelet flips over. Cook the omelet for a few seconds more to set the second side, then slide it out of the pan. Serve the pancake omelet immediately.

1 **Shredding and salting.** Wash zucchini and trim off the tips and stems. Use a rotary shredder *(above)* or a box grater to shred the zucchini into coarse strips. Place the shreds in a bowl in layers about an inch [2½ cm.] thick; sprinkle each layer lightly with salt.

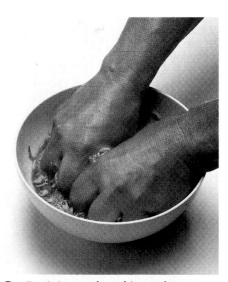

3 **Finishing the omelet.** Sprinkle the surface of the omelet evenly with grated cheese — in this case, Parmesan. Place the pan under a hot broiler. When the surface of the omelet sets and the cheese browns to a light crust — about five minutes — slip the pancake omelet out of its pan and onto a warmed serving dish *(above)*.

4 **Serving the omelet.** Cut the pancake omelet into wedges. Use a wide, flat spatula or a cake server to transfer the wedges to warmed plates and serve at once. Or let the unsliced omelet cool for about 15 minutes to allow the flavor of the spinach to develop, and serve the omelet tepid.

2 **Draining and cooking.** After about 30 minutes, squeeze the zucchini well *(above)*. Rinse the shreds under cold water and squeeze them until dry. Stirring often, sauté the zucchini in oil or butter over medium heat for six or seven minutes, until the shreds have given up most of their moisture.

Improvising Gratins

Layered with other ingredients and then coated with a sauce, pancake omelets provide a substantial base for a gratin assembly. A topping of grated cheese or bread crumbs—or both—completes the preparation; the surface colors lightly when the dish is finished in an oven.

Such omelet gratins invite improvisation. Although cheese will usually play some part, the other elements can be as varied as their availability and your own imagination suggest. In the demonstration shown here, zucchini-flavored omelets are combined with grated Cheddar cheese and strips of roasted and peeled red and green sweet peppers; the dish is coated with a tomato sauce *(recipe, page 166)*. You could substitute mushrooms, asparagus, fennel or spinach for the zucchini, and anchovy fillets or strips of ham could replace the peppers.

For an even heartier dish, combine flat plain omelets *(pages 60-61)* with pieces of roast chicken or turkey or cooked white-fleshed fish, and coat them with a cream-enriched white sauce *(page 34-35)*.

1 **Starting the assembly.** Grate the cheese and prepare the sauce and garnishes in advance. Cook zucchini pancake omelets *(pages 62-63)*. Butter an ovenproof dish, and sprinkle the bottom with a little of the cheese. Add the omelets in a single layer, overlapping them to fit neatly. Place a few pepper strips on top.

2 **Completing the layers.** When all of the omelets are arranged in the dish, scatter over them any remaining pepper strips. Sprinkle the omelets with a layer of grated Cheddar cheese. Spoon the tomato sauce over them *(above)*. Finally, sprinkle on a little more grated cheese —mixed, if you like, with an equal quantity of fresh bread crumbs.

3 **Baking the gratin.** Put the dish into an oven preheated to 375° F. [190° C.]. Allow about 15 minutes for the cheese to melt into the sauce. If the top has not begun to color, place the dish briefly under a hot broiler. Serve from the dish *(above)*.

Molding a Multilayered Loaf

One of the most unusual of all omelet dishes is the loaf assemblage demonstrated at right and on the following two pages. It is composed of variously flavored pancake omelets layered in a mold, bound together with a custard—in this case, eggs and cream mixed with puréed sorrel—and baked in the oven *(recipe, page 132)*. During cooking, the egg in the sorrel mixture sets and holds the omelets together. After cooking, the loaf should cool for about an hour; the heat within it will continue to cook the mixture, firming it sufficiently for easy unmolding.

The omelet flavorings should be selected for color as well as taste. In this demonstration, five different flavorings ranging from bright green spinach to jet-black olives are each used in two pancake omelets, making 10 in all. Stacked alternately, the omelets make a repeated pattern of five different bands.

The sorrel cream used to bind the loaf combines an attractive, pale green color with a refreshingly sharp taste. If sorrel is not available, try mixing the eggs and cream with puréed peas *(page 32)* or a sprinkling of fines herbes—or simply use a plain omelet mixture of beaten eggs and seasonings.

The omelets should be cooked in a pan whose bottom diameter roughly corresponds to that of the mold in which the loaf will be cooked. The mold itself should have a flat bottom and straight sides. It could be a large charlotte mold, a small casserole or a heavy saucepan with an ovenproof handle. To ensure gentle, even heat, the mold is set in a large pan and the loaf cooked in a water bath.

If you do not wish to serve the cooled loaf immediately after unmolding, you can cover it with plastic wrap to keep it from drying out, and refrigerate it for four or more hours.

1 **Assembling the ingredients.** First, prepare the five flavorings: counterclockwise from top left, a stew of tomatoes, garlic, onions, and peppers; black olives, pitted and chopped; sliced mushrooms, sautéed in butter; sautéed, shredded zucchini *(box, page 63)*; and parboiled spinach, chopped and sautéed in butter. In a large bowl, lightly beat eggs *(above)*; add pepper.

2 **Cooking the omelets.** Spoon half of one flavoring into a soup plate. Stir in a small ladleful of the beaten eggs; salt to taste. Cook the omelet, turning it when the underside is firm *(page 63)*. Make a second omelet with the remaining half of the flavoring. Repeat for the four other flavorings, to make a total of 10 omelets. Stack differently flavored omelets separately.

3 **Preparing the sorrel cream.** Whisk in more eggs to supplement any beaten egg that may remain after the omelets are assembled. Pour in heavy cream. Wilt shredded sorrel in butter *(page 33)*. For extra smoothness, purée it into the egg mixture through a sieve with a nonreactive plastic or stainless-steel mesh. Season, then whisk the purée into the eggs and cream.

4 **Filling the mold.** Generously butter a round mold of approximately the same diameter as the omelets—in this case, a deep casserole. Line the bottom of the mold with buttered parchment or wax paper. Ladle some sorrel cream into the mold. Add the omelets, alternating the colors. Press each omelet down and pour a ladleful of sorrel cream over it before adding the next.

7 **Loosening the loaf.** Peel away and discard the uppermost circle of parchment paper covering the top. Let the loaf cool in its mold for about one hour, until it is just tepid. Run the blade of a knife around the inside edge of the mold to loosen the loaf.

8 **Unmolding the loaf.** Invert a round serving plate over the mold. Grip the mold and plate firmly and turn them over together. You should hear the omelet loaf slip onto the plate with an audible slap. Set the plate on a work surface and carefully lift the mold away from the loaf. Peel off the second circle of paper.

5 **Preparing the water bath.** Cover the stacked omelets with more sorrel cream, so that the top omelet is almost submerged. For the water bath, place the mold on a wire rack in a large pan. Cover the top of the mold with a second circle of buttered parchment paper. Then carefully pour boiling water into the pan to immerse the bottom two thirds of the mold.

6 **Cooking the loaf.** Place the water bath in an oven preheated to 375° F. [190° C.]. Bake the loaf for about 45 minutes, until the sorrel cream binder has set and the loaf springs back instantly when you prod the top gently with your finger. Remove the water bath from the oven, and lift out the mold.

9 **Serving.** Garnish the unmolded loaf with simple decorations. In this instance, a ribbon of chopped fresh parsley encircles the rim, and chopped black olives garnish the center. The loaf may be eaten either tepid or cold. For serving, cut it into wedges or crosswise slices.

Separating Yolks and Whites for a Soufflé Effect

By separating the yolks and whites of eggs and beating them independently, you can create an omelet mixture that will rise on cooking and assume something of the light, puffy texture of a soufflé *(pages 80-81)*. Simply seasoned with salt and pepper or flavored with a savory sprinkling of cheese or fresh or dried herbs *(recipe, page 120)*, such a mixture is cooked like a plain omelet in butter on top of the stove.

Soufflé omelets, as these creations are called, owe their lightness to the air that is incorporated into the whites during beating. Eggs separate best right out of the refrigerator, but whites expand to maximum volume if they are first allowed to reach room temperature. You may use a rotary or electric beater, but working with a large wire whisk will speed the process by exposing as much of the egg white to the air as possible. Although a glass, ceramic or stainless-steel bowl will serve, a bowl made of unlined copper will react with the whites to create stronger air bubbles.

To ensure that trapped air is not lost, the whites should be blended with the yolks immediately after beating. Combine them gently by hand or with a rubber spatula and cook the mixture at once, before the bubbles break down and the liquid that is held in suspension settles to the bottom of the bowl.

As with any omelet, the soufflé kind must be cooked quickly in a buttered pan hot enough to set the underside before the top dries. Because of its bulky fluffiness, the mixture will require a larger pan than used for plain omelets; the three-egg omelet shown calls for a 9- to 10-inch [23- to 25-cm.] seasoned pan.

During cooking, the mixture will swell slightly as the heat of the pan forces the trapped air to expand. Soufflé omelets are consequently too puffy to fold more than once. Use a narrow, flexible spatula to fold the omelet, or tilt the pan so that the omelet slides forward, then jerk it repeatedly until the farther edge of the omelet flips back upon itself *(Step 6)*. The cooked omelet should not be heavily garnished; serve it either on its own or surrounded by a simple sauce *(pages 34-35)*.

1 **Separating the eggs.** Crack each egg against the edge of a small bowl. Pull away half of the shell, leaving the yolk in the other half, and let the white drip into the bowl *(above)*. Pass the yolk gently from one half-shell to the other until all the white has dripped out. Transfer the white to a large bowl and place the yolk in a shallow dish.

2 **Blending the yolks.** Season the yolks with salt and pepper. For extra richness, add heavy cream or, as here, bits of cold butter, allowing 1 tablespoon [15 ml.] for every three egg yolks. With the flat of a fork, beat the yolks until lightly blended *(above)*. Do not worry if some pieces of butter remain whole; they will melt during cooking.

6 **Folding the omelet.** Shake the pan gently from time to time. When the underside has set and slides easily — after about two or three minutes — the omelet is ready for folding. Tilt the pan away from you. With a rhythmical movement of the forearm, jerk the pan forward and upward to fold back the lip of the omelet *(above, left)*. Repeat until the omelet is folded in two *(above, right)*.

3 **Beating the whites.** With a wire whisk, beat the whites slowly in a continuous figure-8 motion. Lift the whisk as you beat, to incorporate air. When the whites begin to change to an opaque froth, beat them rapidly with a circular motion until they are stiff enough to cling to the whisk *(above).*

4 **Folding in the egg yolks.** Using a spatula or your hand, scrape the yolks into the beaten whites *(above).* Gently lift the white foam from the bottom of the bowl over the top of the yolks while turning the bowl with your other hand. Fold with an up-and-over motion until yolks and whites are mixed.

5 **Filling the pan.** Melt some butter in a seasoned pan over medium heat. When the butter is foaming, tip the omelet mixture into the pan. Using a spatula, scrape all of the mixture from the bowl, spread it out evenly and smooth its top surface.

7 **Serving.** Slide the folded omelet onto a warmed plate and serve it immediately. In contrast to the firm and lightly colored surface, the center of the omelet should be soft and creamy, laced with small bubbles of air *(left).*

4

Cheese Cookery
A Range of Roles

Although it does not require cooking to make it palatable, cheese has long had an honored and varied role in cookery. It is a primary flavoring, for instance, in savory custard mixtures, in many of those pastry-encased custards known as quiches, and in countless soufflés and soufflé-like preparations. In addition, cheese is itself the central ingredient in a number of dishes. These include a fondue of melted cheese and wine, and its rustic cousin, Welsh rabbit, as well as softened or melted cheeses presented in various guises—over a base of bread, in a pastry shell, or in wrappers such as pancakes or vine leaves. Cubes of cheese may even be given a protective coating of batter and deep fried.

Cheese for any of these dishes is cooked only to alter its texture or to unite it with other elements. Lengthy cooking or extreme temperatures are thus unnecessary and may in fact cause the cheese's two main components, fat and protein, to separate into an oily slick on a rubbery mass.

The texture of the cheese determines how it is prepared and the range of dishes for which it is suitable. For cooking purposes, the three main cheese groups are those hard enough to grate or shred, those soft enough to be beaten, and the in-between cheeses that are sliced or cubed.

The hard cheeses flavor soufflés *(pages 76-81)*, sauces and many custards. For thorough blending, a very hard cheese such as Parmesan should be grated fine *(page 13)*. Less hard cheese such as Gruyère must be coarsely grated or shredded into thin strips, because the cheese would quickly clog a grater's smallest holes.

Very soft cheeses, when beaten, combine smoothly with sauces, eggs, cream or softened butter. They add bulk and mild flavor to a savory custard *(pages 72-73)* or pie, and can be the primary ingredient in fillings for pancakes such as blintzes. Among this group are ricotta and simple farmer cheeses *(pages 10-11)*.

Denser cheeses, such as Brie, must be cut up and gently heated to melt them for thorough blending. (The same technique is sometimes used with firm cheeses: For the fondue on pages 82-83, for example, cubes of Gruyère are gently liquefied in wine.) But for dishes such as the casserole at left, where the aim is not to disperse the cheese evenly throughout the dish, the middle range of cheeses can simply be sliced thin and layered to melt in with the other ingredients as the dish cooks.

A wedge cut from a piping hot cheese casserole reveals layers of mozzarella, bread and tomato sauce. The casserole was baked until the cheese melted, providing a mild background for the herb-scented sauce.

71

Baked Molded Custards

Savory egg custards are much enhanced by flavoring them with cheese—whether grated hard cheese such as Parmesan, which flecks the custard with color and flavor or, as here, fresh farmer cheese, which yields a creamy, homogeneous result. A homemade farmer cheese (pages 10-11) is an excellent choice for a fresh-cheese custard. Also suitable are ricotta or well-drained cottage cheeses enriched with butter or cream. For custard as smooth as satin, the cheese first must be beaten until all lumps disappear.

The mild taste of fresh-cheese custards makes them excellent bases for other flavors (recipes, pages 134-138). Sautéed diced salt pork, added to the cheese custard shown at right, lends an assertive tang; as an alternative, you could use strips of cooked bacon, ham or chicken, or chopped, cooked shrimp. The custard mixture shown in the box on the opposite page includes finely chopped and well-squeezed parboiled lettuce, which contributes a subtly sweet flavor. Zucchini that has been grated, salted, drained and dried (page 63) or finely chopped mushrooms sautéed in butter are other good vegetable flavorings.

Cheese custards of this type can be cooked either in large, plain molds such as the charlotte mold used in the demonstration at right, or in ramekins only large enough for single servings—the choice for the lettuce-flavored custard on the opposite page. Both types of mold should be two thirds immersed in a water bath during baking to keep the custard from overheating and curdling.

A custard in a large mold will take from 40 minutes to an hour to set; because of the lengthy cooking, such a mold should be set on a wire rack in the water bath to keep it away from direct contact with the heat. Small ramekins require only about 15 minutes to cook and do not need the protection of a rack. After cooking, the custards must be cooled until they are firm enough to unmold.

For an extra dimension of flavor and texture, the cooked custard may be coated with warmed cream or served with a savory sauce. For the large custard shown, tomato sauce is used with cream. A white sauce flavored with cheese is another possibility.

1 **Preparing flavorings.** Cut the rind from a piece of salt pork, then chop the pork into even-sized pieces. Fry the pieces until lightly browned, then drain them on paper towels. Butter a deep charlotte mold; line the bottom of the mold with a circle of buttered wax or parchment paper. Scatter the pork over the bottom of the mold.

2 **Mixing cheese and eggs.** Beat fresh cheese—in this case, farmer cheese—with seasonings such as salt, pepper and grated nutmeg. Beat in softened butter. In a separate bowl, beat eggs until they are well blended, then pour them into the cheese mixture and beat the mixture to combine the ingredients thoroughly.

5 **Cooking the custard.** Bake the custard in a preheated 325° F. [160° C.] oven for at least 40 minutes, or until the top turns a golden brown and a skewer inserted in the center comes out clean. Remove the water bath from the oven and lift out the mold.

6 **Unmolding the custard.** Let the custard cool and settle for 10 to 15 minutes. To loosen the custard, run a knife around the inside of the mold. Hold an inverted serving dish over the mold, then reverse the dish and mold together. Lift away the mold and peel the circle of paper off the custard.

3 **Filling the mold.** Little by little, stir hot milk into the custard until the mixture has the consistency of light cream. Ladle the mixture into the mold, leaving at least 1 inch [2½ cm.] at the top: The custard will rise slightly as it cooks.

4 **Preparing the water bath.** Set the filled mold on a wire rack inside a large ovenproof pot. Pour enough boiling water down the side of the pan to immerse two thirds of the mold.

Filling the ramekins. Butter and line the ramekins and place them in a shallow baking dish. Fill the ramekins almost to their rims with a custard — in this case, a cheese custard with lettuce. Pour in boiling water to two thirds of the ramekins' depth. Bake in a 325° F. [160° C.] oven for 15 minutes, until firm. Cool, unmold *(Step 6)* and serve.

7 **Serving the custard.** In separate saucepans over gentle heat, warm tomato sauce *(page 35)* and heavy cream. Spoon the tomato sauce into the serving dish around the sides of the custard; pour the cream over the top. Serve the custard in wedges.

Quiche: Custard in a Case

Baked in a pastry shell, a cheese-flavored custard becomes a *quiche au fromage*—an open-faced cheese tart whose filling and shape can be extensively varied.

The filling, for instance, may be one of the fresh-cheese custards demonstrated on pages 72-73, or it could be an egg custard flavored with a shredded or grated firm cheese such as Emmentaler, Cheddar or the combination of Gruyère and Parmesan used here *(recipe, page 146).* Frequently the cheese custard includes additional flavorings: vegetables ranging from chopped, sautéed onion to sliced, parboiled asparagus, meats such as the sautéed bacon pieces in this demonstration, or fish or shellfish—smoked salmon, for instance, or fresh crab *(recipes, pages 145-149).*

The shell, usually made from a simple short-crust pastry *(demonstration, page 37; recipe, page 167),* can be shaped by any of several methods. You can bake the quiche in a standard piepan or, for individual servings, in tartlet shells that are unmolded after baking. For a particularly handsome presentation, the custard is encased in a large free-standing shell made by molding the pastry in a false-bottomed tart pan such as the one employed in this demonstration.

Any pastry shell for a quiche should be partially baked for 10 minutes before it is filled with the custard mixture and cooked; partial baking sets the shell and prevents the liquid custard from making it soggy. When prebaking, line the empty shell with wax or parchment paper or aluminum foil and fill it with raw rice, dried beans or, as here, dried chick-peas. The weight of this filling keeps the bottom of the shell flat and the sides from collapsing before the pastry has set. The lining and weight can be removed together when the prebaking is completed.

As extra insurance against sogginess, crisp the interior by returning the empty shell to the oven for five minutes. Then, to underscore a cheese-flavored custard, you can paint the interior with beaten egg, sprinkle it with grated cheese, and bake it briefly.

1 Reinforcing the shell. Roll out chilled short-crust pastry. Roll the pastry onto the pin and unroll it over a false-bottomed tart pan. Press the pastry into the pan and trim the edges, leaving a border about 1 inch [2½ cm.] wide. Fold this border into the pan — it should touch but not overlap the bottom of the shell — and press it against the sides *(above)* to form a double tart-shell wall.

2 Trimming the pastry. Rotate a rolling pin over one section of the tart-pan rim: The pan's scalloped edges will cut off excess pastry. Turn the pan and repeat this process until all of the excess pastry has been trimmed. With your fingers, again gently press the walls of the pastry shell against the sides of the tart pan. Refrigerate the shell for 30 minutes to firm the pastry.

5 Mixing the custard. Beat the eggs until they are foamy, then stir in heavy cream, salt and pepper. Add the cheese — in this instance, a half-and-half mixture of grated Parmesan and shredded Gruyère — and mix well.

6 Filling and baking the tart. Fry bacon pieces until they are crisp and drain them on paper towels. Sprinkle the pieces over the bottom of the tart shell. Return the tart pan to the baking sheet and ladle the egg-and-cheese mixture over the bacon, filling the shell to within about ¼ inch [6 mm.] of the rim. Bake in a 375° F. [190° C.] oven for 25 minutes, or until the top of the quiche is puffed and lightly browned.

3 **Partially baking the shell.** Line the pastry shell with parchment paper and fill it with dried chick-peas *(above)*. Set the pan on a baking sheet and bake in a preheated 400° F. [200° C.] oven for about 10 minutes, until the pastry shrinks slightly. Remove the paper and chick-peas, prick the bottom to let steam escape from the pastry, and bake for five more minutes.

4 **Sealing the shell.** Quickly paint the bottom of the shell with a little beaten egg. Sprinkle shredded cheese — Emmentaler, in this case — over the egg wash and return the pan to the oven for about three minutes to set the sealer. Slide the pan off the baking sheet and onto a rack to cool for 30 minutes.

7 **Serving.** To unmold the quiche, set the tart pan on top of a coffee can or, as shown, a crock. The rim will slip free of the quiche; guide it down gently with your hand *(above)*. Transfer the quiche — still resting on the bottom of the tart pan — to a serving platter. Cut it into wedges and serve at once *(right)*, or let it cool for about 20 minutes, cut it and serve it tepid. The quiche loses its puff as it cools, but the flavor is unaffected.

An Airy Medium for Cheese

A gold-crusted, feather-light soufflé is one of the most appealing culinary vehicles for cheese. Like many soufflés, this version begins as a white sauce enriched with egg yolks; cheese added to the sauce diffuses its flavor through the mixture. Beaten egg whites, added last, give the soufflé its lightness: In the oven, the whites expand and the soufflé puffs up.

The best soufflé cheeses are well flavored, with a low moisture content and firm texture: Gruyère, Jarlsberg, Emmentaler, Edam, Gouda and Cheddar are all excellent choices (recipes, pages 139-142). They may be used alone or with a sharp cheese such as Parmesan or sapsago. To keep the strong-flavored cheese from dominating, it should be used discreetly; in this demonstration, Gruyère is accented with a sprinkle of Parmesan.

The ratio of sauce and cheese to eggs is critical. As a general rule, 1¼ cups [300 ml.] of white sauce and 1¼ cups of grated or shredded cheese call for four eggs. Additional egg whites are often added—in the proportion of one extra white to every four eggs—to give a lighter result. Varying the proportions more drastically than this could produce a mixture that is either too heavy to rise properly or too light to hold its shape.

The egg whites will rise to their greatest volume if they are brought to room temperature and are then beaten with a wire whisk in a copper bowl. To keep the beaten egg whites from deflating, they should be immediately and gently combined with the cheese-flavored soufflé base (Step 6). The soufflé will be puffiest if baked at once, but it can sit half an hour if protected by an upturned pot and kept at room temperature.

Soufflés require moderate to high heat to puff up correctly, browning on top but staying creamy and saucelike at the center. The exact cooking time and temperature depend partly on the size of the soufflé, partly on the consistency desired. A large soufflé baked in a moderate oven usually takes 30 to 40 minutes, whereas individual soufflés cooked at higher heat require only half that time. For a very moist consistency, reduce the cooking time and increase the oven temperature. For a firmer, drier texture, increase the time and reduce the temperature.

1 Preparing the cheese. Shred or grate cheese into the smallest possible pieces its texture will allow. Shred firm cheese — such as the Gruyère shown here — against the medium-sized holes of a box grater. Grate harder cheeses — such as the Parmesan at left, above — against the smallest holes.

2 Lining the dish. Generously butter a straight-sided ovenproof dish. To lend extra flavor and texture to the soufflé crust, sprinkle the buttered dish with a few spoonfuls of grated cheese; tip and roll the dish until it is well coated (above). Shake out and reserve any excess cheese for use in the sauce.

6 Folding in egg whites. Spoon the sauce gently into the bowl containing the remaining beaten egg whites. With a rubber or wooden spatula or your hand, carefully fold the whites into the sauce. Be careful not to overmix: A few streaks of unmixed egg whites are preferable to a heavy soufflé.

7 Shaping a cap. Pour the mixture into the prepared dish; the dish should be between half and three quarters full. If you want the center of the soufflé to rise in a high cap, run your thumb around the edge of the soufflé (above) to make a groove about 1 inch [2½ cm.] deep. Bake the soufflé for 35 to 40 minutes in a preheated 375° F. [190° C.] oven.

3 **Making a white sauce.** Heat milk just to boiling and set it aside. Melt the butter in a heavy pan. Stir in the flour and cook the roux for two to three minutes. Add the heated milk to the roux *(above)*, whisking briskly to prevent lumps from forming. Season with salt, pepper and grated nutmeg. Cook the sauce uncovered over very low heat for about 10 minutes, stirring it from time to time. Let it cool slightly.

4 **Enriching the sauce.** Separate room-temperature eggs and transfer the whites to a large bowl, preferably of copper. Off the heat, drop all of the yolks but one into the sauce, reserving the final yolk for another use. Whisk the yolks into the sauce *(above)*. Stir in the cheese.

5 **Lightening the sauce.** With a wire whisk, beat the whites until they form firm but not dry peaks. To lighten the sauce and thus make it easier to incorporate into the bulk of the whites, gently mix about a quarter of the beaten egg whites into the sauce with the whisk *(above)*.

8 **Serving the soufflé.** The soufflé is ready when it has risen well above the rim of the dish and its top is golden *(left)*. Serve it without delay. Make sure each helping includes some of the crust and some of the moist center *(above)*.

Sturdy Soufflé Puddings Steeped in Sauce

Although the classic baked cheese soufflé *(page 77)* is a dramatic dish, it is a supremely fragile one. By altering the soufflé's composition and cooking the mixture in a moist atmosphere, you can produce a sturdier version—one that can be baked in advance, unmolded and then reheated. A coating of sauce applied before reheating will soak into the soufflé, saturating it with extra flavor.

Like the classic soufflé, this variation begins with a white-sauce base. If you like, you may follow the usual procedure of cooking equal quantities of flour and butter to make a roux, then adding milk. Or cook the flour and milk together, then beat in the butter, as shown here *(recipe, page 165)*. This method allows you to use a smaller proportion of butter; it is especially appropriate if you intend to serve the soufflé with cream or a rich sauce.

Although the classic soufflé is often made with more whites than yolks, one or more extra yolks are incorporated into this version to confer extra solidity. The yolk-enriched sauce base is flavored with white Cheddar in this demonstration, although any fairly firm, assertive cheese could be substituted. Instead of relying exclusively on cheese for flavoring, you can replace some of the cheese with an equal quantity of cooked, chopped mushrooms, spinach, ham or fish.

Here, the soufflé mixture is contained in small individual molds, although a large dish can be used if the cooking time is adjusted accordingly. The first cooking may take place as much as two to three hours in advance of serving. It is done in a water bath put in the oven. The moist heat keeps the soufflés from puffing up as dramatically as those baked with dry heat, yet it produces a firm, springy texture that enables the soufflés to withstand unmolding.

The soufflés made here are unmolded onto a bed of grated Cheddar, then topped with cream and more cheese *(recipe, page 140)*. For a contrast of flavor, you could accompany the soufflés with a tomato or velouté sauce *(recipes, pages 165-166)*.

1 Whisking milk into flour. Put the flour into a heavy saucepan. In a separate pan, scald the milk and let it cool slightly. Off the heat, add it gradually to the flour, whisking to prevent lumps. Add a little salt, pepper and grated nutmeg, then stir the mixture over medium heat until it becomes smooth and thickens.

2 Adding butter. Remove the pan from the heat. Cut butter into small pieces and add them to the flour-and-milk mixture. Whisk the sauce until all of the pieces of butter are incorporated.

6 Lifting out the soufflés. When the soufflés are firm and springy to the touch, remove the pan from the oven. Using a spatula, carefully lift the ramekins out of the water bath. Allow the soufflés to cool for a few minutes before unmolding them from the ramekins.

7 Unmolding the soufflés. Butter an ovenproof serving plate and grate half of the remaining cheese onto it. With your fingers, gently ease each soufflé free from the sides of its ramekin *(above)*, or run a knife around it. Unmold the soufflés onto your hand and place them on the bed of cheese.

3 **Grating cheese.** Choose a fairly hard cheese — Parmesan, for example, or the white Cheddar shown above. Using the medium-sized or small holes of a grater, according to the hardness of the cheese, grate half the cheese into the pan *(above)*, then whisk it into the sauce.

4 **Adding egg whites.** Separate eggs, adding one extra yolk for every two whole eggs. Beat all of the yolks into the sauce. In a large bowl, preferably of copper, beat the egg whites until they form soft peaks *(Step 3, page 69)*. Fold the whites gently into the soufflé base.

5 **Filling ramekins.** Butter ceramic ramekins. Spoon enough soufflé mixture into each ramekin to fill it by two thirds *(above)*. Set the ramekins on a rack in a large pan. Pour hot water into the pan until it comes two thirds of the way up the sides of the ramekins. Cook the soufflés in a preheated 350° F. [180° C.] oven for about 20 minutes.

8 **Adding cream.** Pour or spoon heavy cream over the soufflés on the plate, immersing them as deep as the plate permits — up to about half of their depth. Sprinkle more grated cheese over the top of each soufflé.

9 **Serving the soufflés.** Bake the soufflés in their coating of cream for another 20 minutes at 350° F. [180° C.], until the cream is almost completely absorbed and the melted cheese has gilded the tops of the soufflés. The soufflés will puff up slightly during baking; serve them quickly, straight from the oven.

A Soufflé Wrapping for a Savory Filling

A soufflé mixture spread thin in a wide, shallow pan will develop a firm yet light texture when baked, and will lose little of its airiness when unmolded. Such a soufflé is flexible enough to be rolled around a creamy stuffing flavored with cheese or other ingredients. It can then be briefly returned to the oven so that it will heat through and regain its lost volume before being served in slices.

In the roll demonstrated, the soufflé mixture is flavored with Parmesan and Gruyère cheeses; the filling is ricotta, beaten with cream and garnished with chopped parsley and chunks of sweet red pepper. Instead of peppers, you could use sautéed zucchini, parboiled young peas or stewed, drained tomatoes. Other possible fillings include a *duxelles* mixture of chopped shallots and mushrooms stewed in butter *(recipe, page 142)*, or a base of cream cheese, cottage cheese or white sauce enlivened with blue or smoked cheese or grated Parmesan.

The composition of the soufflé base is similar to that of the soufflé on pages 76-77, except that an equal number of egg whites and yolks are used. This proportion gives the soufflé enough substance to be rolled without cracking or breaking. Even so, the soufflé is quite fragile and must be handled with care.

To facilitate the unmolding, a buttered baking pan (a jelly-roll pan is used here) should be lined with well-buttered wax or parchment paper. The soufflé is turned out onto a towel to ensure gentle handling. As the filled soufflé is rolled, the towel serves to distribute pressure evenly along the length of the rolled edge. The towel is then used to lift the soufflé into an ovenproof dish. There the soufflé is topped with melted butter and grated cheese, which will form a crust during the second phase of baking.

1 Filling the baking pan. Butter a jelly-roll pan. Line the bottom and sides with buttered wax or parchment paper, keeping the buttered surface inward. Prepare a soufflé mixture *(pages 76-77)*, using an equal number of egg yolks and whites. Pour the soufflé mixture into the pan, spreading it into a uniform layer with a spatula.

2 Unmolding the soufflé. Bake the soufflé at 350° F. [180° C.] for 15 minutes, or until it is puffy and lightly golden. Remove the pan from the oven and cover it with a towel big enough to overlap the edges on all sides. Grasp the towel-covered pan and reverse it so the soufflé rests on the towel. Carefully lift the pan off the soufflé *(above)*.

5 Lifting the roll. When the soufflé and filling have been completely rolled up, lift the roll, still on its towel, onto a buttered ovenproof gratin dish. Carefully slide the roll onto the dish, positioning it so that the seam side is underneath.

6 Topping the roll. Melt some butter and spoon it over the roll. Grate a small amount of the same cheese used to flavor the soufflé and sprinkle the cheese over the roll, distributing it evenly so that it will form a uniform crust.

3 **Spreading the filling.** Allow the soufflé to cool on the towel for a few minutes. Peel off the paper lining. Since the edges of the soufflé tend to be more brittle than the rest and might crack when rolled, trim about ½ inch [1 cm.] off the two shorter sides. Prepare a filling — ricotta beaten with heavy cream is shown. Spoon the filling onto the soufflé (above) and spread it in an even layer with a spatula. Leave a margin of about 1 inch [2½ cm.] on all sides so that the filling does not ooze out when the soufflé is rolled.

4 **Rolling the soufflé.** Sprinkle the top of the filling with chopped parsley and with sweet red peppers that have been roasted until charred on all sides, left to cool under a damp towel, peeled, seeded and chopped. Roll up the soufflé, using the towel to apply uniform pressure along the rolled edge. To avoid a gap in the center, start the roll with as tight a fold as possible.

7 **Serving the soufflé.** Return the roll to the 350° F. [180° C.] oven to heat the soufflé and its filling through. Remove the roll when a light crust has formed on top — approximately 10 to 12 minutes. Serve the roll cut into slices.

Fondue: Molten and Mellow

Among dishes in which cheese holds center stage, the simplest consists of cheese that is melted into a thick sauce and served—for a contrast of texture—with crusty bread. To prevent the fat and protein in the cheese from separating, the melting must be done as gently as possible: The cheese is diced or shredded, and cooked in a little wine or beer, which not only keeps the cheese from direct contact with the heat, but also contributes a pleasant, subtle flavor. The cooking vessel should be a heavy one set on top of a heat-diffusing pad so that the liquid can be held at the barest simmer.

Other details of preparation depend on how the dish is to be served. A Swiss fondue (the word means "melted" in French) is generally made with Gruyère, sometimes mixed with Emmentaler or Appenzeller, and includes a generous amount of dry white wine (demonstration, right; recipe, page 151).

The fondue comes to the table in its cooking vessel, which is set on a portable heat source to keep the cheese hot and molten. Each diner swirls chunks of bread in the pot to coat them with cheese. Because such prolonged exposure to heat increases the risk of the cheese separating, a little potato flour or all-purpose flour is stirred in before serving: The grains of starch hold the cheese in suspension in the wine and help to keep the mixture stable.

If a smaller quantity of cheese is melted in just a splash of liquid and presented at once, in individual portions, a binder is not necessary. A case in point is Welsh rabbit. This venerable dish—now often referred to as Welsh rarebit—was no doubt christened in ironic reference to the toasted cheese that constituted dinner when a Welsh hunter failed to bag any game. It is made with mature Cheddar, or a similar sharp-flavored cheese, and beer (box, right; recipe, page 153). The melted mixture is simply poured over toast or fried bread; it can then be briefly popped under the broiler to brown the top lightly before serving.

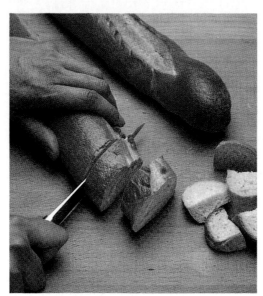

1 **Cutting the bread.** Use a crusty French loaf that has begun to dry out and is firm enough to cut up neatly. With a large, sharp knife, cut the bread into thick slices (above). Halve or quarter the slices into bite-sized chunks.

2 **Flavoring the pot.** To give the fondue a faint flavor of garlic, cut a peeled garlic clove in half and rub its cut surfaces all over the inside of the cooking vessel — traditionally, an earthenware pot. Discard the clove.

A Blend of Cheddar and Beer

1 **Melting cheese in beer.** Put a heavy pan on a heat-diffusing pad over medium heat. Add a small chunk of butter and pour in beer or, as shown here, dark ale. Season with salt and pepper. When the beer is warm, add grated Cheddar. Worcestershire sauce and prepared mustard add flavor.

2 **Serving the melted cheese.** Stir constantly while the cheese melts. As soon as the mixture is thick and creamy, pour it over hot buttered toast, set on heatproof serving plates. Slip the Welsh rabbit under a preheated broiler for a few seconds, or until the top is browned lightly.

3 **Adding the cheese.** Trim the rind off the cheese — Gruyère is used above — and cut it into small dice. Put the pot on top of a heat-diffusing pad over medium heat and pour in dry white wine. Season it with pepper and a little nutmeg. When the wine is warm but not yet simmering, add the cheese.

4 **Stirring the fondue.** As the cheese melts, stir it constantly with a wooden spoon to ensure that it is evenly heated, scraping the bottom of the pot to keep the mixture from sticking. Adjust the heat so that the mixture bubbles very gently.

5 **Adding a binder.** In a cup or small bowl, dissolve a little potato flour in kirsch or white wine. When the cheese has melted completely, stir in the flour and wine to stabilize the fondue. Simmer the fondue for a minute or two longer in order to blend the flavors.

6 **Serving the fondue.** Transfer the pot of fondue to a portable heat source set on the dining table. Adjust the flame to maintain the fondue at a gentle simmer. Give each guest a long-handled fork and some bread pieces. To eat the fondue, spear a piece of bread on the fork, dip it into the pot, lift it out and immediately turn it to coat it with the melted cheese and prevent dripping.

Contrasting Layers Fused in the Oven

When layered with complementary ingredients and baked, cheese melts and unites a casserole with its flavor and texture. A substantial vegetable such as potato or eggplant, or a starchy ingredient such as bread, rice or pasta, gives the casserole body, while a sauce contributes moistness. Lightly beaten egg, poured over the assembly, binds it as it cooks.

The way a cheese is prepared for layering will depend on its texture. Soft cheeses—ricotta or a blue cheese, for example—are spread or crumbled into the casserole. Semisoft cheeses such as mozzarella or Port-Salut are sliced ¼ inch [6 mm.] thick. Firm cheeses such as Parmesan or Cheddar are shredded or grated.

You may vary the ingredients to taste. In this demonstration (recipe, page 139), mozzarella cheese is accompanied with milk-soaked bread and a tomato sauce. Thinly sliced potatoes could replace the bread. Instead of tomato sauce, you could use a spinach purée enriched with cream, or an herb-flavored white sauce.

1 **Moistening the bread.** Cut firm, homemade-type white bread into thin slices; do not trim off the crusts. Butter a large, shallow casserole dish. Moisten each slice of bread by soaking it briefly in a dish of milk, then place it in the casserole to make a neat layer covering the bottom. In this case, the slices form an overlapping pattern; alternatively, they could be cut into smaller pieces and fitted into the casserole side by side.

4 **Mixing the binder.** In a mixing bowl, whisk five or six eggs until well blended. Beat in freshly grated Parmesan cheese (above). Pour the mixture evenly over the topmost bread layer. With a long-tined fork, pierce through the layers in several places to enable the egg mixture to penetrate all of the layers.

5 **Adding a final topping.** Let the casserole stand for a few minutes so that the egg mixture permeates the bread. Dribble the remaining tomato sauce over the top for a decorative effect (above). Dot the surface with small pieces of butter, which will melt and help to brown the top during cooking.

2 **Adding sauce.** Ladle a sauce — in this example, a tomato sauce *(page 35)* — over the bread to cover it completely in a thick layer. For extra flavor, sprinkle the sauce with herbs. Dried oregano is used here; crumble the leaves of the herb in your fingers and scatter the pieces over the layer of sauce.

3 **Arranging the cheese.** Spread the cheese — in this instance mozzarella, sliced ¼ inch [6 mm.] thick — neatly on top of the tomato sauce to cover it almost completely *(above)*. Alternate layers of milk-soaked bread, herb-sprinkled sauce and mozzarella until the casserole is nearly full, ending with a layer of bread. Reserve a little sauce for a topping *(Step 5)*. Use a spoon or spatula to press down the top layer and compact the assemblage.

6 **Baking and serving.** Bake the casserole, uncovered, in a preheated 350° F. [180° C.] oven for about one hour, until the top is lightly browned. Cut the casserole into wedges *(right)*. Serve the casserole either hot or warm, accompanied by a green salad.

A Choice of Pastry Containers

Pastry makes attractive containers for melted-cheese mixtures and provides, in addition, a crisp textural contrast to the soft filling. The pastry itself is formed as shown on page 37; the ingredients in the pastry mixture will vary, however, with the type of casing you choose.

The free-form pastry casing demonstrated at right, for instance, will need a crust strengthened with eggs in order to hold its shape (recipe, page 147).

For this casing, sheets of unbaked pastry are closely molded and sealed around a filling of cheese and ham bound with egg. The cheese is a mixture of ricotta, chosen for its smooth body; Parmesan, for its strong, nutty flavor; mozzarella, for its melting qualities; and provolone, for its piquancy. The Parmesan is grated, the provolone and the mozzarella are simply cubed. The mozzarella softens during the lengthy cooking time needed to bake the crust, but the provolone remains firm enough to add a distinctive textural note to the pie.

A similar effect could be achieved with a variety of other cheeses: Any fresh white cheese could be used instead of ricotta, Cheddar instead of Parmesan, Fontina instead of mozzarella. Or you could completely change the dish's character by replacing the provolone with a blue cheese, or by studding the mixture with chopped vegetables, salted and drained if they exude liquid, as tomatoes do. Any mixture for a casing of this type should be fairly dense and firm, so that it does not seep out during cooking.

If you form and prebake an open tart shell (pages 74-75), the filling mixture can be a liquid one that will firm up with additional baking. In the bottom demonstration, a partially baked pastry shell is filled with Brie that has been melted by gentle heating in a water bath and then moistened with cream and egg (recipe, page 143). Brief baking is sufficient to set the cheese filling and color the crust.

A Free-form Pie

1 **Mixing the cheese.** Cut mozzarella and provolone into small dice. In a large bowl, mix the diced cheese with diced cooked ham, a lump of fresh cheese — in this case, ricotta — and grated Parmesan. Stir into the mixture a little chopped parsley, beaten egg, and salt and pepper.

2 **Putting the filling in place.** Make a short-crust dough and divide it into two slightly unequal portions. Roll the larger portion into a round about ¼ inch [6 mm.] thick. Trim it to make a circle. Drape the circle around the rolling pin and transfer it to a baking sheet. Spoon the filling onto the dough (above).

An Open Tart with a Melted Filling

1 **Preparing the cheese.** Cut the rind from a ripe piece of soft cheese — in this example, Brie. Cut the cheese into chunks and put them in a pan. Stand the pan on a rack in a larger pan half-filled with simmering water (above). Add cream gradually to the cheese and stir until the cheese has melted smoothly.

2 **Adding beaten egg.** Beat eggs and gradually stir them into the melted cheese. Remove the mixture from the heat and flavor with salt and a little sugar. If you like, add a pinch of saffron, dissolved in a spoonful of boiling water, and a little ground ginger.

3 **Enclosing the filling.** Pat the filling into a neat circle, leaving a margin of dough 1½ inches [4 cm.] wide all around. Roll the second piece of dough into a circle and trim it. Drape it loosely around the rolling pin, then unroll it to cover the filling. Brush the edge of the top layer with beaten egg or water.

4 **Sealing the dough.** Fold the exposed rim of the bottom layer of dough back over the edge of the top layer. Then fold this tripled rim up against the enclosed filling. To flute the edge, press in with a forefinger while pushing an adjacent section out with your thumb. Slit the pie lid to let steam escape.

5 **Baking and serving the pie.** For an attractive glaze, brush the top of the pie with egg yolk mixed with water, and score the glaze with the tines of a fork. Bake in a 375° F. [190° C.] oven for about one hour, until the pastry crisps. Using two wide spatulas, transfer the pie to a dish; serve it hot or cold.

3 **Filling the pastry case.** Line a tart pan with a removable base with short-crust dough and partially bake it, as demonstrated on page 75, Step 3. Then pour the cheese-and-egg mixture into the pastry case *(above)*.

4 **Baking and serving the tart.** Bake the tart in a preheated 375° F. [190° C.] oven for 30 minutes, until the filling puffs and the surface is golden brown. Lift the tart from its mold *(Step 7, page 75)* and slide it onto a serving plate. Present the tart hot, tepid or cold, cutting wedges just before serving it.

Surprise Parcels with Savory Centers

Small pieces of firm, well-flavored cheese become delectably soft when baked or fried, but they require some form of protection to keep them in shape and prevent their surfaces from melting as they cook. Cheese pieces to be baked can be wrapped in leaves and thus transformed into savory surprise parcels. Because the leaves provide moisture, they are particularly useful for cheese that is beginning to dry up and might otherwise be thrown away.

The leaves best suited to wrapping cheese are grapevine leaves: They have a unique aroma and a mildly astringent flavor that attenuates the sharpness of a cheese past its prime. Fresh leaves have the best color, but they are likely to be tough, even after cooking; most diners prefer to discard them before they eat the cheese. Preserved leaves are generally tender enough to eat; they should be covered with boiling water and soaked for half an hour to remove the taste of brine before you wrap them around the cheese. Lettuce and spinach leaves, blanched briefly to make them supple, can also serve as wrappers.

Leaves will not adhere to cubes of cheese (right, bottom) that are deep fried. Instead, the cubes should be coated with protective layers of flour, eggs and bread crumbs. Cook the cubes in olive oil for its delicate, fruity flavor, or in an oil with an unassertive taste—corn or peanut oil, for example—so that the flavor of the cheese is unchallenged.

To ensure that the coating cooks to crispness, the oil should be deep enough to cover the cubes and must be maintained at a temperature of 350° to 375° F. [180° to 190° C.]. If you do not have a deep-frying thermometer, test the temperature by dropping a cube of bread into the pan: The oil should sizzle and the bread should crisp almost immediately. To prevent fluctuations in the temperature of the oil, introduce the cold pieces of cheese to the pan one by one and fry them in batches, taking care not to crowd the pan. Drain the cubes of cheese thoroughly before serving them.

A Shiny Wrapping of Leaves

1 **Preparing the cheese.** With a sharp knife pare the rind from pieces of cheese—a goat's-milk cheese that has begun to dry up is shown here. Cut away any mold on the cheese surface. Small cheeses should be cut into halves or quarters; cut large cheeses into ¾-inch [2-cm.] cubes.

2 **Wrapping the cheese.** Wash fresh grapevine leaves in cold water and dry them with paper towels. Snap off the stems. Place a piece of cheese about 1 inch [2½ cm.] from the base of each leaf. Fold the sides of the leaf over the cheese, tucking in the edges neatly; roll up the leaf to form a package.

Crunchy Crumb Coating for Cubes

1 **Cutting cubes of cheese.** With a sharp knife, remove the rind from a large block of cheese—Fontina, in this case. Cut through the cheese to make slices about ¾ inch [2 cm.] thick. Cut each slice into strips ¾ inch wide, then slice across the strips to cube the cheese.

2 **Coating the cubes.** With your fingers, turn each cube first in flour, then in beaten egg. Finally, place the cube on a pile of dry bread crumbs. Sprinkle some more crumbs over the top and sides of the cube, patting them into place evenly. Set the cubes aside for a few minutes to firm the coating.

3 **Cooking the parcels.** Arrange the cheese parcels compactly in an oiled ovenproof dish, with the loose ends of each wrapping tucked well under the cheese. To prevent the leaves from charring, brush the parcels with olive oil. Put the dish in a preheated 450° F. [230° C.] oven for about 15 minutes.

4 **Serving the cheese.** When the vine leaves start to darken and the parcels feel soft when pressed, remove the dish from the oven. Serve the leaf-wrapped cheese hot — accompanied, if you like, by slices of bread that have been crisped in the oven for five minutes.

3 **Deep frying the cubes.** Half-fill a deep saucepan with oil. Heat the oil to 350° F. [180° C.]. With a slotted spoon, lower the cheese cubes one at a time into the oil (above); be careful not to crowd the pan. The cubes will be ready in three or four minutes, when their coatings have turned a rich golden brown. Drain them on paper towels.

4 **Serving the fried cheese.** Arrange the drained cubes on an ovenproof dish. Place the dish in a preheated 250° F. [120° C.] oven to keep the cheese hot while you fry more batches. When all of the cubes are fried and drained, arrange them on a napkin and serve, while they are soft and creamy inside (above).

Pancake Packages

Wafer-thin pancakes, wrapped around fresh cheese, form envelopes of flavor known as blintzes. In this classic of Middle European cuisine, the pancakes are twice-cooked: After the parcels are filled, they are returned to the skillet to heat the cheese and crisp the wrappers.

Because these pancakes absorb moisture, the filling must be made with a dry cheese such as farmer, ricotta or un-creamed cottage cheese. If the cheese seems stiff, some sour cream or creamed cottage cheese may be added before the cheese is sieved to make it smoother. The mixture is then bound with egg yolks (recipe, page 158).

The pancake batter contains a high ratio of eggs, yielding flexible, crepelike cakes. To ensure tenderness, mix the ingredients just enough to moisten them, then let the batter stand to relax the flour's gluten—a resilient network of protein molecules.

The pancakes are fried on only one side, then folded around the filling with the uncooked surface facing out. When the parcels are fried, the uncooked side will brown without toughening. Serve blintzes hot with sour cream, berries or preserves, or cinnamon and sugar.

1 **Preparing the filling.** Place a strainer over a bowl. With a wooden spoon, force the cheese — in this case, farmer cheese moistened with a small amount of creamed cottage cheese — through the strainer. Stir in egg yolks, melted butter and sugar. Salt to taste.

2 **Making the pancake.** Prepare the batter and let it rest for an hour. Heat a heavy skillet or crepe pan; brush the pan with a film of melted butter. Ladle in about 3 tablespoons [45 ml.] of batter and quickly tilt the pan to spread it in a thin layer. Cook the pancake for 20 to 30 seconds, just until the top sets.

3 **Stacking the pancakes.** Loosen the cooked pancake with a spatula, if necessary, and slide it onto a plate. Brush the pan with more butter if it looks dry. Continue to make pancakes, stacking one on top of the other.

4 **Filling the blintzes.** Lay a pancake, cooked side up, on a flat surface. Place a spoonful of filling just above the center of the pancake (left). Fold the sides of the pancake toward the middle so that they overlap (center). Fold down the top to seal in the filling (right), then roll the pancake toward you.

5 **Frying the blintzes.** Place the blintzes, seam sides down, in a heated pan brushed with butter. Fry them for four or five minutes, regulating the heat so the blintzes brown slowly and evenly. When the underside is done, use two spatulas to turn each blintz (above), and cook for another four or five minutes. Serve at once.

Anthology of Recipes

Drawing upon the cooking traditions and literature of more than 32 countries, the editors and consultants for this volume have selected 220 published recipes for the Anthology that follows. The selections range from the simple to the unusual—from homely Welsh rabbit to an elegant Roquefort quiche baked in a yeast-pastry shell.

Many of the recipes were written by world-renowned exponents of the culinary art, but the Anthology also includes selections from rare and out-of-print books and from works that have never been published in English. Whatever the sources, the emphasis in these recipes is always on fresh, natural ingredients that blend harmoniously.

Since many early recipe writers did not specify amounts of ingredients, sizes of pans or even cooking times and temperatures, the missing information has been judiciously added. In some cases, instructions have been expanded. Where appropriate, clarifying introductory notes have also been supplied; they are printed in italics. Modern terms have been substituted for archaic language, but to preserve the character of the original recipes and to create a true anthology, the authors' texts have been changed as little as possible.

In keeping with the organization of the first half of the book, the Anthology begins with dishes based on whole eggs, continues to those made with beaten eggs (and in some cases, cheese as well), and concludes with dishes that feature cheese.

Recipes for standard preparations—white sauce, shortcrust pastry and stock among them—appear at the end of the Anthology. Unfamiliar cooking terms and uncommon ingredients are explained in the combined General Index and Glossary.

Apart from the primary components—eggs, cheese and elements that are mentioned in the recipe titles—all recipe ingredients are listed in order of use, with both the customary United States measurements and the new metric measurements provided in separate columns. The metric quantities supplied here reflect the American practice of measuring such solid ingredients as flour or sugar by volume rather than by weight, as European cooks do.

To make the quantities simpler to measure, many of the figures have been rounded off to correspond to the gradations that are now standard on metric spoons and cups. (One cup, for example, equals precisely 240 milliliters; wherever practicable in these recipes, however, a cup's equivalent appears as a more readily measurable 250 milliliters.) Similarly, weight, temperature and linear metric equivalents are rounded off slightly. Thus the American and metric figures are not equivalent, but using one set or the other will produce equally good results.

Fried Eggs

To Fry an Egge as Round as a Ball

The author has adapted this recipe from one that she found in an Elizabethan cookbook.

To serve 4

4 to 8	eggs	4 to 8
1 lb.	lard	½ kg.

Heat the lard in a very deep frying pan until it spits when a small piece of bread is dropped into it. With a large wooden spoon, stir the lard until a great pit is swirling in the center of the pan. Continue stirring and drop an egg into the center, stirring around the egg until it is cooked through. Remove gently with a slotted spoon and place the egg into a warmed casserole. Proceed with each egg until they are all cooked. It may take two people to cook eggs this way, one to crack and drop the egg, the other to stir. Serve at once.

RUTH ANNE BEEBE
SALLETS, HUMBLES & SHREWSBERY CAKES

Eggs Clementine

Oeufs à la Clementine

To serve 4

4	eggs	4
4	slices bread, fried in butter	4
½ cup	shredded Gruyère cheese	125 ml.
¼ cup	dry white wine	50 ml.
	salt	
	cayenne pepper	
4 tbsp.	butter	60 ml.

Arrange the fried bread in an ovenproof serving dish. Melt the cheese in a saucepan with the wine; season it with salt and cayenne. Pour this mixture onto the fried bread. Fry the eggs in hot butter, and place each egg on a slice of the fried bread. Put the dish into a preheated 400° F. [200° C.] oven, or under a broiler, for two minutes to glaze the tops of the eggs.

LE CORDON BLEU

Toasted Omelet

To serve 2

4	eggs, beaten until frothy	4
1	large onion, finely chopped	1
2 tbsp.	chopped fresh coriander leaves	30 ml.
2	fresh green chilies, stemmed, seeded and finely chopped	2
	salt	
4	slices bread with the crusts removed	4
⅓ cup	oil	75 ml.

Mix the eggs with the onion, coriander, chilies, and salt to taste. Soak the bread in this mixture for about five minutes until it is slightly soft. Heat the oil in a large skillet and fry the bread. Distribute the remaining egg mixture equally on top of the slices. Fry the bread slices on both sides until they are golden brown. Serve immediately.

PREMILA LAL
THE EGG & CHEESE COOK-BOOK

Rancher-Style Eggs

Huevos Rancheros

Tomatillos are green ground cherries, sometimes called husk tomatoes, available in cans in Latin American food stores. The oils in chilies may irritate your skin; handle them carefully and wash your hands immediately after chopping them.

To serve 4

8	eggs, fried	8
8	tortillas	8
12	tomatillos, coarsely chopped	12
5 tbsp.	lard	75 ml.
1	onion, chopped	1
1	garlic clove, chopped	1
1	sprig fresh coriander, chopped	1
1 or 2	fresh hot chilies, stemmed, seeded and chopped	1 or 2
	salt	

Using a mortar and pestle, pound the tomatillos and garlic together with the coriander and chilies. Fry the onion in 2 tablespoons [30 ml.] of lard until they are soft. Add the tomatillo mixture and simmer the sauce for 10 minutes. Fry the tortillas in the remaining lard until they become soft. Drain them and place the tortillas on a warmed platter. Place one fried egg on top of each tortilla. Pour the tomatillo sauce over the eggs. Serve while the eggs are still hot.

NURI FONSECA
RECETAS DE AMERICA LATINA

Spanish Fried Eggs

Huevos Fritos a la Española

To serve 4

4	eggs	4
½ cup	olive oil	125 ml.
1	large onion, chopped	1
4	medium-sized ripe tomatoes, peeled and chopped	4
3	green peppers, halved, seeded, deribbed and chopped	3
	salt	
	toasted bread, cut into triangles (optional)	

Heat 4 tablespoons [60 ml.] of the oil in a saucepan and cook the onion, tomatoes and peppers in it until slightly softened. Season with salt, cover and cook slowly for 40 minutes, or until the vegetables are cooked to a thick purée. Place the purée in a warmed serving dish.

Fry the eggs in the remaining oil; break them into a cup first if desired and slide them into the hot oil.

When they are cooked, place the eggs on top of the purée to serve. If desired, garnish with triangles of toasted bread.

MARIA PILAR JEREZ
TU COCINA

Eggs the Antidame Way

The title of this 18th Century recipe probably indicates that the ingredients were considered rather strong for refined feminine tastes.

To serve 6

10	eggs	10
⅓ cup	olive oil	75 ml.
2 tbsp.	finely chopped fresh parsley	30 ml.
2 tbsp.	finely cut fresh chives	30 ml.
2	salt anchovies, filleted, soaked in water for 30 minutes, drained, patted dry and finely chopped	2
1 tbsp.	capers, rinsed and finely chopped	15 ml.
	salt and pepper	
	grated nutmeg	
	fresh lemon juice	

Pour the olive oil into a heatproof serving dish and break six of the eggs into it. Cook over low heat until the whites of the eggs are just set, the yolks still soft.

Meanwhile, separate the yolks and whites of the four remaining eggs. Whip the whites stiff. Put the yolks with the parsley, chives, anchovies and capers and beat them all together; season with salt, pepper, a little nutmeg and lemon juice. Fold in the egg whites, then put this composition over the other eggs that are already in the dish, and bake in a preheated 400° F. [200° C.] oven until the top is slightly set; a moment is enough. When they are done enough, serve hot.

VINCENT DE LA CHAPELLE
THE MODERN COOK

Eggs with Shrimp Sauce

Uova alla Salsa di Gambero

These eggs may be prepared in individual egg dishes, the sauce poured over when they are half-cooked, and finished under a broiler. The recipe serves six as a first course.

The original version of this recipe calls for prawns —crustaceans about the size of large shrimp but with the appearance of tiny lobster tails. The tails are sometimes available frozen in the United States.

To serve 3

6	eggs	6
5 oz.	raw unshelled shrimp	150 g.
5 tbsp.	butter	75 ml.
1 tbsp.	olive oil	15 ml.
2 tbsp.	finely chopped onion	30 ml.
2 tbsp.	chopped fresh parsley	30 ml.
	salt	
½ oz.	pine nuts, toasted and pounded in a mortar	15 g.
5 or 6 tbsp.	hot water	75 or 90 ml.

Melt 2 tablespoons [30 ml.] of the butter in a pan with the oil. Fry the onion and parsley gently until the onion is transparent, about 10 minutes. Add the shrimp and a pinch of salt, and cook for 10 minutes. Add the pine nuts and cook for another five minutes. Add the hot water, cover and simmer over very low heat for 30 minutes. Pound the contents of the pan in a mortar and press the mixture through a sieve. Reheat the sieved sauce.

Cook the eggs in the remaining butter until the whites are barely set. Slip the eggs onto a warmed serving dish and pour the reheated sauce over them before serving.

G. B. AND GIOVANNI RATTO
CUCINIERA GENOVESE

Chard Croquettes with Egg Yolk and Butter Sauce

Ovi in Sublisi

To roast almonds, place blanched almonds on a baking sheet in a preheated 400° F. [200° C.] oven for 10 minutes, or until lightly browned.

To serve 3 or 4

4	eggs, beaten	4
¼ lb.	Swiss chard, ribs removed, leaves parboiled for 3 minutes, squeezed dry and chopped (½ cup [125 ml.])	100 g.
2 tbsp.	butter or olive oil	30 ml.
1	scallion, chopped	1
1 tsp.	chopped fresh sweet marjoram leaves and flowers	5 ml.
1 tbsp.	chopped roasted almonds	15 ml.
	salt and pepper	
¼ tsp.	ground cinnamon	1 ml.
⅔ cup	milk	150 ml.
1 cup	flour	¼ liter
⅔ cup	freshly grated Parmesan cheese, or ½ cup [125 ml.] shredded provolone cheese	150 ml.
1 cup	dry bread crumbs	¼ liter
	olive oil for deep frying	

Egg yolk and butter sauce

2	egg yolks	2
16 tbsp.	unsalted butter (½ lb. [¼ kg.]), diced	240 ml.
1 tbsp.	cold water	15 ml.
3 tbsp.	flour	45 ml.
2½ cups	tepid water, lightly salted	625 ml.
1 tbsp.	strained fresh lemon juice	15 ml.
	salt and pepper	

For the croquettes, first heat the butter or oil in a saucepan and add the chard, scallion, marjoram, almonds, salt, pepper and cinnamon. Stir in the milk, and cook over low heat until the liquid is almost completely absorbed. Add about 1 tablespoon [15 ml.] of the flour, half of the beaten eggs and all of the cheese, and mix well. Cook for a minute or two longer until the mixture is thick, then allow it to cool.

Shape the mixture into eight to 12 small cylinders, roll them in the remaining flour, then in the remaining eggs, and finally in the bread crumbs. Deep fry these croquettes a few at a time in oil preheated to 365° F. [185° C.] until golden brown, two to three minutes. Drain on absorbent paper, and keep the croquettes warm while you prepare the sauce.

For the sauce, stir the egg yolks and cold water in a bowl. Over low heat, melt 4 tablespoons [60 ml.] of the butter in a heavy saucepan, add the flour and stir until the mixture begins to bubble. Off the heat, whisk in the tepid salted water; return the pan to the heat and whisk again until the mixture boils. Remove from the heat to cool for a minute, then add the egg yolks and return the pan to the heat. Whisk until the sauce thickens slightly. Do not let it boil.

Off the heat, add the lemon juice and the remaining butter, and whisk steadily until the sauce is smooth. Correct the seasoning and serve the sauce immediately as an accompaniment to the croquettes.

IPPOLITO CAVALCANTI
CUCINA TEORICO-PRATICA

Poached and Mollet Eggs

Eggs in Cream

Uovi alla Crema

To serve 4

8	eggs	8
1 cup	heavy cream	¼ liter
	salt and freshly ground pepper	

Pour the cream into a large enameled-iron gratin dish and place it over high heat. Boil the cream until it has reduced by half. Reduce the heat, break the eggs into the cream, season with salt and pepper, and cook until the eggs are almost set. Place the dish under the broiler for about two minutes to finish cooking the egg whites; the yolks should stay soft.

IL CUOCO PIEMONTESE RIDOTTO ALL'ULTIMO GUSTO

Eggs Poached in Wine

Uova in Camicia al Vino

This is a real connoisseur's dish that one rarely comes across these days, and then only in the old families of Versilia. If red wine is used instead of the white wine called for, the dish becomes less delicate.

	To serve 6	
12	eggs	12
2 cups	dry white wine	½ liter
3	onions, sliced	3
2	garlic cloves	2
	thyme	
½	bay leaf	½
	salt and pepper	
	grated nutmeg (optional)	
3 tbsp.	butter, kneaded with 1 tsp. [5 ml.] of flour	50 ml.
12	slices firm-textured white bread, fried in butter	12

Pour the wine into a saucepan and add the onions, garlic, a pinch of thyme, the bay leaf, salt, pepper and, if desired, a touch of nutmeg. Bring the mixture to a boil, reduce the heat and simmer for 15 minutes.

One at a time, break the eggs into a small cup and slide them into the wine, gently spooning the white over the yolk, as for poached eggs. Cook no more than three eggs at a time. The wine should barely simmer. After about three minutes, remove the eggs with a slotted spoon and keep them warm.

When all of the eggs are cooked, remove the bay leaf and purée the wine mixture through a fine sieve into a clean pan. Whisk the kneaded butter into the wine, and cook it over low heat until this sauce is reduced and thickened to a creamy consistency. Place a poached egg on each piece of fried bread and pour the sauce over the eggs.

MARIÙ SALVATORI DE ZULIANI
LA CUCINA DI VERSILIA E GARFAGNANA

Poached or Soft-boiled Eggs with Fines Herbes

Oeufs Mollets Fines Herbes

These can be made either with poached eggs or *oeufs mollets*—soft-boiled eggs—that is, eggs put in boiling water and boiled for four to five minutes, steeped in cold water and shelled. The white is cooked and the yolk remains soft without being runny.

This is one of those excessively (and deceptively) simple dishes which can make the reputation of a good cook; the process takes only about two minutes, so provided that the eggs are prepared beforehand and the herbs ready-chopped, the dish can be made at the last minute.

	To serve 1	
2	eggs, poached or soft-boiled	2
1 tbsp.	chopped fresh herbs, such as parsley, chives and tarragon	15 ml.
1 tbsp.	butter	15 ml.
	fresh lemon juice	

Melt the butter, put in the eggs and sauté them without letting the butter burn. Sprinkle in the herbs and a squeeze of lemon juice, and serve immediately.

ELIZABETH DAVID
FRENCH COUNTRY COOKING

Eggs in Red Wine

Oeufs au Vin Rouge

	To serve 6	
12	eggs, at room temperature	12
1 quart	red wine	1 liter
2 tbsp.	rendered goose fat (or substitute butter)	30 ml.
2	shallots or 1 onion, sliced	2
2	carrots, sliced	2
2	leeks, white parts only, sliced	2
3	garlic cloves, crushed to a paste	3
1 tbsp.	flour	15 ml.
1	bouquet garni	1
	salt and pepper	
1 tbsp.	vinegar	15 ml.

Melt the goose fat in a saucepan and add the shallots or onion, the carrots, leeks and garlic. Cook for 10 minutes, or until the vegetables are softened. Sprinkle in the flour, mix well, and stir in the wine. Add the bouquet garni and season this sauce mixture with salt and pepper. Cook, uncovered, over low heat for 45 minutes, or until the sauce is reduced by half. Discard the bouquet garni.

Bring a large saucepan of water to a simmer and add the vinegar. Poach the eggs, four at a time, in this liquid for four to five minutes, using a slotted spoon to wrap the whites over the yolks. Remove and drain the eggs, and trim the whites neat. To serve, slide the eggs gently into the wine sauce.

HENRI PHILIPPON
QUERCY PÉRIGORD

Poached Eggs in Wine Sauce

Oeufs en Matelote

To serve 4

4	eggs, poached	4
½ cup	dry white wine	125 ml.
¼ lb.	fresh button mushrooms (about 1⅓ cups [325 ml.])	125 g.
¼ lb.	pearl or small boiling onions, peeled (about 1 cup [¼ liter])	125 g.
4 tbsp.	butter	60 ml.
1 tbsp.	flour	15 ml.
½ cup	beef stock (recipe, page 164)	125 ml.
2	egg yolks, beaten	2
4	slices bread, toasted	4

Sauté the mushrooms and onions in the butter for about five minutes, or until they begin to soften. Sprinkle in the flour, and stir in the stock and wine. Cook, uncovered, over low heat for 20 minutes, or until the onions are tender and the sauce is thickened.

Remove the pan from the heat and cool the sauce slightly. Stir the egg yolks into the sauce. Heat the sauce gently for a minute or two to thicken it without letting it boil.

Arrange a poached egg on each slice of toast, pour the sauce over the eggs, and serve.

A. B. DE PÉRIGORD
LE TRÉSOR DE LA CUISINIÈRE ET DE LA MAÎTRESSE DE MAISON

Eggs, Cheese and Truffles

Oeufs, Fromage et Truffes

To serve 4

8	eggs	8
2 oz.	Fontina cheese, cut into small pieces (about ¼ cup [50 ml.])	50 g.
1	fresh white truffle, very thinly sliced	1
4 tbsp.	butter	60 ml.
	salt and pepper	
	grated nutmeg	

Melt the butter in a large skillet set over low heat, add the cheese and let it melt. Add the slices of truffle and mix well. Break the eggs onto the cheese and truffles and season them with salt, pepper and a pinch of nutmeg. Let the eggs set—about five minutes—then serve.

F. AND T. RARIS
LES CHAMPIGNONS, CONNAISSANCE ET GASTRONOMIE

Eggs with Green Herb Sauce

To serve 6

6	eggs	6
1 cup	fresh chervil, parsley, chives, tarragon and watercress leaves, blanched for 1 minute in boiling water	¼ liter
6	capers, rinsed	6
1	oil-packed flat anchovy fillet, rinsed and patted dry	1
1¼ cups	white sauce (recipe, page 165)	300 ml.
6	slices bread, fried in butter	6

Pound the herbs in a mortar with the capers and anchovy. Pass the mixture through a sieve, and stir it into the white sauce. Poach the eggs in simmering water. Arrange each poached egg on a square of fried bread, and pour a portion of the sauce over each.

A. KENNEY HERBERT
FIFTY BREAKFASTS

Eggs with Mixed Vegetables

Uova alla Giardiniera

To serve 4

8	eggs, freshly poached and still warm	8
1	onion, chopped	1
1 cup	freshly shelled peas	¼ liter
1	small celery heart, halved, cored and chopped	1
4 tbsp.	butter	60 ml.
2 tbsp.	chopped fresh parsley	30 ml.
1 tsp.	chopped fresh marjoram	5 ml.
	salt	

Melt half of the butter in a saucepan and cook the onion until soft. Add the peas, celery, parsley and marjoram; cover and cook over very low heat until the peas are tender, about 20 minutes. Add a tablespoon [15 ml.] of water to the pan after the first 10 minutes if the pan looks dry. Off the heat, swirl in the remaining butter and season to taste.

Pour the vegetable mixture into a serving dish, arrange the poached eggs on top and serve.

VINCENZO CORRADO
IL CUOCO GALANTE

Eggs Poached in Tomatoes

Uova al Pomodoro

	To serve 6	
12	eggs	12
2 lb.	very ripe plum tomatoes, peeled and chopped	1 kg.
¼ cup	olive oil	50 ml.
1	garlic clove, chopped	1
	salt and pepper	
5 or 6	fresh basil leaves, each torn into 2 or 3 pieces	5 or 6

Heat the oil in a large saucepan, preferably one made of terra cotta. When it is hot, sauté the garlic lightly until pale golden in color. Add the tomatoes and cook them over low heat for about 15 minutes. Check to be sure they are very soft and of a saucelike consistency, and if necessary cook them a little longer; do not add any water or broth. Add salt and pepper to taste.

Add the basil to the saucepan. Carefully break the eggs into the tomato sauce. Sprinkle salt and pepper over the eggs; let them poach for about eight minutes. Bring the eggs to the table in the pan.

GIULIANO BUGIALLI
THE FINE ART OF ITALIAN COOKING

Doctor's Eggs

Oeufs du Docteur

	To serve 6	
6	eggs	6
2 tbsp.	butter	30 ml.
4	shallots, very finely chopped	4
1 cup	chopped fresh mushrooms	¼ liter
4	lettuce leaves, cut into thin shreds	4
⅓ cup	dry white wine	75 ml.
¾ cup	veal stock (recipe, page 164), boiled until syrupy and reduced to 4 tbsp. [60 ml.]	175 ml.
1 cup	heavy cream	¼ liter
1 tbsp.	chopped fresh chervil	15 ml.
1 tbsp.	chopped fresh tarragon	15 ml.
	rough puff pastry (recipe, page 166)	

Roll out the dough to form an oval, using the trimmings to make a border around the edge. Place the oval on a floured baking sheet and bake it in a preheated 400° F. [200° C.] oven until it is puffed and golden, about 15 to 20 minutes. Put the pastry on a large serving dish and keep it warm.

Heat the butter and cook the shallots in it until they are soft but not brown. Add the mushrooms and lettuce leaves. Moisten with the wine, then cook the mixture over medium heat until the liquid is reduced by half. Add the reduced stock and the cream, and continue cooking until the sauce is lightly thickened.

Poach the eggs in a pan of simmering water, drain them, and arrange them on the pastry shell. Add the chervil and tarragon to the sauce and cover the eggs with it.

70 MÉDECINS DE FRANCE
LE TRÉSOR DE LA CUISINE DU BASSIN MÉDITERRANÉEN

Poached Eggs with Sorrel Juice Sauce

Oeufs au Jus d'Oseille

If desired, the eggs may be served on slices of fried or toasted bread, with the sauce poured over them.

	To serve 6	
6	eggs, poached	6
1¼ cups	chopped fresh sorrel	300 ml.
	salt and pepper	
	grated nutmeg	
2 tbsp.	butter, cut into small pieces	30 ml.
2	egg yolks	2
1 cup	veal stock (recipe, page 164)	¼ liter

In a mortar, pound the sorrel well, extracting all of the juice from it. Whisk the juice with all of the remaining ingredients except the poached eggs. Put the mixture in a saucepan and stir it over low heat until lightly thickened; it must not boil. Arrange the poached eggs in a warmed serving dish, pour the sauce over them and serve.

MARIN
LES DONS DE COMUS

Eggs Poached in Creole Sauce

To serve 3

6	eggs	6
¼ cup	finely chopped green pepper	50 ml.
¼ cup	finely chopped scallions	50 ml.
½ cup	chopped fresh mushrooms	125 ml.
1 tsp.	salt	5 ml.
4	medium-sized tomatoes, peeled, seeded, chopped and cooked until soft, or puréed raw through a food mill	4
1	garlic clove, crushed to a paste	1
1 tbsp.	sugar	15 ml.
2 tbsp.	olive oil	30 ml.
¼ tsp.	pepper	1 ml.
¼ cup	chopped fresh parsley	50 ml.

Mix together all of the ingredients except the eggs, and place them in a broad saucepan. Bring to a boil and cook for five minutes. Turn off the heat. Break the eggs into a saucer and slip them one at a time into the sauce. Let them stand for five minutes, or until the whites are just set. Serve each egg with a portion of the sauce.

SUE TRIBUS
THE WONDERFUL WORLD OF BREAKFAST

Eggs in Caul

Oeufs en Crépines, à Ce que l'On Veut

Pork caul is a fatty stomach membrane, used as a natural casing and obtainable at butcher shops. In place of the stewed onions, you may use any other diced cooked vegetables or meats, their cooking juices reduced and thickened. Serve the dish with a sauce of your choice.

To serve 4

5	eggs, 4 poached, 1 beaten	5
4	pieces of pork caul, each about 6 inches [15 cm.] square	4
5 tbsp.	butter	75 ml.
1⅓ cups	chopped onions	325 ml.
2	salt anchovies, filleted, soaked in water for 30 minutes, patted dry and chopped	2
3	egg yolks	3
3 tbsp.	heavy cream	45 ml.
	salt and pepper	

Melt the butter, add the onions, and cook over very low heat until soft but not colored, about 30 minutes. Stir in the chopped anchovies. Beat together the egg yolks and cream and, off the heat, stir them into the onion mixture. Return to low heat and cook, stirring, until well thickened. Season.

Trim any ragged edges from the poached eggs. Lay the pieces of caul on a flat surface and brush them with beaten egg. Place a spoonful of the onion mixture on each piece of caul, make a hollow in the mixture with the back of the spoon, and slip a poached egg upside down into each hollow. Mound the remaining mixture around the eggs, and wrap the edges of the caul over the top to seal. Turn the packages over, seam sides down, onto a baking sheet and bake in a preheated 425° F. [220° C.] oven for about 10 minutes, or until the caul is golden on top.

MENON
LES SOUPERS DE LA COUR

Brains in Red Sauce

Cervelles Sauce Rouge

The original version of this recipe called for sheep brains, which are rarely available except from slaughterhouses.

To serve 6

6	eggs	6
4	calf's brains, soaked in cold water for 1 hour and membranes removed	4
1 cup	water	¼ liter
	salt	
2	dried red chilies	2
3 tbsp.	chopped fresh coriander leaves (or 1 tsp. [5 ml.] coriander seeds, crushed)	45 ml.
4	garlic cloves	4
1 tbsp.	paprika	15 ml.
½ cup	oil	125 ml.

Put the brains in a saucepan with the water. Salt them, and add the chilies, coriander and garlic. Dissolve the paprika in the oil and add it to the pan.

Cook the brains over low to medium heat for 20 minutes, or until they are cooked through but still firm. Three minutes before taking the pan from the heat, add the eggs, one by one, and poach them in the sauce.

IRENE LABARRE AND JEAN MERCIER
LA CUISINE DU MOUTON

Eggs Benedict

To serve 6

6	eggs, poached	6
6	thin slices ham	6
3	English muffins, halved, toasted and generously buttered	3
	butter	
½ tbsp.	Madeira (optional)	7 ml.
	hollandaise sauce *(recipe, page 165)*	
	paprika	
	fresh parsley sprigs	

Trim the ham to fit the muffins. Sizzle the ham in a frying pan in a small amount of butter, turn, and add the Madeira, if used. Lay one slice of ham on each muffin half, top with a poached egg, and cover with hollandaise sauce. Sprinkle with paprika and garnish with parsley. Serve hot.

IDA BAILEY ALLEN
BEST LOVED RECIPES OF THE AMERICAN PEOPLE

Mollet Eggs with Haddock

The techniques of cooking and shelling mollet eggs are demonstrated on pages 24-25. The haddock may be baked or poached until it flakes easily.

To serve 4

4	*mollet* eggs, shelled	4
½ lb.	cooked haddock, flaked (about 2 cups [½ liter])	¼ kg.
1 cup	white sauce *(recipe, page 165)*	¼ liter
½ cup	light cream	125 ml.
	salt and pepper	
2	garlic cloves, finely chopped	2
1 tbsp.	vegetable oil	15 ml.

Keep the shelled eggs warm in a bowl of hot water. Bring the white sauce to a boil, stir in the cream and boil rapidly for five minutes. Season to taste with salt and pepper.

Crush the garlic until smooth with ¼ teaspoon [1 ml.] salt, using the flat side of a knife blade. In a saucepan, cook the crushed garlic in the oil for a few minutes, then add the haddock. Beat the mixture over the heat, gradually adding three quarters of the white sauce; check the seasoning. Turn the haddock mixture into a warm serving dish. Remove the eggs from the water, drain them well and arrange them on top. Coat the eggs with the remaining sauce and serve for lunch with toast or garlic bread.

THE EDITORS OF HOUSE & GARDEN
HOUSE & GARDEN'S NEW COOK BOOK

Eggs Poached on Tomatoes and Smoked Herring

Aijja au Hareng Fumé "Lzza bi Ringa"

Harissa is a hot condiment widely used in North African cooking. To make it, combine dried red chilies, chopped garlic, cumin seeds, salt and olive oil in proportions to taste, and pound them together in a mortar or grind them to a smooth paste in a blender or food processor.

To serve 4

4	eggs	4
4	medium-sized tomatoes, peeled and sieved	4
3 oz.	smoked herring, broiled for 5 to 7 minutes, skinned, filleted and crumbled	100 g.
1 cup	water	¼ liter
½ cup	olive oil	100 ml.
1 tbsp.	*harissa*	15 ml.
2 tsp.	paprika	10 ml.
3 or 4	garlic cloves, thinly sliced	3 or 4
1½ tsp.	caraway seeds, pounded to a paste	7 ml.
1	medium-sized sweet red pepper, halved, seeded, deribbed and diced	1
	salt	

Heat the oil in a skillet. Stir in the tomatoes, *harissa*, paprika, garlic and caraway seeds. Add the herring and the water. Simmer the mixture for five minutes, then add the red pepper. Continue cooking over low heat for about 20 minutes, or until you have a thick sauce.

Correct the seasoning and break the eggs, one by one, onto the sauce. Cook until the whites set, and serve hot.

AHMED LAASRI
240 RECETTES DE CUISINE MAROCAINE

Egg Sausage

Natural sausage casings are cleaned beef, lamb or pork intestines. For this recipe, lamb or pork casings may be used. They are available in bulk from wholesalers and in smaller quantities from butchers.

These sausages may be treated like any meat sausage: sautéed or poached, or sliced and eaten cold.

	To serve 4	
6	eggs, beaten until frothy	6
1 tsp.	salt	5 ml.
½ tsp.	white peppercorns, cracked	2 ml.
¼ tsp.	cayenne pepper	1 ml.
1 tsp.	finely cut fresh chives	5 ml.
1 tsp.	finely chopped onion	5 ml.
1 tsp.	finely chopped green pepper	5 ml.
1 tsp.	finely chopped olives	5 ml.
1 cup	heavy cream	¼ liter
2	lamb or pork sausage casings, each 8 inches [20 cm.] long, thoroughly rinsed with cold water	2

Add to the eggs all of the ingredients except the cream and the sausage casings. Beat in the cream.

Tie one end of each sausage casing very tightly with string. Use a large funnel to fill the casings with the egg mixture, being careful not to let air pockets form. Leaving about 2 inches [5 cm.] of the casing unfilled to allow for expansion, tie off the ends. Bring a large pot of water to a rolling boil and drop in the filled casings. Remove from the heat and let the sausages stand in the cooking liquid for 30 to 45 minutes, occasionally stirring with a spoon (which avoids punctures) so that the filling does not separate.

Have a pot of cold water ready, and when the sausages are firm, remove them from the hot water and drop them into the cold water. Let them stand for 30 minutes. Store in the refrigerator; they will keep for a few days.

MEL MARSHALL
THE DELECTABLE EGG AND HOW TO COOK IT

Hard-boiled Eggs

Dot Heart Eggs

Any number of servings can be boiled at the same time, as this Chinese way of boiling eggs enables them to be kept, if necessary without refrigeration, for a day or two. In the tropics, I have found it better to immerse them in fresh water and keep them in the refrigerator as they become too salty with keeping. They are eaten for breakfast, taken on picnics or used for snacks, known as "dot hearts," or hunger appeasers. The eggs are almost soft again after this prolonged boiling.

	To serve 12	
12	eggs	12
1½ tsp.	salt	7 ml.
2 tsp.	tea leaves	10 ml.
	thinly pared peel of 1 tangerine	

In a thick saucepan, boil the eggs in water for one hour. Drain them, immerse them in cold water until cool, then tap gently to crack the shells, but do not peel them. Return the eggs to the saucepan with fresh water just to cover, bring to a boil and add the salt, tea and tangerine peel. Simmer over very low heat for two hours. Remove the saucepan from the heat, but leave the eggs in the water. Serve hot or cold.

MARY SLATER
CARIBBEAN COOKING FOR PLEASURE

Gratin of Chopped Eggs

Oeufs au Gratin

	To serve 4	
7	eggs, 6 hard-boiled and chopped, 1 lightly beaten	7
1 tbsp.	chopped fresh parsley	15 ml.
1	garlic clove, crushed to a paste	1
	salt and pepper	
1 cup	white sauce *(recipe, page 165)*, cooled	¼ liter
2 tbsp.	butter	30 ml.
¼ cup	dry bread crumbs	50 ml.
2 tbsp.	olive oil	30 ml.

Mix the chopped eggs with the parsley and garlic; season with salt and pepper. Stir the beaten egg into the white sauce, and mix the sauce with the chopped eggs.

Spoon the mixture into a buttered shallow ovenproof dish. Dot the top with the butter, and sprinkle it with the bread crumbs. Bake in a preheated 350° F. [180° C.] oven for 20 minutes, or until the mixture is firm but not dried out. Before serving, sprinkle the top with the oil.

E. AURICOSTE DE LAZARQUE
CUISINE MESSINE

Baked Stuffed Eggs
Oeufs Gratinés

To serve 4

8	eggs, hard-boiled	8
2	egg yolks, beaten	2
1 cup	fresh white bread crumbs	¼ liter
¼ cup	chopped mixed herbs	50 ml.
1 cup	shredded Gruyère cheese	¼ liter
4 tbsp.	butter, softened	60 ml.
1 tbsp.	heavy cream	15 ml.
	salt and pepper	

Mix the beaten egg yolks with the bread crumbs in a small bowl. Halve the hard-boiled eggs lengthwise while they are still warm and place the hard-boiled yolks in the bowl with the bread-crumb mixture. Add the herbs, cheese and 2 tablespoons [30 ml.] of the butter, and mix well. Stir in the cream to make a soft consistency. Season with salt and pepper.

Use half of the yolk mixture to stuff the egg whites, and spread the remaining mixture in the base of a buttered gratin dish just big enough to hold the egg halves. Place the stuffed eggs on top, dot with the remaining butter and cover with foil. Bake in a preheated 400° F. [200° C.] oven for five to six minutes. Remove the foil and return the eggs to the oven for one minute to brown the tops.

NINETTE LYON
LES OEUFS

Eggs Ponce de Leon

To serve 4 to 6

6	eggs, hard-boiled	6
2 tbsp.	butter	30 ml.
½	onion, diced	½
1 tbsp.	flour	15 ml.
2 cups	tomato juice	½ liter
½ cup	chopped celery	125 ml.
¼ cup	chopped green peppers	50 ml.
½ cup	mushrooms	125 ml.
	salt and pepper	
½ tsp.	Worcestershire sauce	2 ml.
½ cup	white sauce (recipe, page 165)	125 ml.
	cracker crumbs	

Chop the whites of the eggs, and mash the yolks. Brown the onion in 1 tablespoon [15 ml.] of the butter, add the flour and blend well. Put in the tomato juice, celery and peppers, and cook slowly until done. Add the mushrooms, the seasoning and the Worcestershire sauce. When this is all done, add the white sauce, the egg yolks and the chopped egg whites. Place in a shallow buttered casserole. Sprinkle with cracker crumbs, dot with the remaining butter and bake in a preheated 375° F. [190° C.] oven until brown—about 10 to 15 minutes. Serve hot.

LILLIE S. LUSTIG, S. CLAIRE SONDHEIM AND SARAH RENSEL (EDITORS)
THE SOUTHERN COOKBOOK OF FINE OLD RECIPES

Old-fashioned Egg Pie
Tourte d'Oeufs à l'Ancienne

To serve 4 to 6

6	eggs, hard-boiled and sliced	6
2 cups	sliced, fresh mushrooms, sautéed in 3 tbsp. [45 ml.] of butter for 5 minutes	½ liter
	salt and white pepper	
1 cup	white sauce (recipe, page 165)	¼ liter
1	egg yolk, beaten	1

Crepe batter

¼ cup	flour	50 ml.
	salt	
1	egg, beaten	1
½ cup	milk or water	125 ml.
2 tbsp.	butter, melted	30 ml.
	rough puff pastry (recipe, page 166, but double the quantities called for)	

To make the crepes, put the flour in a mixing bowl with a pinch of salt. Add the egg, the milk or water and finally, the melted butter, whisking to blend thoroughly. Heat a lightly greased 10-inch [25-cm.] crepe pan or skillet and pour in half of the crepe batter, swirling it around the base of the pan to make a large crepe. Cook for about two minutes on each side until golden brown, then make a second crepe with the remaining batter.

Roll out the pastry in two rounds and use one to line a 10-inch quiche pan. Place a crepe in the lined pan. Mix the eggs, mushrooms, salt and pepper, and white sauce, and fill the pie with this mixture. Cover with the second crepe, then with the second round of pastry, sealing the edges well. Brush the top with the egg yolk, score decoratively with a fork, and bake in a preheated 425° F. [220° C.] oven until golden and crusty, about 40 minutes. Serve bubbling hot.

ÉDOUARD M. NIGNON
LE LIVRE DE CUISINE DE L'OUEST-ÉCLAIR

Hard-boiled Eggs with Basil and Parmesan Sauce

Oeufs Durs au Pistou

French pistou, like the Italian pesto sauce, must be made from fresh basil. Dried basil will not give the authentic flavor.

	To serve 4	
4	eggs, hard-boiled	4
¼ cup	chopped fresh basil	50 ml.
½ cup	freshly grated Parmesan cheese	125 ml.
3	garlic cloves, coarsely chopped	3
	salt and pepper	
7 to 10 tbsp.	olive oil	105 to 150 ml.

Halve the eggs lengthwise and arrange them on a plate. Crush the garlic with ¼ teaspoon [1 ml.] of the salt in a mortar and add the basil, pounding until you have a smooth paste. Gradually add the cheese and oil alternately until the sauce has the consistency of thick cream. Add pepper and more salt to taste, spoon the sauce over the eggs and allow them to marinate for at least 30 minutes before serving.

NINETTE LYON
LES OEUFS

Mushroom Baked Eggs

Oeufs au Gratin

	To serve 4	
8	eggs, hard-boiled	8
1 cup	chopped fresh mushrooms	¼ liter
1	shallot, finely chopped	1
1 tbsp.	chopped fresh parsley	15 ml.
⅓ cup	tomato sauce (recipe, page 166)	75 ml.
	salt and pepper	
3 tbsp.	butter, melted	45 ml.
2 tbsp.	dry bread crumbs	30 ml.

Halve the eggs lengthwise. Remove the yolks and mash them with the mushrooms, shallot and parsley. Add the tomato sauce, salt and pepper, and 1 tablespoon [15 ml.] of the butter. Cook the mixture for a few minutes.

Arrange the egg whites in a gratin dish. Stuff them with the cooked yolk mixture. Sprinkle the tops with the bread crumbs, then with the remaining butter. Bake in a preheated 400° F. [200° C.] oven for about 15 minutes, or until the eggs are golden on top. Serve hot.

LA CUISINE LYONNAISE

Hard-boiled Eggs in Onion Sauce

Oeufs à la Provençale

Rocambole is also known as giant garlic because of the size of its stems, not its bulbs. Its bulbs have brown skins and flesh and are somewhat milder in taste than garlic.

	To serve 4	
8	eggs, hard-boiled and sliced	8
2	scallions, chopped	2
2	shallots, chopped	2
3 tbsp.	chopped rocambole, or substitute garlic	45 ml.
2 tbsp.	butter	30 ml.
1 tbsp.	flour	15 ml.
3 tbsp.	finely chopped fresh parsley	45 ml.
	salt and pepper	
	grated nutmeg	
¼ cup	heavy cream	50 ml.
¾ cup	oil	175 ml.
6 tbsp.	strained Seville orange juice	90 ml.

Melt the butter in a heavy saucepan, stir in the flour, and add the parsley, scallions, shallots and rocambole or garlic. Season with salt, pepper and nutmeg, and stir in the cream and oil. Cook over low heat, stirring, until the mixture forms a smooth, thick sauce—about 15 minutes.

Correct the seasoning, stir in the orange juice, add the sliced eggs and continue to cook until the eggs are heated through. Serve hot.

MARIN
LES DONS DE COMUS

Eggs in Onion Sauce

Oeufs à la Tripe

The name of this dish indicates its similarity in texture to tripe and onions. To give the sauce extra body and color, stir in two or three raw egg yolks and 1 tablespoon [15 ml.] of chopped fresh parsley just before the sliced eggs are added.

	To serve 6	
12	eggs, hard-boiled and sliced into rounds	12
6	onions, thinly sliced	6
8 tbsp.	butter	120 ml.
	salt and pepper	
1 tbsp.	flour	15 ml.
1 cup	light cream	¼ liter

In a saucepan, melt the butter, add the onions, and season them with salt and pepper. Cook over low heat until the onions are soft and golden, but not browned—eight to 10 minutes. Sprinkle in the flour and pour in the cream. Turn up the heat to bring the sauce to a boil, then reduce the heat at once and cook, stirring, for 25 to 30 minutes. Add the sliced eggs and heat them briefly in the sauce without allowing the mixture to boil. Serve very hot.

JULES BRETEUIL
LE CUISINIER EUROPÉEN

Hard-boiled Eggs with Potatoes and Shallots

Oeufs Durs aux Pommes de Terre et aux Échalotes

	To serve 4	
5	eggs	5
4	medium-sized potatoes	4
3	shallots, finely chopped	3
7 tbsp.	butter	100 ml.
	salt and pepper	
3 tbsp.	wine vinegar	45 ml.

Boil the potatoes in their skins until just tender. Hard-boil the eggs. Plunge them into cold water, then shell them and put them into hot water to keep warm.

Preheat the oven to 300° F. [150° C.]. Melt 2 tablespoons [30 ml.] of the butter in a skillet over medium heat. Add the shallots, cover and cook gently until they are soft and golden, about 10 minutes.

Meanwhile, peel the potatoes and slice them ½ inch [1 cm.] thick. Slice the eggs the same way. Arrange the egg and potato slices alternately in a buttered, shallow ovenproof serving dish. Cover the dish with foil, and keep the eggs and potatoes warm in the oven.

When the shallots are done, sprinkle them over the eggs and potatoes. Season with salt and pepper. In the same skillet, cook the remaining butter until it is nut brown, and pour it over the egg mixture. Return the skillet to high heat, add the vinegar and bring it to a boil. Pour it over the eggs and potatoes and serve at once.

MARTINE JOLLY
RÉUSSIR VOTRE CUISINE

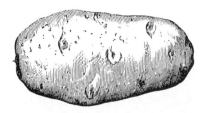

Eggs Marie-Louise

Oeufs Marie-Louise

	To serve 4	
6	eggs, hard-boiled and sliced	6
2	potatoes, boiled, peeled and thinly sliced while still hot	2
½	celeriac, peeled, diced and steamed for 25 minutes until tender	½
2 cups	white sauce *(recipe, page 165)*	½ liter
¼ cup	freshly shredded Gruyère cheese	50 ml.
2 tbsp.	dry bread crumbs	30 ml.

Carefully mix the egg slices, potato slices, and celeriac into the white sauce. Spoon the mixture into a gratin dish, sprinkle with the shredded cheese and bread crumbs, and bake in a preheated 400° F. [200° C.] oven for 20 minutes, or until golden and bubbling.

ÉDOUARD M. NIGNON
LE LIVRE DE CUISINE DE L'OUEST-ÉCLAIR

Egg Pie

Pâté aux Oeufs

	To serve 4	
6	eggs, 5 hard-boiled, 1 beaten	6
4	medium-sized potatoes, boiled, peeled and mashed	4
2 tbsp.	butter	30 ml.
¼ cup	heavy cream	50 ml.
	salt and pepper	
	grated nutmeg	
2 tbsp.	chopped fresh parsley	30 ml.
1 cup	white sauce *(recipe, page 165)*	¼ liter

Shell the hard-boiled eggs and cut them into slices not too thin. Mix the potatoes with the butter and cream; season well with salt, pepper and a very little nutmeg.

Line the bottom of a buttered 1½-quart [1½-liter] casserole with the potato mixture, then make a layer of sliced eggs. Scatter over some parsley and cover with a little white sauce. Continue these layers until the eggs are used up. Let the last layer be a coating of sauce, and cover the top with mashed potatoes. Smooth this over carefully with a wetted knife and mark a neat pattern on top with a fork or the point of a knife; brush over with the beaten egg and bake in a preheated 350° F. [180° C.] oven for about 30 minutes, or until the top is browned.

C. HERMAN SENN
HOW TO COOK EGGS AND OMELETS IN 300 DIFFERENT WAYS

Hard-boiled Eggs
with a Green Sauce

Oeufs Durs à la Farce

Purslane, or portulaca, is a weed common in New England. It is a thickly branched, spreading, fleshy plant with yellow-green flowers. Its small, narrow leaves taste like spinach.

To serve 4

10	eggs, 8 hard-boiled, 2 beaten	10
½ lb.	sorrel, chopped	¼ kg.
½ lb.	Swiss chard, green parts only, chopped	¼ kg.
½ lb.	young spinach, chopped	¼ kg.
1 cup	finely chopped purslane leaves (optional)	¼ liter
2 tbsp.	finely cut fresh chives	30 ml.
2 tbsp.	chopped fresh parsley	30 ml.
4 tbsp.	butter	60 ml.
	salt	
½ tsp.	mixed spices	2 ml.

Melt the butter in a skillet, add the greens and herbs, season with salt and spices, and cook over low heat, stirring occasionally, until the greens are tender and their liquids have been reabsorbed, about 10 to 15 minutes. Add the yolks of four hard-boiled eggs and mix them into the greens, crushing them with a wooden spoon. Off the heat, stir in the beaten eggs. Return this sauce to low heat and stir until it thickens slightly. Chop or slice the four remaining hard-boiled egg whites; halve or quarter the other four hard-boiled eggs. Spread the sauce evenly on a warmed platter and arrange the egg halves or quarters on it. Scatter the chopped or sliced egg whites over the top. Serve hot.

NICOLAS DE BONNEFONS
LES DÉLICES DE LA CAMPAGNE

Gratin of Hard-boiled Eggs
in Creamed Sorrel

Gratin d'Oeufs Dur à la Crème d'Oseille

To serve 4 to 6

6	eggs, hard-boiled and halved	6
10 oz.	sorrel	300 g.
	salt and pepper	
8 tbsp.	butter	120 ml.
¾ cup	fresh bread crumbs	175 ml.
1 cup	heavy cream	¼ liter

If the sorrel is young and tender, cut it into fine shreds and stew it gently, salted, in 3 tablespoons [45 ml.] of the butter.

If older, plunge the leaves first into boiling water and drain them the moment the water returns to the boil. Then stew them in 3 tablespoons of butter, stirring regularly, for about 20 minutes, or until the liquid has evaporated and the sorrel has melted into a purée. Stir in the cream a little at a time, permitting it to absorb the sorrel and thicken before adding more; grind in pepper, and taste for salt.

While the sorrel is stewing, put the bread crumbs to cook in the remaining 5 tablespoons [75 ml.] of butter over low heat, stirring or tossing until they are lightly golden.

Butter a gratin dish just large enough to hold the eggs. Arrange the eggs, cut surfaces up, side by side. Spoon the hot sauce over them, evenly masking all of the eggs. Sprinkle the sautéed bread crumbs regularly over the entire surface, and bake in a preheated 400° F. [200° C.] oven for about 15 minutes, or until the gratin is well heated through and the surface is lightly browned.

RICHARD OLNEY
SIMPLE FRENCH FOOD

Stuffed Eggs in Wine Sauce

Oeufs Farcis à la Bourguignonne

To serve 4

8	eggs, hard-boiled, halved lengthwise, the yolks separated from the whites	8
2	egg yolks	2
1 tbsp.	chopped fresh parsley	15 ml.
2 tbsp.	chopped scallion	30 ml.
	salt and pepper	
	mixed spices	
	grated nutmeg	
2 cups	fresh bread crumbs, soaked in ½ cup [125 ml.] heavy cream	½ liter
8 tbsp.	butter, softened	120 ml.
Wine sauce		
1 cup	red wine	¼ liter
½ cup	diced, lean cooked ham	125 ml.
1	small onion, finely chopped	1
2	shallots, finely chopped	2
2 tbsp.	butter	30 ml.
1 tbsp.	flour	15 ml.
1 cup	stock (recipe, page 164), cooked, uncovered, until it is reduced by half	¼ liter
1	truffle, sliced	1

To make the sauce, brown the ham, onion and shallots in half of the butter in a saucepan. Add the wine and simmer until the liquid is reduced by half. Melt the remaining butter in another pan and stir in the flour to make a roux. Press the reduced wine mixture through a sieve into the roux, stirring to make a smooth sauce. Add the reduced stock. Simmer the sauce over very low heat, removing the skin that forms on the top, until it is lightly thickened—about 15 minutes.

Meanwhile, pound the parsley and onion with the salt, pepper, mixed spices and a very little nutmeg to form a paste. Then pound in the hard-boiled and raw egg yolks, the bread crumbs and butter. Force this paste through a sieve.

Stuff about half of the egg whites with the mixture, mounding it up to give the whites the shape of whole eggs. (Reserve the rest of the whites for another use.) Spread the remaining stuffing in a buttered shallow gratin dish, and arrange the stuffed eggs on top.

Place the dish of eggs in a preheated 325° F. [170° C.] oven for about 15 minutes to brown the eggs lightly without letting them dry out. Add the truffle to the sauce and serve it very hot to accompany the dish of eggs.

GASTON DERYS
LES PLATS AU VIN

Hard-boiled Eggs Deep-fried in Minced Pork Coating

Yuk Yerng Chung-Dahn

To serve 4

4	eggs, hard-boiled	4
1½ cups	pork, very finely chopped	375 ml.
½ tsp.	salt	2 ml.
1 tbsp.	soy sauce	15 ml.
2 tsp.	rice wine or dry sherry	10 ml.
2	scallions, finely chopped	2
1 tbsp.	cornstarch	15 ml.
	vegetable oil for deep frying	
1	head lettuce, shredded	1

Add the salt, soy sauce, rice wine or sherry, scallions and cornstarch to the pork. Mash and stir the mixture to a very smooth consistency.

Coat each egg with a quarter of the pork mixture, encasing the egg evenly. Deep fry the eggs in hot oil until golden brown, five to 10 minutes.

Drain, then slice each egg in half lengthwise and arrange the halved eggs on a bed of shredded lettuce.

JOHN D. KEYS
FOOD FOR THE EMPEROR

Upside-down Eggs

Kai Kuam

Fish sauce (nuoc mam is one variety) is a thin brownish sauce produced by fermentation of salted fresh fish. It is extremely salty and smells strongly of fish, but when used in moderation, provides a surprisingly subtle flavor. It is obtainable bottled, as "fish's gravy," at Oriental grocery stores. If duck eggs are not available, the same number of jumbo-sized chicken eggs may be substituted.

In Laos caviar made from the eggs of the giant Mekong River catfish (Pangasianodon gigas) was traditionally used for this dish. But this species has become extremely rare, and even in Laos it would now be normal to substitute another cured fish roe (preferably, but not necessarily, from a fresh-water fish).

To serve 5

10	eggs, hard-boiled and cut in half lengthwise	10
3	duck eggs, beaten	3
½ cup	ground lean pork	125 ml.
2	garlic bulbs, unpeeled	2
5	shallots, unpeeled	5
2 tbsp.	caviar or other cured fish roe	30 ml.
1 to 2 tsp.	fish sauce (optional)	5 to 10 ml.
2 tsp.	ground black pepper	10 ml.
2 tbsp.	finely chopped fresh coriander leaves	30 ml.
2 tbsp.	lard	30 ml.

Sear the ground pork in an ungreased pan until it gives off a good aroma (about two minutes).

Remove the yolks from the hard-boiled eggs. Cook the garlic and shallots in the embers from a charcoal fire, or bake them in a preheated 400° F. [200° C.] oven for 20 minutes, until they are soft. Then peel them and pound them in a mortar with the hard-boiled egg yolks, pork and caviar. Taste. If the taste is not strong enough, add a little fish sauce. Then add half of the pepper and half of the coriander. Mix thoroughly and stuff the mixture into the whites of the hard-boiled eggs. Put the two halves of the eggs together.

Put the lard in a wok or large frying pan and set it on high heat. When the lard is hot, dip the stuffed eggs in the beaten duck eggs and fry them until they are golden.

Arrange the fried stuffed eggs on a serving dish, garnish them with the remaining black pepper and coriander leaves and serve them, either hot or lukewarm.

PHIA SING
TRADITIONAL RECIPES OF LAOS

Egg Croquettes with Bacon

To serve 2

5	eggs, 4 eggs hard-boiled and chopped, 1 egg beaten	5
½ cup	chopped cooked ham or fried bacon (optional)	125 ml.
2 tbsp.	butter	30 ml.
4 tbsp.	flour	60 ml.
⅔ cup	milk	150 ml.
	salt and pepper	
¼ cup	dry bread crumbs	50 ml.
	fat for deep frying	

Melt the butter in a saucepan, add 2 tablespoons [30 ml.] of the flour, then add the milk by degrees and cook for five to 10 minutes, or until the sauce is thick. Add the chopped eggs and the ham or bacon if liked. Season to taste.

Let the mixture cool, and form it into small rolls. Flour, egg and crumb these, and deep fry them in hot fat for two minutes, or until the croquettes are golden brown. Serve with mixed vegetables.

SHIRLEY M. HANSON (EDITOR)
FOOD FOR THOUGHT

Creamed Eggs with Shrimp

Huevos de Montevideo

To serve 6

6	hard-boiled eggs, chopped	6
½ cup	shelled, deveined, cooked shrimp	125 ml.
2 tbsp.	butter, melted	30 ml.
¼ cup	dry mustard	50 ml.
1 cup	cream	¼ liter
1 tsp.	chopped fresh parsley	5 ml.
	salt and pepper	
½ cup	shredded mozzarella cheese	125 ml.

Mix the butter with the shrimp, mustard, cream, parsley, and salt and pepper to taste. Place the chopped eggs in a buttered ovenproof dish and pour the butter-shrimp mixture over them. Sprinkle the top with the shredded cheese. Bake in a preheated 400° F. [200° C.] oven for 10 minutes, or until the cheese starts to brown. Serve immediately.

NURI FONSECA
LATINOAMERICA EN SU COCINA

A Fricassy of Eggs: Lady Powis's Receipt

This recipe is from a book, subtitled "Secrets of a Seventeenth-century Housewife," that was recently reissued in a compilation by Madeleine Masson.

To serve 6

6	eggs, hard-boiled and thinly sliced	6
6	egg yolks	6
4 tbsp.	butter	60 ml.
⅔ cup	dry red or white wine	150 ml.
1	salt anchovy, filleted, soaked in water for 30 minutes, drained, patted dry and chopped	1
1 tsp.	fines herbes	5 ml.
1 tsp.	grated onion	5 ml.
1 tsp.	freshly grated lemon peel	5 ml.
	grated nutmeg	

Put the sliced eggs into a frying pan with the butter and, when they are hot, pour off the butter, and put to them claret or white wine which you like best, all but 1 tablespoon [15 ml.], with the anchovy, herbs, onion and lemon peel. Let all boil up, then have in readiness the egg yolks well beaten with 1 tablespoon of wine and some nutmeg, put into the pan and cook a little to thicken and serve it up.

REBECCA PRICE
THE COMPLEAT COOK

Baked Eggs

Eggs on Toast

The author of this 1923 recipe suggests that the dish was often called "ox eyes" —presumably because of its appearance.

To serve 4

8	eggs	8
8	slices white or brown bread, toasted	8
	butter	
	salt and pepper	
½ cup	heavy cream	125 ml.

Stamp out a round from each slice of toast, and cut out the centers of the rounds with a smaller cutter so as to form rings of toast. Spread a little fresh butter over the rings, and place them on a well-buttered baking dish. Break an egg carefully into each ring of toast, season with a little salt and pepper, and pour a spoonful of cream around each egg. Bake in a preheated 350° F. [180° C.] oven for about 10 minutes, or until the whites begin to set. Great care must be taken that the eggs do not get overcooked and, above all, that the yolks are not disturbed during the process of cooking. Send the dish to the table as hot as possible.

C. HERMANN SENN
BREAKFAST DISHES AND SAVOURIES

Eggs with Shrimp

Les Oeufs Meulemeester

To cook the shrimp required in this recipe, simmer ½ lb. [¼ kg.] of fresh shrimp in salted water for five minutes. Drain the shrimp and peel them.

This recipe from Bruges, Belgium, is several centuries old and is much appreciated in Holland and Flanders.

	To serve 4	
6	eggs	6
¼ lb.	cooked shrimp	125 g.
5 tbsp.	butter, 1 tbsp. [15 ml.] cut into small pieces	75 ml.
1 tbsp.	Dijon mustard	15 ml.
1 tsp.	chopped mixed fresh parsley and chervil	5 ml.
	salt and pepper	
1 cup	heavy cream	¼ liter
½ cup	shredded Gruyère cheese	125 ml.

Immerse the eggs in boiling water, boil them for seven minutes and plunge them into cold water. Peel immediately.

Melt 4 tablespoons [60 ml.] of the butter in a saucepan over low heat, and quickly slice the warm eggs into the butter. Add the shrimp, mustard, parsley and chervil, and season with salt and pepper. Add the cream, and slide the pan back and forth rapidly until all of the ingredients are thoroughly combined.

Pour this mixture into a buttered gratin dish. Sprinkle the surface with the shredded Gruyère cheese and dot with the cut-up pieces of butter. Set under the broiler or in a preheated 475° F. [240° C.] oven for five minutes, or until the top is browned and bubbling. Serve immediately.

PAUL BOUILLARD
LA CUISINE AU COIN DU FEU

Slovakian-Style Eggs

Eier auf Slowakische Art

	To serve 4	
8	eggs, the yolks separated from the whites, and the whites stiffly beaten	8
8	slices white bread, toasted	8
1¼ cups	milk	300 ml.
	salt and pepper	

Soak the toast in the milk for one minute, then arrange the slices side by side in a large, shallow, buttered baking dish. Season the egg whites with salt and spread them on the toast. With a teaspoon, make a depression over the center of each slice of toast; place a yolk in each depression. Sprinkle the yolks with salt and pepper. Bake in a preheated 350° F. [180° C.] oven for about 15 minutes, or until the egg yolks are set. Serve immediately.

ELEK MAGYAR
KOCHBUCH FÜR FEINSCHMECKER

Egg Yolks on Toast

Rossi d'Uvo al Canapè

	To serve 6	
6	egg yolks	6
6	slices firm-textured white bread, cut 1 inch [2½ cm.] thick, and the crusts removed	6
4 tbsp.	butter	60 ml.
1 cup	white sauce (recipe, page 165)	¼ liter
½ cup	freshly grated Parmesan cheese	125 ml.
¼ tsp.	ground cinnamon or grated nutmeg	1 ml.
	salt	

Make a hollow in the center of each slice of bread, being careful not to cut all of the way through. Fry the bread cases in the butter until they are golden. Place them in an oven-proof serving dish, and put an egg yolk into each hollow. Heat the sauce gently and stir in the cheese, cinnamon or nutmeg, and a pinch of salt. Cool the sauce slightly, and pour it over the bread and yolks.

Bake in a preheated 350° F. [180° C.] oven for 15 minutes, without allowing the yolks to become hard. Serve hot.

PELLEGRINO ARTUSI
LA SCIENZA IN CUCINA E L'ARTE DI MANGIAR BENE

Baked Eggs in Curds

	To serve 6	
6	eggs	6
2 cups	cottage or curd cheese, beaten well	½ liter
2 tbsp.	butter, melted	30 ml.
1 tsp.	cayenne pepper	5 ml.
1 tsp.	ground cumin	5 ml.
¼ tsp.	ground turmeric	1 ml.
	salt and pepper	
	fresh coriander leaves, finely chopped	

Pour equal amounts of melted butter into six individual ovenproof bowls. To the beaten cheese curds, add the cayenne pepper, cumin, turmeric, and salt and pepper. Beat until thoroughly blended. Spoon the cheese into the individual bowls. Break one egg into each bowl and bake in a preheated 450° F. [230° C.] oven for about 10 minutes, or until the eggs are well set. Sprinkle with the coriander leaves and serve immediately.

PREMILA LAL
THE EGG & CHEESE COOK-BOOK

Cantal Eggs

Oeufs à la Cantalienne

	To serve 4	
8	eggs, the yolks separated from the whites, and the whites stiffly beaten	8
½ cup	shredded Cantal cheese	125 ml.
	salt and pepper	
3 tbsp.	heavy cream	45 ml.

Butter a round, fairly deep gratin dish. Salt and lightly pepper the egg whites, and spread them in the dish. Make eight dents in the whites, with the back of a spoon, and put a yolk in each dent. Cover the yolks with cream, then sprinkle the whole surface with the cheese. Bake in a preheated 350° F. [180° C.] oven for 10 minutes.

EUGÉNIE BRAZIER
LES SECRETS DE LA MÈRE BRAZIER

Eggs with Cream in Ramekins

Oeufs à la Crème en Cocotte

	To serve 4	
4	eggs	4
¼ cup	heavy cream	50 ml.
4 tbsp.	butter, cut into small pieces	60 ml.
	salt and pepper	

Heat four ramekin dishes in a 350° F. [180° C.] oven for five minutes. Bring the cream to a boil and pour a tablespoon [15 ml.] of it into each ramekin. Break an egg into each dish and season with salt and pepper. Top each egg with 1 tablespoon of the cut-up butter.

Set the ramekins in a roasting pan and pour in enough hot water to come halfway up the sides. Cook the eggs on top of the stove or in a preheated 350° F. [180° C.] oven for 10 minutes, or until the whites of the eggs are set and the yolks are still soft.

MARIE BISSON
LA CUISINE NORMANDE

Eggs Baked with Cheese

Oeufs Gratinés au Fromage

Any firm mild-flavored cheese may be used to prepare this dish: Gruyère, Emmentaler, Edam, Cheddar, Muenster or Monterey Jack.

	To serve 2	
4	eggs	4
¼ lb.	cheese, grated or shredded	125 g.
2	medium-sized onions, finely chopped	2
5 tbsp.	butter	75 ml.
4	slices firm-textured white bread, cut into 3- to 4-inch [8- to 10-cm.] rounds and fried in butter	4
1 cup	beef stock (recipe, page 164)	¼ liter
	freshly ground pepper	

Fry the onions in 2 tablespoons [30 ml.] of the butter until they are soft and transparent, about 15 minutes. Fill the base of a deep round dish with the onions and place the fried bread croutons on top. Pour in enough stock to nearly cover the bread. Break an egg onto each crouton and sprinkle the eggs with the cheese. Season with pepper. Melt the remaining butter and pour it over the eggs. Place the dish in a preheated 425° F. [220° C.] oven, or under a hot broiler, until the cheese melts and the eggs are just set (about seven minutes). Serve hot.

PROSPER MONTAGNÉ AND A. GOTTSCHALK
MON MENU

Swiss Eggs in a Shell

To serve 4 to 6

6	eggs	6
1½ cups	shredded Emmentaler cheese	375 ml.
6 or 7	thin slices fresh white bread, buttered on both sides	6 or 7
	butter, softened	
	salt and pepper	
¾ cup	cream	175 ml.
4 tbsp.	grated Parmesan cheese	60 ml.

To form a shell, fit the bread slices into a 9-inch [23-cm.] pie plate like a pinwheel, with the slices overlapping and radiating from the center so that their outer corners project in points beyond the rim. Fill in the center of the shell with the last slice. Set the shell in a preheated 475° F. [250° C.] oven for five minutes to toast it lightly. Remove the shell, then reduce the oven heat to 350° F. [180° C.].

Sprinkle the shell with the Emmentaler cheese. Break the eggs into the shell over the cheese. Sprinkle with salt and pepper to taste. Pour the cream over the eggs. Sprinkle the top with the Parmesan. Bake until the eggs are set, about 10 minutes.

RUTH CONRAD BATEMAN
I LOVE TO COOK BOOK

Black Beans and Eggs

To serve 6

6	eggs	6
1½ cups	dried black beans, soaked in water overnight and drained	375 ml.
	salt and pepper	
1 cup	finely chopped onions	¼ liter
2	garlic cloves, finely chopped	2
1	bay leaf	1
¼ tsp.	basil	1 ml.
1 cup	shredded Cheddar cheese	¼ liter
2 tbsp.	dry sherry	30 ml.

Cover the beans with water, bring to a boil, boil for 10 minutes, cover and simmer for two hours or more, until tender. Now add salt, pepper, the onions, garlic, bay leaf and basil.

Remove the beans from the heat and let them stand at room temperature for about three hours. Or cool the beans and refrigerate them overnight.

Warm up the beans and mash them well with a fork. If the mixture does not mash easily, cook it until it does. Then stir in the cheese, reduce the heat and stir again until the cheese melts. Add the sherry.

Distribute the bean mixture among six buttered ramekins. Make a hollow in the center of each filled ramekin and slide an egg into each hollow. Bake in a preheated 350° F. [180° C.] oven for 10 to 15 minutes, until the eggs are firm.

CAROL COLLVER THURBER
THE CALYPSO COOKBOOK

Eggs Baked with Savoy Cabbage and Caraway

If the crinkly-leaved Savoy cabbage is not available, a green cabbage may be substituted.

In the summer, use green beans, scallions and tomatoes for a lighter texture, and flavor them with fennel.

To serve 4

8	eggs	8
1	Savoy cabbage, tough outer leaves discarded, halved, cored and shredded	1
1 tbsp.	caraway seeds	15 ml.
2 tbsp.	olive oil	30 ml.
1	onion, thinly sliced	1
1	garlic clove, finely chopped	1
4	medium-sized ripe tomatoes, peeled and chopped	4
1 cup	sour cream	¼ liter

Put the cabbage into a saucepan with the oil, onion, garlic, tomatoes and half of the caraway seeds. Cover the pan and set it over medium heat for 20 minutes, stirring occasionally. Take the pan from the heat, cool the cabbage a little and stir in half of the sour cream.

Put the cabbage into a large, shallow ovenproof dish and make eight indentations in it. Break the eggs into these. Mix the remaining sour cream and caraway seeds together and spoon them over the eggs, covering the yolks if possible.

Cover the dish completely with buttered or oiled foil and put it into a preheated 400° F. [200° C.] oven for 20 minutes, or until the egg whites are set, but the yolks still liquid.

GAIL DUFF
GAIL DUFF'S VEGETARIAN COOKBOOK

Baked Eggs with Carrots

Oeufs à la Mont-Bry

To serve 6

6	eggs	6
8 to 10	medium-sized carrots, julienned	8 to 10
2 tbsp.	butter	30 ml.
	salt and pepper	
	sugar (optional)	
½ cup	heavy cream	125 ml.

Cook the carrots with the butter until they are soft but not brown, about 15 minutes, keeping the heat low and adding a few drops of water occasionally. Add seasoning to taste and, if desired, a very little sugar.

When the carrots are cooked, butter six individual oven-proof dishes and divide the carrots among them. Break an egg into each dish and cover it with cream. Stand the dishes in a shallow baking pan partly filled with hot water. Put them into a preheated 350° F. [180° C.] oven and bake for about 10 minutes, or until the whites are firm and the yolks are still soft. Season again lightly after removing from the oven, and serve the eggs hot.

CAROLINE MIQUEL
LES BONNES RECETTES DE TANTE CAROLINE

Eggs Glaz'd with Cucumbers

Despite its name, the cookbook from which this recipe is anthologized was published in 1733.

Eggs may be prepared in the same way with chicory, lettuce, celery, asparagus tips, peas or artichoke bottoms.

To serve 4 or 8

8	eggs	8
6	small cucumbers, peeled, quartered lengthwise, seeded and sliced	6
	salt and pepper	
2	onions, sliced	2
½ cup	vinegar	125 ml.
½ cup	water	125 ml.
3 tbsp.	butter	45 ml.
1 tbsp.	flour	15 ml.
1 cup	veal or chicken stock (recipe, page 164)	¼ liter
	grated nutmeg	

Marinate the cucumbers with salt, pepper, the onions, vinegar and water for about two hours. Drain the cucumbers thoroughly and dry them in a cloth. Put them in a pan with 2 tablespoons [30 ml.] of the butter, and fry them until they are lightly colored. Sprinkle them with the flour and wet them with the stock. Simmer them for five minutes, skim the sauce and taste for seasoning.

Arrange this ragout in a large shallow ovenproof dish. Break your eggs at equal distances among the cucumbers, and season the top of each egg with a little salt and nutmeg. Place the dish in a preheated 425° F. [220° C.] oven for 10 minutes, or until the eggs are just set. When your eggs are done and not hard, serve hot.

VINCENT DE LA CHAPELLE
THE MODERN COOK

Eggs in Cases with Mushrooms

To serve 6

6	eggs	6
¼ lb.	fresh mushrooms, trimmed, trimmings reserved	125 g.
2 cups	milk	½ liter
2	egg yolks, lightly beaten	2
2 cups	fresh bread crumbs	½ liter
	salt and pepper	
¼ tsp.	ground allspice	1 ml.
1 tbsp.	butter	15 ml.
1 tbsp.	flour	15 ml.
3 tbsp.	toasted dry bread crumbs	45 ml.

Stew the mushrooms in 1 cup [¼ liter] of the milk for about 15 minutes over low heat. Drain them, reserving the milk, and chop them up small.

Add the egg yolks to the milk and cook, stirring, over low heat until the mixture thickens without coming to a boil. Stir in the chopped mushrooms and the fresh bread crumbs to make a mixture with the consistency of a stuffing. Season with salt and allspice.

Line six well-buttered china ramekins with this mixture, leaving a hollow in the center of each, into which break a fresh egg. Set the dishes in a shallow pan with hot water 1 inch [2½ cm.] deep around them and bake them in a preheated 350° F. [180° C.] oven for 10 minutes, or until the whites of the eggs are set.

For the sauce, simmer the mushroom trimmings in the remaining milk for 20 minutes. Season with a pinch each of salt and pepper. Strain the mixture. Work the butter and flour together, and whisk it into the broth. Cook until the sauce thickens. Coat the top of each egg with the sauce, dust with toasted bread crumbs and serve.

A. KENNEY HERBERT
FIFTY BREAKFASTS

Maria Luigia's Eggs with Cheese

Uova al Formaggio alla Maria Luigia

	To serve 4	
8	eggs	8
¼ cup	heavy cream	50 ml.
3 tbsp.	freshly grated Parmesan cheese	45 ml.
1	small onion, very finely chopped	1
	pepper	

Put the cream into a large shallow ovenproof dish, break the eggs into the cream, sprinkle them with the cheese and lastly, add the onion. Bake in a preheated 350° F. [180° C.] oven for about 10 minutes, or until the whites are set and the yolks still soft. Season with pepper to taste, and serve.

FERRUCCIO BOTTI
GASTRONOMIA PARMENSE OSSIA PARMA CAPITALE DEI BUONGUSTAI

Butcher's Wife Eggs

Oeufs sur le Plat à la Bouchère

	To serve 6	
6	eggs	6
¼ lb.	lean beef, finely chopped	125 g.
	salt and pepper	
4 tbsp.	butter, melted	60 ml.
⅓ cup	tomato sauce *(recipe, page 166)*	75 ml.

Butter six individual shallow ovenproof egg dishes. Season the meat with salt and pepper, and make a ring of meat in the base of each dish. Break an egg into each ring. Spoon a little melted butter on top of each yolk, then bake in a preheated 450° F. [230° C.] oven for 10 minutes, or until the whites are cooked but the yolks still soft. Salt and pepper the eggs, and pour a little tomato sauce around each one.

PROSPER MONTAGNÉ AND A. GOTTSCHALK
MON MENU

Baked Eggs in a Crust with Watercress

	To serve 4	
4	large eggs	4
4	bread cases	4
2	large bunches watercress, trimmed	2
12 tbsp.	unsalted butter	180 ml.
	salt and pepper	
3	large scallions	3
2 tbsp.	flour	30 ml.
1½ cups	milk	375 ml.
	grated nutmeg	

Melt 4 tablespoons [60 ml.] of the butter and, using a pastry brush, coat the bread cases inside and out with the butter. Place the cases on a baking sheet and bake them for 10 minutes in a preheated 350° F. [180° C.] oven.

Bring a small saucepan of salted water to a boil. Select 16 handsome watercress sprigs and set them aside for garnish. Throw the remaining watercress and the scallions into the water and blanch for one minute. Drain and refresh them under cold water. Wrap the greens in an old kitchen towel and squeeze them very hard until they are dry. Purée in a food processor or blender and set aside.

Melt 2 tablespoons [30 ml.] of butter in a small saucepan. Stir in the flour and whisk over low heat for four minutes. Slowly stir in 1 cup [¼ liter] of the milk, season with salt, pepper and nutmeg, then cook over low heat for 15 minutes. Then add the watercress-and-scallion purée and let the sauce simmer another 10 minutes. It should be very thick.

Use two thirds of this sauce to coat the interiors of the bread cases. Break an egg into each hollow and return the cases to the oven for 10 to 12 minutes. (The whites of the eggs should set; the yolks should remain liquid.)

Place the saucepan containing the remaining watercress sauce over low heat. Whisk in the remaining milk and bring to a boil. Remove the pan from the heat and whisk in the remaining butter. Taste for seasoning.

Pour the sauce onto four warm dinner plates. Set a baked egg case in the middle of each prepared plate and garnish the plates with the reserved sprigs of watercress.

JUDITH OLNEY
COMFORTING FOOD

Tomatoes Stuffed with Eggs

Paradais Rosii Umplute cu Oua

To serve 4

4	small eggs	4
4	large ripe tomatoes	4
	salt	
6 tbsp.	butter, melted	90 ml.
	freshly ground black pepper	
⅓ cup	freshly grated Parmesan cheese	75 ml.
1 tbsp.	finely cut fresh fennel leaves	15 ml.
1 tbsp.	chopped fresh parsley	15 ml.
¼ cup	heavy or sour cream (optional)	50 ml.

Slice off the stem ends of the tomatoes, reserving these lids, and scoop out the pulp, seeds and ribs. Sprinkle the insides with salt, and invert the tomatoes in a colander to drain for 10 to 15 minutes.

Arrange the tomatoes in a well-buttered baking dish just large enough to hold them upright. Pour a little melted butter into each tomato case. Sprinkle with pepper. Break each egg into a saucer and slide it into a tomato case. Sprinkle the top with the cheese, parsley and fennel. Pour in the rest of the butter and replace the cut-off tomato lids.

Bake in a preheated 350° F. [180° C.] oven for about 20 minutes; the cheese should bubble up to the top of the tomatoes, and the skins should be almost ready to burst. Serve the tomatoes sprinkled with the baking-dish juices and herbs, and the cream, if desired.

ANISOARA STAN
THE ROMANIAN COOKBOOK

Bacon and Eggs in a Mug

To serve 4

8	eggs, 4 beaten	8
½ cup	shredded Gruyère cheese	125 ml.
	salt and pepper	
½ cup	crisp, crumbled bacon	125 ml.
1 tbsp.	chopped fresh parsley	15 ml.
½ cup	chopped, sautéed fresh mushrooms	125 ml.
4 tbsp.	heavy cream	60 ml.
4 tbsp.	butter	60 ml.

Use 2 tablespoons [30 ml.] of the butter to grease the interiors of four medium-sized ovenproof coffee mugs, and sprinkle the bottoms and sides of the mugs with some of the grated cheese. Season the beaten eggs and divide them among the mugs. Mix the bacon, parsley and mushrooms together and spoon this mixture in a neat layer over the beaten eggs.

Break an egg into each mug, season it, and pour a tablespoon [15 ml.] of cream over each egg yolk. Cover the eggs with the remaining cheese and place a morsel of the remaining butter on top.

Put the mugs in a pan containing 1½ inches [4 cm.] of hot water and cook the eggs, loosely covered with foil, either over low heat or in a preheated 300° F. [150° C.] oven for 10 to 12 minutes, or until the whites of the eggs are set. The yolks should remain soft. At no time should the water boil. Place the mugs under the broiler for a brief moment so the cheese can begin to brown.

JUDITH OLNEY
COMFORTING FOOD

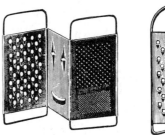

Baked Eggs, Navarre-Style

Huevos al Plato a la Navarra

Chorizo is a spicy pork sausage flavored with paprika and garlic and is sold at Mexican or Latin American food stores.

This recipe calls for shallow individual earthenware dishes of the kind used throughout Spain for *Huevos al Plato.*

To serve 4

8	eggs	8
4	ripe tomatoes, peeled and chopped	4
2 tbsp.	butter	30 ml.
	salt and pepper	
2 tbsp.	chopped fresh parsley	30 ml.
8	slices *chorizo*	8
¼ cup	shredded Gruyère cheese	50 ml.

Cook the tomatoes in the butter for 15 minutes, or until they form a thick purée. Season them with salt and pepper and add the parsley.

Butter four individual baking dishes and divide the tomato sauce among them. Break two eggs into each dish and place a slice of the *chorizo* beside each yolk. Sprinkle the cheese over the eggs.

Bake them in a preheated 350° F. [180° C.] oven for 15 to 20 minutes. The yolk should remain soft.

ANA-MARÍA CALERA
365 RECETAS DE COCINA VASCA

Grilled Eggs with Lamb

To make the coconut milk called for in this recipe, pour about ⅓ cup [75 ml.] of boiling water over 2 tablespoons [30 ml.] of freshly grated coconut. After five minutes, strain through a cloth, pressing to extract all of the milk.

	To serve 6	
6	eggs	6
2 lb.	lean boneless lamb, cubed	1 kg.
8 oz.	cottage cheese	¼ kg.
	salt	
	ghee	
4	large onions, thinly sliced and 1 slice coarsely chopped	4
¼ cup	coconut milk	50 ml.
¼ tsp.	ground saffron, dissolved in 1 tbsp. [15 ml.] milk	1 ml.

Ginger paste

¼-inch	slice fresh ginger root, peeled	6-mm.
1	onion, finely chopped	1
10	garlic cloves, crushed to a paste	10

Masala

6	dried red chilies, stemmed and seeded	6
8	whole cardamoms, the pods removed and discarded	8
2	peppercorns	2
¼ tsp.	cumin seeds	1 ml.
¼-inch	slice turmeric root (or substitute ½ tsp. [2 ml.] ground turmeric)	6-mm.
1 tbsp.	coriander seeds	15 ml.
1-inch	stick cinnamon	2½-cm.
1	onion, chopped	1

Prepare the ginger paste and *masala* by pounding the ingredients for each in a mortar or putting them through a food grinder or processor. Set aside in separate bowls.

Blend the lamb with the cheese and a little salt. Set aside for one hour. Heat a little ghee and in it fry the coarsely chopped onions for 10 minutes, or until light brown. Add the ginger paste and fry until dark brown. Add the lamb mixture and cook over medium heat until the meat is almost tender, about 15 minutes. Remove from the heat.

In another pan, heat some more ghee and fry the onion slices lightly, then add the *masala*. When the slices are golden brown, add the lamb mixture and cook until tender. Pour in the saffron and mix well. Add salt to taste and break the eggs over the lamb. Place under the broiler and cook until the eggs set. Serve immediately.

PREMILA LAL
THE EGG & CHEESE COOK-BOOK

Eggs with Calf's Brains

Oeufs en Cocotte Sagan

	To serve 6	
6	eggs	6
2	calf's brains	2
	ice water	
2 tbsp.	fresh lemon juice	30 ml.
1 cup	chicken stock *(recipe, page 164)*	¼ liter
½ cup	heavy cream	125 ml.
4 tbsp.	butter, melted	60 ml.
	salt and freshly cracked black pepper	
¼ cup	freshly grated Parmesan cheese	50 ml.

Prepare the brains by soaking them in ice water to cover, mixed with the lemon juice, for about 30 minutes. Drain them and remove all of the membranes, using a small paring knife. Pat them dry with a paper towel.

Put the brains in a little pan and cover them with the stock. Simmer over low heat for 10 minutes. Drain them, cool slightly, and chill them for a few minutes in the refrigerator. Cut them into ½-inch [1-cm.] cubes, mix them with half of the cream and half of the melted butter, and season with salt and pepper.

Have ready six ramekins or cocottes and a shallow pan of hot water about ½ inch [1 cm.] deep. Fill each ramekin halfway with the brains and break one egg on top. Sprinkle with a little salt and pepper. Spoon the remaining cream over the eggs and sprinkle with the cheese and the remaining butter. Set the ramekins in the pan of hot water and bake for six minutes in a preheated 350° F. [180° C.] oven. Remove from the oven. Place each hot ramekin on a folded napkin on a plate. Serve at once.

DIONE LUCAS AND MARION GORMAN
THE DIONE LUCAS BOOK OF FRENCH COOKING

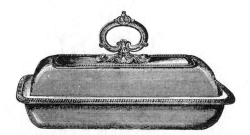

Egg Mold with Rémoulade Sauce

Pain d'Oeufs, Sauce Rémoulade

This dish can be prepared in advance, since it is eaten cold. All that remains to be done just before serving the meal is to make the sauce.

To serve 4		
6 to 8	eggs	6 to 8
1 tbsp.	butter, melted	15 ml.
	salt	

Rémoulade sauce		
2	egg yolks	2
	salt	
⅔ cup	olive oil	150 ml.
	fresh lemon juice	
1	shallot, finely chopped	1
1 tbsp.	chopped fresh parsley	15 ml.
1 tbsp.	chopped fresh chervil	15 ml.
2 tsp.	chopped fresh tarragon	10 ml.
5	capers, rinsed and chopped	5
1 or 2	oil-packed flat anchovy fillets, rinsed, patted dry and finely chopped	1 or 2
	white pepper	
½ tsp.	Dijon mustard	2 ml.

Butter a straight-sided, small (about 2-cup [½-liter]) mold. To do this more easily, pour a little melted butter into the bottom of the mold and allow it to cool, then use a knife to spread additional softened butter on the sides of the mold. Break enough eggs into the mold to fill it almost to the rim, though not more than eight eggs. Take care to prevent the yolks from breaking. Sprinkle each egg with a little salt. When the mold is full, place it in a pan of hot water and bake it in a preheated 350° F. [180° C.] oven for 30 minutes, or until the mass of eggs has set completely. Let the mold cool for 15 minutes, then turn the eggs out onto a small dish, cover with an inverted bowl and refrigerate.

Fifteen minutes before serving, prepare the sauce. Place the egg yolks in a mortar with a pinch of salt, and stir with a pestle, turning always in the same direction. Pour in the olive oil, drop by drop, until the sauce is quite thick and firm and comes away from the sides of the mortar. Continuing to stir, add a few drops of lemon juice. Finish the sauce by stirring in the shallot, herbs, capers and anchovies, white pepper, and mustard. To serve, cover the egg mold with a thick layer of the sauce.

MME. JEANNE SAVARIN (EDITOR)
LA CUISINE DES FAMILLES

Eggs on a Savory Base

Oeufs au Gratin

	To serve 4	
4	eggs	4
7 tbsp.	butter	105 ml.
1½ cups	fresh bread crumbs	375 ml.
1	salt anchovy, filleted, soaked in water for 30 minutes, drained, patted dry and chopped	1
1 tbsp.	chopped fresh parsley	15 ml.
1 tbsp.	finely cut fresh chives	15 ml.
1	shallot, finely chopped	1
6	egg yolks, beaten	6
	salt and pepper	

Melt 4 tablespoons [60 ml.] of the butter in a skillet, add the bread crumbs, and cook, stirring, until the butter is absorbed. Off the heat, stir in the anchovy, parsley, chives, shallot and egg yolks. Spread the mixture in a buttered heatproof gratin dish. Cook over low heat until the mixture begins to set, about five minutes, then break the whole eggs on top. Season with salt and pepper. Cook in the hot oven for a few minutes, or slide the dish under a hot broiler until the whites set, then serve.

NOUVEAU MANUEL DE LA CUISINIÈRE BOURGEOISE ET ÉCONOMIQUE

Eggs Baked with Oysters Normandy

Oeufs au Plat à la Normande

	To serve 4	
8	eggs	8
24	live oysters, shucked and their liquor reserved	24
½ cup	heavy cream	125 ml.
	salt and pepper	

Put 2 tablespoons [30 ml.] of cream with salt and pepper to taste into each of four small ovenproof dishes. Put six oysters in each dish and pour a bit of their liquor over them.

Break the eggs over the oysters—two to each dish—and bake them in a preheated 350° F. [180° C.] oven for 10 minutes, or until the whites are set, but the yolks are still liquid. Serve the eggs in their baking dishes.

MARIE BISSON
LA CUISINE NORMANDE

Scrambled Eggs

Francis Picabia's Eggs
Oeufs Francis Picabia

To serve 4

8	eggs, mixed well with a fork	8
	salt	
16 tbsp.	butter (½ lb. [¼ kg.]), cut into small pieces	240 ml.

Add salt, but no pepper, to the eggs. Pour them into a saucepan and put it over very, very low heat. Keep turning the eggs with a fork while very slowly adding the pieces of butter. It should take 30 minutes to prepare this dish, which does not scramble but thickens to a suave consistency.

ALICE B. TOKLAS
THE ALICE B. TOKLAS COOK BOOK

Eggs with Cheese
Uovi al Formaggio

Savoy cheese is also sold as tomme de Savoie; it is a soft cheese from the Savoy region of France. Tallegio or Bel Paese are two suitable alternatives.

To serve 3

6	eggs, beaten	6
¼ lb.	Savoy cheese, shredded (about 1 cup [¼ liter])	125 g.
1 tbsp.	butter	15 ml.
1 tbsp.	chopped fresh parsley	15 ml.
2 tbsp.	chopped scallion	30 ml.
	grated nutmeg	
⅓ cup	dry white wine	75 ml.
3	slices white bread with the crusts removed, cut into strips	3

Put the cheese, butter, parsley, scallion, a pinch of nutmeg and the wine in a saucepan. Simmer over low heat, stirring constantly until the cheese has melted. Add the eggs, mix well, and continue to cook over low heat until the eggs are just set. Pour the mixture into a warmed serving dish and arrange the strips of soft bread around the edge.

IL CUOCO PIEMONTESE RIDOTTO ALL'ULTIMO GUSTO

Scrambled Eggs with Dandelion

Dandelion is not only good as a salad, but also delicious cooked and used with eggs. The hearts only are used; all the coarser, big leaves should be removed and only a small portion of the root—carefully scraped—left, just enough to keep the small leaves together. They should be well washed, then well dried.

To serve 4

8	eggs, beaten with salt and pepper	8
8	dandelion hearts, chopped	8
4 tbsp.	butter	60 ml.

Melt the butter in a saucepan over low heat. Stir in the dandelion hearts and cook them until they begin to wilt. Pour in the eggs, and cook and stir until they are scrambled.

MARCEL BOULESTIN AND ROBIN ADAIR
ONE HUNDRED AND TWENTY WAYS OF COOKING EGGS

Swiss Eggs
Oeufs à la Bonne Suisse

To serve 4 to 6

6	eggs, the yolks separated from the whites, and the whites stiffly beaten	6
½ lb.	Gruyère cheese, shredded (about 2 cups [½ liter])	¼ kg.
4 tbsp.	butter	60 ml.
1 cup	dry white wine	¼ liter
2 tbsp.	chopped fresh parsley	30 ml.
2 tbsp.	chopped scallions	30 ml.
	pepper	
	grated nutmeg	
3	slices firm-textured white bread, cut into strips and fried in butter until golden	3

Put the cheese, butter, wine, parsley, scallions, pepper and nutmeg into a saucepan. Place the saucepan on a trivet in a larger pan partly filled with hot water. Stir over low heat until the cheese melts. Add the egg yolks and whites, and cook them as you would scrambled eggs. Transfer the eggs to a serving dish and garnish them with the strips of fried bread. Serve hot.

LE MANUEL DE LA FRIANDISE

Scrambled Eggs with Cheese and Wine

La Fondue

To serve 4

6	eggs	6
½ cup	shredded Gruyère cheese	125 ml.
1 cup	dry white wine	200 ml.
1	garlic clove, chopped	1
4 tbsp.	butter, softened	60 ml.
	salt and pepper	

Put the wine and garlic in a saucepan and boil the mixture until the garlic is soft and the wine reduced by half, about 15 minutes. Strain the liquid and let it cool.

Beat the eggs with the cheese, butter, reduced wine, and salt and pepper to taste. Cook the mixture over low heat, stirring it continuously with a fork. When the eggs begin to set, remove the pan from the heat and continue to stir for two minutes, or until the eggs are set.

MENUS PROPOS SUR LA CUISINE COMTOISE

Eggs with Gruyère Cheese

Oeufs au Fromage

To serve 4

6	eggs, beaten	6
1¼ cups	shredded Gruyère cheese	300 ml.
2 tbsp.	butter	30 ml.
	salt and pepper	
2 tbsp.	chopped fresh parsley	30 ml.
2 tbsp.	finely cut fresh chives	30 ml.
⅔ cup	dry white wine	150 ml.
4 tbsp.	fried bread crumbs or small croutons (recipe, page 166)	60 ml.

Put together in a saucepan the cheese, butter, salt and pepper, parsley, chives and wine. Cook gently, stirring, until the cheese has melted.

Add the eggs, stirring continuously over low heat until the mixture becomes thick and creamy. Transfer it to a serving dish and garnish with the bread crumbs or croutons.

NOUVEAU MANUEL DE LA CUISINIÈRE BOURGEOISE ET ÉCONOMIQUE

Scrambled Eggs with Eggplant

Rántotta Törökparadicsommal

This Bulgarian-influenced dish is still part of the everyday repertoire in southern Hungary. Sometimes it is made with onion and tomato purée, without garlic and dill.

To serve 10

10	eggs	10
3	small or 2 medium-sized eggplants, diced	3
4 tbsp.	butter	60 ml.
1	garlic clove, crushed to a paste	1
1 tsp.	finely cut fresh dill	5 ml.
	ground mace	
	salt and pepper	

Melt the butter and sauté the eggplants. When they are soft, add the garlic and cook for a few minutes more. Sprinkle with the dill and a pinch each of mace and pepper.

Beat the eggs lightly and add salt to taste. Pour the eggs over the eggplants and cook the mixture over low heat, stirring continuously, until the eggs are scrambled.

GEORGE LANG
THE CUISINE OF HUNGARY

Scrambled Eggs with Mustard

Oeufs à la Robert

To serve 4

8	eggs, beaten	8
1 to 2 tsp.	Dijon mustard	5 to 10 ml.
4 tbsp.	butter	60 ml.
1	onion, chopped	1
¼ cup	degreased meat roasting juices, or ½ cup [125 ml.] meat stock (recipe, page 164), boiled until it is reduced by half, and cooled	50 ml.
	salt and pepper	

Melt 2 tablespoons [30 ml.] of the butter and gently cook the onion in it until soft. Dice the remaining butter and add it to the eggs with the meat juices, salt and pepper, and the onion. Pour the mixture into a heavy saucepan and cook it over very low heat, stirring all the time with a wooden spoon, until the eggs are scrambled to a creamy consistency. When the eggs are almost ready, stir in mustard to taste.

MENON
LES SOUPERS DE LA COUR

Eggs Scrambled with Tomato and Basil

Brouillade de Tomates au Basilic

	To serve 4	
8 to 10	eggs, beaten	8 to 10
4	tomatoes, peeled, seeded and coarsely chopped	4
1	handful fresh basil leaves and flowers, chopped	1
	salt	
3 or 4	garlic cloves, flattened with the side of a knife blade	3 or 4
1	bouquet garni of bay leaf, thyme and a celery rib, or 1 pinch of crumbled mixed herbs	1
½ tsp.	sugar	2 ml.
¼ cup	olive oil	50 ml.
4 tbsp.	butter, cut into small pieces	60 ml.

Cook the tomatoes, salted, with the garlic, bouquet garni or the mixed herbs, and the sugar in the olive oil over low heat—tossing the mixture from time to time—until the free liquid is evaporated and the tomatoes seem only to be coated with oil. Discard the garlic and the bouquet garni.

Add the butter to the eggs, season to taste, beat the mixture lightly with a fork and, with a wooden spoon, stir it into the tomato mixture, keeping it over low heat and continuing to stir constantly. When the eggs begin to thicken, add the basil, chopped at the last minute to prevent it from blackening. Remove the eggs from the heat just before the desired consistency is achieved and continue stirring.

RICHARD OLNEY
SIMPLE FRENCH FOOD

Wild Onions and Eggs

The author has adapted this recipe from The Indian Cook Book, which was published in 1933 by the Indian Women's Club of Tulsa, Oklahoma.

Wild onions are a native American plant that, until now, have always defeated domestication. If you are lucky enough to find a place where wild onions grow, you will be able to secure, year after year, enough for the household. They freeze well. If you cannot find any, you may substitute one bunch of scallions, a piece of garlic the size of a small Spanish peanut and 1 tablespoon [15 ml.] of cut fresh chives. Mash the garlic with salt. Chop scallions and chives together, then mix with the garlic salt. This mixture will fairly resemble the flavor of wild onions.

	To serve 8	
8	eggs	8
2	bunches wild onions, 10 to 12 in each bunch	2
4	thick bacon slices, cut into ½-inch [1-cm.] strips	4
2 tbsp.	water	30 ml.
½ cup	milk	125 ml.
	salt and freshly ground black pepper	

Wash the onions, remove the outer leaves and peel the roots. Cut the green parts into 2-inch [5-cm.] lengths, then coarsely chop them. Place the chopped onions in a cold frying pan along with the pieces of bacon and fry over medium heat, stirring once in a while, until the bacon starts to turn brown and the onion becomes limp. Add the water and a sprinkling of salt, and continue cooking for another 10 to 15 minutes.

Beat the eggs with the milk and salt and pepper to taste, then add the eggs to the onion mixture. Scramble fast and serve immediately.

LOUIS SZATHMÁRY
AMERICAN GASTRONOMY

Eggs in Stewed Vegetables

Chachoucka

A spicy dish from Africa. Sometimes okra is added to the other vegetables.

	To serve 4	
8	eggs	8
2	medium-sized onions, sliced	2
⅓ cup	olive oil	75 ml.
2	medium-sized green or red peppers, broiled, peeled, seeded and cut into small pieces	2
2	medium-sized tomatoes, peeled and chopped	2
	salt and pepper	

Cook the onions in hot olive oil in a fireproof dish until they are soft. Add the peppers and, after five minutes, the tomatoes. Season with salt and pepper and cook slowly for about 15 minutes, or until the mixture is almost reduced to a pulp. Push the vegetables to the sides of the dish.

Beat the eggs, pour them into the center, and scramble them until cooked; or break them in whole, and cook them until the whites are set.

X. MARCEL BOULESTIN AND A. H. ADAIR
SAVOURIES AND HORS-D'OEUVRE

Scrambles with Wild Rice

To cook the wild rice in this recipe, stir ¼ cup [50 ml.] of rice into 1 cup [¼ liter] of boiling water. Cook covered until the water has been completely absorbed, about 40 minutes.

To serve 4 to 6

8	eggs	8
1 cup	cooked wild rice	¼ liter
¼ cup	chopped celery	50 ml.
¼ cup	chopped green pepper	50 ml.
2 tbsp.	butter	30 ml.
½ cup	light cream	125 ml.
	salt and pepper	

Sauté the celery and the green pepper in the butter in a large skillet set over medium heat. Lightly beat the eggs with the cream; stir in the wild rice.

Pour the egg mixture onto the sautéed vegetables in the skillet and scramble until the eggs are set but still soft, about five minutes. Season with salt and pepper.

BETH ANDERSON
WILD RICE FOR ALL SEASONS COOKBOOK

Satchel Eggs

This dish may be served with any hot, well-flavored sauce, such as tomato sauce (recipe, page 166) or velouté sauce (recipe, page 165).

To serve 4

6	eggs, beaten	6
1	small French loaf or 4 crusty rolls, split lengthwise and the soft centers removed	1
6 tbsp.	butter	90 ml.
	salt and pepper	
½ cup	chopped cooked ham	125 ml.
¾ cup	chopped fresh mushrooms	175 ml.
⅓ cup	shredded Gruyère cheese	75 ml.

Butter the insides of the bread crusts with 4 tablespoons [60 ml.] of the butter. Bake in a preheated 400° F. [200° C.] oven for six to eight minutes, or until they are lightly browned.

Meanwhile, season the eggs with salt and pepper; mix in the ham and mushrooms. Melt the remaining butter and lightly scramble the egg mixture in it. Pile the eggs in one half of the split loaf, top the eggs with the cheese and bake in a preheated 450° F. [230° C.] oven for about five minutes, or until the cheese has melted and browned on top.

Put the empty half-crust on top and serve immediately with a sauce on the side.

MARGARET SHERMAN
THE WINE AND FOOD SOCIETY'S GUIDE TO EGGS

Eggs with Late Summer Vegetables, Bilbao-Style

Pisto a la Bilbaína

To serve 4

4	eggs, beaten	4
7 tbsp.	oil	100 ml.
1	onion, thinly sliced	1
4 to 5	small zucchini, peeled and cubed	4 to 5
3	ripe tomatoes, peeled and mashed	3
1 cup	finely diced cooked ham with its fat	¼ liter
2	garlic cloves, thinly sliced	2
2	green peppers, broiled until the skin blackens and blisters, peeled, seeded and cut into pieces	2
	salt	
4	bread slices, cut into triangles and fried in oil or butter until golden (optional)	4

Heat the oil in a heavy pan. First sauté the onion until the slices are soft, then add the zucchini cubes, cover, and cook them slowly for about five minutes.

Add the tomatoes, ham, garlic and peppers, season with salt to taste, cover, and cook until the zucchini is just tender.

Just before serving, add the eggs to the vegetables and stir until the eggs are set. Serve in a warmed dish, garnished if desired with triangles of fried bread.

ANA-MARÍA CALERA
365 RECETAS DE COCINA VASCA

Golden Tripe

To serve 6

4	eggs	4
5 tbsp.	freshly grated Parmesan cheese	75 ml.
2 lb.	precooked honeycomb tripe, washed	1 kg.
3 cups	court bouillon (recipe, page 164)	¾ liter
1	garlic clove, finely chopped	1
6 to 8 tbsp.	finely chopped fresh parsley	90 to 120 ml.
¼ cup	olive oil	50 ml.
4	slices bacon, finely chopped	4
1	onion, thinly sliced	1
	salt and pepper	

Cover the tripe with the court bouillon and simmer it, covered, for about an hour, or until the tripe is tender. Drain it, reserving the stock, and cut the tripe into 1½-inch [4-cm.] squares. Sauté the garlic and parsley in 2 tablespoons [30 ml.] of the olive oil until the garlic is golden. Remove the garlic and parsley with a slotted spoon.

Add the remaining oil, the bacon and onion, and sauté until the onion slices are limp. Add the garlic mixture, tripe, and salt and pepper to taste. Simmer the mixture for two to three minutes. Add ⅔ cup [150 ml.] of the reserved stock; cover and cook over low heat for about 30 minutes.

Just before serving, beat the eggs together with the cheese. Pour the egg mixture over the tripe; stir lightly and cook until the eggs are just set, about one or two minutes. The eggs should have a creamy consistency. Serve at once.

JANA ALLEN AND MARGARET GIN
INNARDS AND OTHER VARIETY MEATS

Eggs Scrambled with Cream

Oeufs Brouillés à la Crème

To serve 6

8	egg yolks, beaten	8
2	egg whites, beaten	2
1¼ cups	heavy cream	300 ml.
4 tbsp.	butter	60 ml.
3 or 4	fresh mushrooms, coarsely chopped	3 or 4
1	bouquet garni	1
1	thin slice cooked ham, cut into julienne	1
2 oz.	veal trimmings, diced	60 g.
⅔ cup	veal stock (recipe, page 164)	150 ml.
2 or 3 tbsp.	veal or other meat roasting juices, degreased (optional)	30 or 45 ml.
	salt and pepper	
	grated nutmeg	
1 cup	croutons (recipe, page 166)	¼ liter

Over low heat, melt 1 tablespoon [15 ml.] of butter and sauté the mushrooms, bouquet garni, ham and veal until all of the meat is well browned. Add the stock, let it boil until it is nearly reduced to syrup, then add the cream and simmer, stirring often, until the liquid is reduced by about half.

Pass the mixture through a sieve, pressing firmly to extract all flavor from the residue. Gradually stir into this sauce the roasting juices, egg yolks and whites. Season to taste with salt, pepper and grated nutmeg.

Stirring all the time, cook the mixture in the top of a double boiler over simmering water until the eggs are set but still creamy and soft. Garnish with the croutons.

MARIN
LES DONS DE COMUS

Omelets

Raw Egg Omelet

Omelette aux Oeufs Crus

To serve 4

8	eggs, beaten with salt and pepper	8
3	egg yolks, lightly beaten	3
4 tbsp.	butter	60 ml.
1 tbsp.	finely cut fresh chives or chopped fresh watercress	15 ml.

Heat the butter in a large omelet pan and pour in the eggs. When the omelet is almost set and moves easily in the pan, mix the egg yolks with the chives or watercress and spread this mixture over the omelet. Fold it in half and serve.

FREDERICK ELLES AND SACHA SOSNO
99 OMELETTES ORIGINALES

Flamed Vodka Omelet

Omelette Aletti

To serve 4

8	eggs, the yolks separated from the whites, and the whites stiffly beaten	8
¼ cup	vodka	50 ml.
2 tbsp.	butter	30 ml.
½	onion, chopped	½
1 tsp.	paprika	5 ml.
	salt	
3 to 4 tbsp.	heavy cream	45 to 60 ml.

Heat 1 tablespoon [15 ml.] of the butter in a small pan and gently cook the onion until it is transparent, adding ¼ teaspoon [1 ml.] of the paprika. Allow the onion to cool, then mix it with the remaining butter. Press this paprika-butter mixture through a sieve.

Mix the egg yolks and beaten egg whites together and season with salt. Melt the paprika butter in a skillet and add the eggs. Cook until the omelet is almost set. Mix the cream with the remaining paprika and spread it in the center of the omelet. Fold the omelet into thirds.

Heat the vodka in a ladle or small saucepan, set it alight, and pour it, flaming, over the omelet. Serve immediately.

ROBERT COURTINE
MES REPAS LES PLUS ÉTONNANTS

Egg Symphony

Symphonie d'Oeufs

For the basic techniques of hard-boiling and poaching eggs, see pages 24-25 and 26-27. To prepare a tomato sauce to serve with this dish, peel, seed and roughly chop four medium-sized ripe tomatoes. Season them to taste with salt, pepper and herbs, and simmer them over medium heat until they have reduced to a fairly thick purée —about 20 minutes.

	To serve 4	
14	eggs	14
4 tbsp.	butter	60 ml.
	salt and pepper	

Hard-boil two of the eggs, cool and shell them, and chop them fine. Poach four of the eggs and keep them warm.

Beat the eight remaining eggs together, and season them with salt and pepper. Heat a quarter of the butter in a small omelet pan. When the butter foams, but before it browns, pour in a quarter of the beaten eggs. Cook, pulling the edges of the omelet toward the center, until the entire mixture is set. Slide the omelet out onto a warmed plate, and repeat the operation three times more.

Sprinkle the omelets with the chopped, hard-boiled eggs, and place a poached egg in the center of each. Fold the edges of the omelets over the poached eggs. Serve immediately, with a hot tomato sauce.

EUGÉNIE BRAZIER
LES SECRETS DE LA MÈRE BRAZIER

Cheese and Mint Omelet

Omelette au Brocciu et à la Menthe

The original version of this recipe calls for brocciu, a Corsican fresh sheep's-milk cheese, known as brousse in mainland France. Since neither brocciu nor brousse is available in the United States, Tallegio cheese can be used instead.

	To serve 2	
4	eggs, beaten	4
5 oz.	Tallegio cheese, mashed to a paste with a fork	150 g.
3 or 4	fresh mint leaves, cut into quarters	3 or 4
	salt and pepper	
2 tbsp.	butter or oil	30 ml.

Mix the cheese, mint, and salt and pepper well into the eggs. Heat the butter or oil in an omelet pan, pour in the egg mixture and cook for about one minute, or until the omelet is just set. Roll it as you slide it from the pan.

MARIA NUNZIA FILIPPINI
LA CUISINE CORSE

Puffed Cheese Omelet

	To serve 1	
2	eggs, the yolks separated from the whites	2
	salt	
	Tabasco sauce	
1½ tbsp.	butter, cut into bits	22 ml.
½ cup	finely shredded Cheddar	125 ml.

Add a pinch of salt to the egg whites and two or three drops of Tabasco sauce to the yolks. With a rotary beater, beat the whites rapidly until they form firm, unwavering peaks. Then, using the same beater (do not bother to wash it), beat the yolks long enough to combine them.

With a rubber spatula, scrape the yolks over the whites, and fold the two together until only a few streaks of the whites are apparent. Be careful not to overfold.

Drop the butter bits into a 10-inch [25-cm.] frying pan with a nonstick surface. Set the pan over medium heat. When the butter melts, tip the pan from side to side to coat the bottom and sides evenly.

With the rubber spatula, scrape the omelet mixture into the center of the pan. Then, with a small metal spatula, quickly spread the omelet so that it covers the bottom of the pan. With the tip of the spatula, shape the edges of the omelet to make it as round as possible. Reduce the heat to low.

Cook the omelet for about one minute to firm the underside, then slide the pan gently back and forth across the burner until the omelet moves freely in one foamy mass. Now let the omelet cook for about two minutes more, or until the underside of the omelet is golden brown and the top feels warm, not hot, to the touch.

Immediately remove the pan from the heat and scatter the shredded cheese evenly over the omelet. Grasp the handle of the pan securely and hold the pan tilted, with its far edge just inside the edge of the warmed plate. Insert the metal spatula under the edge of the omelet away from the handle, simultaneously drawing the pan back until about half the omelet has come to rest on the plate while the other half remains in the pan. Now confidently push the tilted pan forward, using its rim to fold the remaining half of the omelet over as it slides from the pan. This forms a puffed, golden-brown crescent, the cheese enclosed within it. Serve the omelet at once on a preheated plate.

MICHAEL FIELD
COOKING ADVENTURES WITH MICHAEL FIELD

Cheese and Jelly Omelet

Tortilla de Jalea con Queso

To serve 4

4	eggs, the yolks separated from the whites	4
3½ oz.	cheese, cut into cubes	100 g.
¼ cup	milk	50 ml.
	salt	
1 tbsp.	melted butter	15 ml.
	guava or other fruit jelly	

Combine the cheese cubes with the milk and cook, stirring occasionally, over low heat until the cheese melts. Remove from the heat and cool the mixture slightly. Beat the egg yolks with the salt and add them slowly to the milk. Salt to taste. Beat the egg whites until stiff and gently fold them into the mixture, being careful to keep it slightly lumpy.

Melt the butter in a medium-sized ovenproof skillet. Pour in the egg mixture and cook over low heat until the omelet rises slightly and the bottom sets, about five minutes. Then bake in a preheated 325° F. [160° C.] oven for 15 minutes, or until the omelet is dry and golden on top. Remove it from the oven and place it on a flat serving dish. Spread jelly on one side of the omelet and fold it in half; then spread more jelly on top. Serve immediately.

NURI FONSECA
LATINOAMERICA EN SU COCINA

Asparagus Omelet

Aumelette d'Asperges

To serve 4

8	eggs, beaten	8
7 or 8	medium-sized asparagus spears (about ½ lb. [¼ kg.]), tough ends removed and stalks cut into pea-sized pieces	7 or 8
5 tbsp.	butter	75 ml.
1 tbsp.	flour	15 ml.
	salt and pepper	
1 tbsp.	chopped fresh parsley	15 ml.
2 or 3	chopped scallions	2 or 3
½ cup	heavy cream	125 ml.

Heat half of the butter and stir in the flour. Add the asparagus, salt, pepper, parsley and scallions. Cook gently for about 10 minutes, or until the asparagus is tender but still firm. Then stir in the cream, bring it to a boil and remove the skillet from the heat.

Heat the remaining butter in a large omelet pan. Mix the eggs well into the asparagus. Pour the mixture into the pan and cook it for about three or four minutes, until the omelet is brown on the bottom. Reverse it immediately onto a warmed plate for serving, or place it under the broiler for a minute or two to set the top before serving.

L'ESCOLE PARFAITE DES OFFICIERS DE BOUCHE

Broad Bean Omelet

Omelette de Fèves Vertes

There are many variations on this recipe, and other vegetables, first sweated in butter, then gently simmered in cream, may be used in place of the broad beans. These include mushrooms, garden peas, asparagus tips, artichoke bottoms, white or black truffles, spinach and sorrel.

To serve 2

4	eggs, beaten	4
2 lb.	young broad beans, shelled and peeled	1 kg.
2 tbsp.	butter	30 ml.
1 tbsp.	chopped fresh parsley	15 ml.
2 tsp.	finely cut fresh chives or finely chopped scallions	10 ml.
1 cup	heavy cream	¼ liter
	salt and pepper	
2	egg yolks	2

In half of the butter, gently sauté the broad beans with the parsley and chives or scallions. Add ½ cup [125 ml.] of the cream, season lightly with salt and pepper, and cook over low heat for about 10 minutes, or until the beans are soft. Set aside off the heat.

Beat half of the remaining cream into the eggs; salt to taste. Heat the remaining butter in a small omelet pan, pour in the eggs and make a flat omelet, cooking about two to three minutes until the eggs are set but the center creamy. Slip the omelet onto a warmed serving plate.

Beat the egg yolks with the remaining cream and stir them into the creamed beans. Return the beans to low heat, stirring until the sauce thickens. Do not let the sauce boil. Pour the sauced beans over the omelet, and serve.

MASSIALOT
LE CUISINIER ROIAL ET BOURGEOIS

Artichoke Omelet

This is a Roman specialty and one of the best. According to the century-old method, roast-meat drippings are the fat used for cooking it, and may replace olive oil here.

To serve 6

6	eggs, beaten	6
2 or 3	plump tiny artichokes, spiky leaves and chokes removed, bottoms quartered	2 or 3
3 tbsp.	strained fresh lemon juice	45 ml.
2 tbsp.	olive oil	30 ml.
	salt and pepper	
1 tsp.	chopped fresh parsley	5 ml.

Before cooking the artichokes, let them stand for a few minutes in a bowl of cold water, with the lemon juice added to prevent them from going black.

Now drain, and cook them in a medium-sized omelet pan with the olive oil, salt, pepper and a dash of water if the pan threatens to cook dry.

When the artichokes are cooked (about 10 minutes), pour in the eggs with the parsley. Cook over medium-low heat for about five minutes longer, so that the eggs are mixed with the artichokes and nearly set. The omelet is ready.

SOPHIA LOREN
IN THE KITCHEN WITH LOVE

Roman Omelet

Uova alla Romana

The original recipe calls for provatura, a fresh Roman cheese made from water-buffalo milk. It is not available in the U.S.

To serve 4

8	eggs	8
4 tbsp.	butter	60 ml.
2 lb.	broad beans, shelled and peeled (3 cups [¾ liter])	1 kg.
¼ lb.	small boiling or pickling onions	125 g.
1 tbsp.	chopped fresh herbs (savory, marjoram, parsley)	15 ml.
	salt and pepper	
	ground allspice	
2 tbsp.	heavy cream	30 ml.
2 oz.	Tallegio or Bel Paese cheese, sliced	60 g.

Melt half of the butter in a saucepan and add the broad beans, onions, herbs and seasonings. Cover and cook gently for 15 to 20 minutes, or until the vegetables are tender. Beat together the eggs and cream, and stir in the cheese and the vegetable mixture.

Heat the remaining butter in a large omelet pan and, when the butter foams, pour in the egg mixture. Cook for five minutes, or until the omelet is set. Place the omelet under the broiler briefly to cook the top. Serve the omelet unfolded.

VINCENZO CORRADO
IL CUOCO GALANTE

Cauliflower Frittata

Frittata di Cavolfiore

To serve 4

6	eggs, beaten	6
1	small cauliflower (about 10 oz. [300 g.]), trimmed, cored, broken into florets, boiled until just tender and finely chopped	1
4 tbsp.	butter	60 ml.
1 tbsp.	olive oil	15 ml.
	salt and pepper	
2 tbsp.	freshly grated Parmesan cheese	30 ml.

Heat the butter and oil in a medium-sized omelet pan, put in the cauliflower, and season it with salt and pepper. Cook the cauliflower gently until it has absorbed the butter and oil. Beat the eggs with the cheese and a pinch of salt. Pour them over the cauliflower, and cook until the omelet is set. It should not be necessary to turn it.

PELLEGRINO ARTUSI
LA SCIENZA IN CUCINA E L'ARTE DI MANGIAR BENE

Lettuce Omelet

As the lettuce for the omelet, you can use Bibb, Boston hearts or buttercrunch hearts.

To serve 2

4	eggs, beaten	4
1	small lettuce, coarsely sliced	1
2 tbsp.	butter	30 ml.
	salt and pepper	
2 or 3 tbsp.	white sauce *(recipe, page 165)*	30 or 45 ml.

Sauté the lettuce in half of the butter until softened. Season it with salt and pepper, and combine it with the white sauce.

Melt the remaining butter in a medium-sized omelet pan. Pour the eggs into the pan and let the omelet cook until almost set. Put the lettuce filling into the center of the omelet, fold it over and serve.

NARCISSA CHAMBERLAIN
THE OMELETTE BOOK

Leek Omelet

Omelette aux Poireaux

To serve 4		
8	eggs	8
4 or 5	leeks, white parts only	4 or 5
2 tbsp.	heavy cream	30 ml.
	salt and pepper	
2 tbsp.	butter	30 ml.

Cook the leeks in a few spoonfuls of water for 10 minutes. Drain the leeks, and boil the cooking liquid until it is reduced to about 1 tablespoon [15 ml.]. Chop the leeks fine; stir the cream into the leeks.

Beat the eggs with salt, pepper, and the reduced cooking liquid. Melt the butter in a large omelet pan. When the butter is hot, pour in the beaten eggs and allow them to set. Spread the leeks down the center of the omelet, and fold the omelet over the leeks just before you turn it out of the pan.

FREDERICK ELLES AND SACHA SOSNO
99 OMELETTES ORIGINALES

Cold Frittata, Country-Style

Frittata Fredda alla Rustica

To serve 4		
6	eggs	6
1	small eggplant, peeled and cut into slices ½ inch [1 cm.] thick	1
	salt and pepper	
3	artichokes, outer leaves discarded, sliced into water acidulated with fresh lemon juice	3
½ cup	olive oil	125 ml.
2	green peppers, broiled until the skin blackens and blisters, peeled, seeded and cut into thin strips	2

Sprinkle the eggplant slices with salt and let them stand in a colander for one hour. Drain and pat the eggplant dry. Drain the artichoke slices well on absorbent paper.

Heat half of the oil in a skillet, and when it is hot add the artichokes and eggplant. Cover and cook over low heat for 30 minutes or until very tender, adding a little water if needed.

In a bowl, beat the eggs with a pinch of salt and a little pepper. Remove the artichokes and eggplant from the pan and drain them well on absorbent paper. Chop them and add them to the eggs with the pepper strips. Mix well.

In a 10-inch [25-cm.] skillet, heat the remaining oil until it sizzles. Pour in the egg-and-vegetable mixture and cook until the eggs are set. Turn the *frittata* out onto a serving platter. Cool and then cut into small wedges. Serve cold.

WAVERLEY ROOT
THE BEST OF ITALIAN COOKING

Eggs in a Greatcoat

Uova in Surtout

To serve 6		
13	eggs, 7 hard-boiled and quartered, 6 beaten	13
8 tbsp.	butter	120 ml.
2 tbsp.	chopped fresh parsley	30 ml.
2 tbsp.	chopped scallion	30 ml.
1 cup	chopped fresh mushrooms	¼ liter
1 tbsp.	finely cut fresh chives	15 ml.
1 tbsp.	flour	15 ml.
1 cup	milk	¼ liter
	salt and freshly ground pepper	
¼ cup	dry bread crumbs	50 ml.

Melt 2 tablespoons [30 ml.] of the butter in a saucepan over low heat. Put in the parsley, scallion, mushrooms and chives, and cook until the vegetables are soft. Mix the flour with the milk and stir them into the pan. Season with salt and pepper. Bring the sauce to a boil and stir it until it thickens, about five minutes. Add the egg quarters, cook for a moment, and then arrange the eggs and sauce in a heated shallow serving dish, 8 inches [20 cm.] in diameter.

Heat 2 tablespoons of the butter in a large omelet pan, pour in the beaten eggs and cook until this omelet is set, turning it to brown both sides lightly. Place the omelet over the eggs and sauce so that sauce and eggs are completely hidden. Melt the remaining butter and brush a little of it over the top of the omelet. Sprinkle with bread crumbs, pour on the rest of the butter and put the dish under the broiler for a minute or two to brown the crumbs.

IL CUOCO PIEMONTESE RIDOTTO ALL'ULTIMO GUSTO

Dried Mushroom Omelet

L'Omelette aux Cèpes Secs ou aux Mousserons Secs

	To serve 4	
8	eggs, lightly beaten	8
2 oz.	dried cepes or field mushrooms, soaked in hot water for 2 hours, rinsed in warm water, drained and diced	60 g.
¼ cup	olive oil	50 ml.
1	shallot, chopped	1
½	garlic clove, chopped	½
½ cup	diced cooked ham	125 ml.
	salt and pepper	
2 tbsp.	butter	30 ml.

Heat the oil in a skillet and cook the shallot for five minutes, or until softened. Add the mushrooms, garlic and ham, and cook, stirring, for 10 minutes, or until the mushrooms are soft. Cool the mixture slightly.

Stir the mushroom mixture into the eggs, season to taste, and let the eggs stand for 30 minutes.

Melt the butter in a large omelet pan, pour in the egg mixture, and cook until the omelet is almost set but still creamy in the center. Fold the omelet as you slide it onto a warmed serving dish.

ALBIN MARTY
FOURMIGUETTO: SOUVENIRS, CONTES ET RECETTES DU LANGUEDOC

Lyons Onion Omelet

Omelette Lyonnaise

	To serve 4	
8	eggs, beaten with ¼ cup [50 ml.] water	8
2	onions, thinly sliced	2
2 tbsp.	chopped fresh parsley	30 ml.
3 tbsp.	butter	45 ml.
	salt and pepper	
¼ cup	white wine vinegar	50 ml.

Heat the butter in a large omelet pan over low heat, and in it brown the onions, mixed with the parsley. Season them with salt and pepper, then pour the eggs over the onion mixture and cook the omelet until the underneath is brown and the top almost set. Turn it over like a pancake, cook for another minute and transfer it to a warmed serving dish.

Add the vinegar to the hot pan, bring it quickly to the boil and sprinkle it over the omelet just before serving.

FÉLIX BENOIT AND HENRY CLOS JOUVE
LA CUISINE LYONNAISE

Feydeau's Omelet

Omelette Feydeau

	To serve 3	
10	eggs, 7 beaten, 3 poached or soft-boiled	10
1 lb.	fresh mushrooms	½ kg.
10 tbsp.	butter, 6 tbsp. [90 ml.] diced	150 ml.
½ cup	freshly grated Parmesan or Gruyère cheese	125 ml.
2½ cups	white sauce (recipe, page 165)	625 ml.
⅓ cup	heavy cream	75 ml.
1	small truffle, cut into julienne (optional)	1
	salt and pepper	

Put the raw mushrooms through a food processor, then sauté them in 2 tablespoons [30 ml.] of the butter until all of their liquid has evaporated.

Over low heat, add most of the grated cheese to the white sauce. Add 4 tablespoons [60 ml.] of the diced butter, then stir in the cream and the truffle if using.

Add 2 tablespoons of diced butter to the beaten eggs with salt and pepper. Heat the remaining 2 tablespoons of butter in a large omelet pan, then pour in the eggs. Cook until the omelet is almost set, but still liquid on top. Roll the omelet as you slide it onto a warmed ovenproof serving dish. Slit the top of the omelet to form a pocket. Spoon the mushroom purée into the pocket.

Place the poached or soft-boiled eggs on top of the filling. Cover with the cheese sauce, sprinkle with the remaining cheese and put under a hot broiler for two to three minutes, or until the cheese browns.

PROSPER MONTAGNÉ
THE NEW LAROUSSE GASTRONOMIQUE

Mashed Potato Omelet

Omelette Markode

A meat omelet may be cooked in the same way. Replace the potatoes with 1 pound [½ kg.] well-cooked beef or lamb, chopped with onions and spices.

	To serve 4	
8	eggs	8
5	medium-sized potatoes, peeled, halved and steamed for 35 to 40 minutes	5
3	garlic cloves, finely chopped	3
3 tbsp.	chopped fresh parsley	45 ml.
	salt and pepper	
3 tbsp.	olive oil	45 ml.
	lemon wedges or prepared mustard	

In a bowl, crush the potatoes with a fork. Add the garlic and parsley. Beat the eggs into the potatoes, one by one, and season the mixture with salt and pepper.

Heat the oil in a large heavy skillet, pour in the egg mixture and cook over low heat for 15 minutes, or until the underneath is browned and the top almost set.

Take the skillet off the heat, cover it with an inverted plate, turn it over so that the omelet falls onto the plate, and slide the omelet back into the skillet. Cook the second side for 10 minutes, or until browned. Serve hot or cold, with lemon wedges or mustard.

IRÈNE AND LUCIENNE KARSENTY
LA CUISINE PIED-NOIR

Grated Potato and Cheese Omelet

La Râpée

	To serve 2	
2	eggs, beaten	2
2	medium-sized potatoes, peeled and grated (about 1¼ cups [300 ml.])	2
	salt and pepper	
1 tbsp.	finely chopped onion	15 ml.
1	garlic clove, finely chopped	1
2 tbsp.	finely shredded Gruyère cheese	30 ml.
2 tbsp.	butter	30 ml.

Mix together the eggs, potatoes, salt and pepper, onion, garlic and cheese. Melt the butter in a medium-sized omelet pan, pour in the egg mixture and cook for five minutes on each side, or until golden and firm.

ÉDOUARD M. NIGNON
LE LIVRE DE CUISINE DE L'OUEST-ÉCLAIR

Swiss Stuffed Omelets

Omelettes Farcies à la Suisse

The rolled, stuffed omelets may alternatively be sprinkled with bread crumbs and melted butter and broiled, or dipped in beaten egg, then in crumbs and fried in butter.

	To serve 6	
7	eggs, beaten	7
⅔ cup	heavy cream	150 ml.
	salt	
8 tbsp.	butter	120 ml.
3	thick slices white bread with the crusts removed, cut into strips	3
2	egg yolks, beaten	2
¼ cup	freshly grated Parmesan cheese	50 ml.
Sorrel stuffing		
½ lb.	fresh sorrel, stemmed and shredded	¼ kg.
2 tbsp.	butter	30 ml.
⅓ cup	heavy cream	75 ml.
	salt	
1½ cups	fresh white bread crumbs	375 ml.
½ cup	freshly grated Parmesan cheese	125 ml.
3	hard-boiled egg yolks, mashed	3

Mix the beaten eggs with 3 or 4 tablespoons [45 or 60 ml.] of the cream and a pinch of salt. Heat 2 tablespoons [30 ml.] of butter in a large omelet pan and make seven thin, flat omelets with the egg mixture, stacking them in reserve while you make the stuffing.

For the stuffing, cook the sorrel in the butter until it is melted to a purée. Add the cream, season with salt, and simmer until slightly thickened. Off the heat, stir in the bread crumbs, cheese and egg yolks.

Spread out six of the omelets on a clean cloth, divide half of the stuffing among them and roll them up. Fry the bread strips slowly in 4 tablespoons [60 ml.] of the butter until they are golden. Dip one side of each strip into the beaten egg yolks, and arrange the strips—dipped sides outward—to form a wall around the edge of a shallow ovenproof dish just large enough to hold the omelets. Cut the stuffed omelets in half crosswise and arrange them in the dish; fill any gaps and cover the tops of the omelets with the remaining stuffing. Pour the rest of the cream over the top.

Place the remaining omelet flat on top of the dish as a cover. Sprinkle it with the cheese, dot with the remaining butter and bake in a preheated 350° F. [180° C.] oven for 30 minutes, or until the top omelet is golden.

LOUIS AUGUSTE DE BOURBON
LE CUISINIER GASCON

Sorrel Omelet
Omelette à l'Oseille

To serve 2

4	eggs, beaten with salt and pepper	4
3 oz.	fresh young sorrel leaves, stems and middle ribs removed, finely cut with a knife	90 g.
½	garlic clove, chopped	½
1 tbsp.	chopped fresh chervil	15 ml.
2 tbsp.	butter	30 ml.

Mix the sorrel with your eggs, and add the garlic and chervil. Melt the butter in a medium-sized omelet pan. Pour in the eggs and allow them to set. The omelet should be made rather thick so that, the inside being less cooked, the sorrel that is there remains almost raw. This gives it a peculiar acid taste, extremely pleasant and fresh.

X. MARCEL BOULESTIN
SIMPLE FRENCH COOKING FOR ENGLISH HOMES

Omelet Sandwich with Sorrel Filling
Omelette à la Gendarme

To serve 4

6	eggs, 4 beaten, the yolks of 2 separated from the whites	6
½ lb.	sorrel, finely chopped (about 2 cups [½ liter])	¼ kg.
6 tbsp.	butter	90 ml.
¼ cup	heavy cream	50 ml.
1 cup	fresh bread crumbs	¼ liter
⅔ cup	freshly grated Parmesan cheese	150 ml.
	salt and pepper	
4	slices firm-textured white bread, cut into fingers and fried in butter	4

Cook the sorrel in 2 tablespoons [30 ml.] of the butter until it is reduced to a purée. Beat the two egg yolks with the cream and stir them into the sorrel with most of the bread crumbs and cheese, reserving about 2 tablespoons of each.

Heat 1 tablespoon [15 ml.] of the butter in a large omelet pan. Season the four beaten eggs with salt and pepper, and pour half of the egg mixture into the pan. Cook until just set, and slide the omelet onto a serving dish.

Lightly beat the two egg whites, dip the fried bread fingers into the whites and arrange them around the edge of the omelet. Spread the sorrel mixture on the center of the omelet. Heat another tablespoon of butter in the omelet pan and make another thin omelet with the remaining egg mixture.

Slip this omelet over the filling, moist side uppermost, so that the sorrel is completely hidden.

Melt the remaining butter and sprinkle it on top, then sprinkle on the remaining bread crumbs and cheese. Bake in a preheated 450° F. [230° C.] oven for about five minutes, then place the omelet under a preheated broiler for a minute or two to brown the top.

MENON
LES SOUPERS DE LA COUR

Spinach Omelet from Nice
Omelette Niçarde aux Épinards

To serve 4

8	eggs, beaten	8
¼ lb.	Swiss chard, leaves chopped (about 1½ cups [375 ml.])	125 g.
1½ cups	chopped fresh spinach	375 ml.
8 tbsp.	olive oil	120 ml.
⅓ cup	freshly grated Parmesan cheese	75 ml.
1 tbsp.	chopped fresh parsley	15 ml.
1 tbsp.	chopped fresh basil	15 ml.
2	garlic cloves, chopped	2

Cook the chard and spinach in half of the olive oil until the oil is completely absorbed. Cool the mixture slightly, and add it to the eggs with the cheese, parsley, basil and garlic.

Heat the remaining oil in an omelet pan that will make an omelet two fingers thick (an 8-inch [20-cm.] pan). Pour in the egg mixture and cook over medium heat for 10 minutes, or until the omelet is set.

C. CHANOT-BULLIER
VIEILLES RECETTES DE CUISINE PROVENÇALE

California Omelet

To serve 3 or 4

6	eggs, lightly beaten	6
1	small garlic clove, crushed to a paste	1
4 tbsp.	olive oil	60 ml.
12	large ripe olives, pitted and chopped	12
½ cup	heavy cream	125 ml.
2	tomatoes, peeled, seeded and diced	2
1	avocado, halved, pitted, peeled and diced	1

Heat the garlic in 2 tablespoons [30 ml.] of the oil. Remove the garlic, add the olives and cream, and heat them gently. Heat the remaining oil in a large omelet pan, pour in the eggs and cook until they are set and the underside is brown. Add the tomatoes and avocado to the cream mixture just as the omelet is nearing completion. As soon as the vegetables are heated (no cooking please!), pour one third of the mixture onto the omelet.

Fold the omelet, turn it onto a hot platter and pour the rest of the vegetable mixture around the omelet.

HELEN BROWN
HELEN BROWN'S WEST COAST COOK BOOK

Green Tomato Frittata

Frittata di Pomodori Verdi

To flour green tomato slices, pat the cut surfaces dry and place the slices on a flour-covered plate for a few seconds, turning them to lightly coat both sides. Flour the slices as you use them, just before adding them to the hot oil.

	To serve 6	
6	eggs, very lightly beaten with a pinch of salt	6
4	large green tomatoes, cut into slices ½ inch [1 cm.] thick	4
1 cup	olive oil	¼ liter
1 cup	flour	¼ liter
	salt and freshly ground pepper	

Heat all but 1 tablespoon [15 ml.] of the oil in a frying pan. While the oil is heating, flour the tomato slices.

When the oil begins to sizzle, place only as many tomato slices in the pan as will make a single layer. Sauté until golden brown on both sides, then transfer to a paper towel to drain; sprinkle with salt and pepper. Fry the remaining tomato slices in the same way.

Heat the remaining tablespoon of oil in a large omelet pan. When it is hot, add the tomato slices. (The slices are reduced in size from having been sautéed, so they should all fit in one layer.) Pour the eggs over the tomato slices.

When the eggs are well set and the frittata is well detached from the bottom of the pan, place a plate, face down, over the pan. Holding the plate firmly, reverse the pan and turn the frittata out.

Return the pan to the heat. Carefully slide the frittata into the pan to cook the other side. After one minute, reverse the frittata onto a serving dish. Serve either hot or cold.

GIULIANO BUGIALLI
THE FINE ART OF ITALIAN COOKING

Zucchini Flower Omelet

I have seen this omelet turn out more successfully if, instead of cooking the flowers whole, you tear them up into pieces of more or less equal size.

	To serve 2	
4	eggs, beaten	4
4 to 6	zucchini flowers	4 to 6
2 tbsp.	olive oil	30 ml.
	salt	
1 tsp.	chopped fresh parsley	5 ml.

Cook the flowers over low heat in half of the oil and a sprinkling of salt for two to three minutes, or until wilted. Pour them into the eggs, without forgetting to add the parsley.

Heat the remaining oil in a medium-sized omelet pan, pour in the egg mixture and cook the omelet for about five minutes, or until it sets and the underside begins to brown.

SOPHIA LOREN
IN THE KITCHEN WITH LOVE

Zucchini Omelet

Omelette aux Courgettes

	To serve 4	
6	eggs, beaten	6
2	medium-sized zucchini, peeled, 1 diced and 1 cut into thin rounds	2
4 tbsp.	oil or butter	60 ml.
2 tsp.	chopped fresh parsley	10 ml.
1	garlic clove, chopped	1
	salt and pepper	
⅔ cup	tomato sauce *(recipe, page 166)*	150 ml.

Lightly sauté the diced zucchini in 1 tablespoon [15 ml.] of the oil or butter until they are soft; add half of the parsley. Remove them, and sauté the zucchini rounds in an additional tablespoon of oil or butter until they are soft and golden. Sprinkle them with the remaining parsley and the garlic, then set them aside.

Season the eggs with salt and pepper, and add the diced zucchini. Heat 1 tablespoon of oil or butter in a large omelet pan, pour in half of the egg mixture and cook until the omelet is set. Turn it out flat onto a round serving dish and cover it with the zucchini rounds.

Make a second omelet with the rest of the egg mixture and place that on top of the first. Surround the omelet with a ring of tomato sauce.

PROSPER MONTAGNÉ AND A. GOTTSCHALK
MON MENU

Swiss Chard Omelet from Nice

Omelette Niçoise à la Blette

As a variation on this recipe, you may add a few spinach leaves to the chard.

	To serve 4	
8	eggs, beaten	8
about 10	Swiss chard leaves	about 10
3 tbsp.	butter	45 ml.
½	garlic clove	½
½ cup	shredded Gruyère cheese	125 ml.
	salt and pepper	

Heat 1 tablespoon [15 ml.] of the butter and gently cook the chard leaves in it for 10 minutes. Coarsely chop them with the garlic. Add the cheese, salt and pepper to the leaves, and mix this with the eggs.

Melt the remaining butter in a large omelet pan, pour in the egg mixture, and cook the omelet for about five minutes, or until it has set but is still creamy in the middle. Fold the omelet as you slide it from the pan.

BENOIT MASCARELLI
LA TABLE EN PROVENCE & SUR LA CÔTE D'AZUR

Iraq Walnut Omelet

	To serve 3 or 4	
6	eggs, beaten	6
¾ cup	finely chopped walnuts	175 ml.
½ cup	dried currants, soaked in warm water for 15 minutes and drained	125 ml.
¼ tsp.	ground saffron	1 ml.
¼ tsp.	ground turmeric	1 ml.
2 tbsp.	finely cut fresh chives	30 ml.
¼ cup	fresh bread crumbs	50 ml.
	salt and pepper	
1 to 2 tbsp.	butter	15 to 30 ml.

Mix the walnuts, currants, saffron, turmeric, chives, bread crumbs, salt and pepper into the eggs. Melt 1 tablespoon [15 ml.] of the butter in a large omelet pan over high heat and pour the egg mixture into it. When set and brown on one side, add more butter to the pan if necessary, turn the omelet and lightly cook the other side.

NARCISSA CHAMBERLAIN
THE OMELETTE BOOK

Rouen Omelet

Omelette Rouennaise

	To serve 4	
8	eggs, beaten	8
2	duck livers, clinging membrane or fat removed, and thinly sliced	2
	salt and pepper	
¾ cup	red wine	175 ml.
6 tbsp.	butter	90 ml.

Bring half of the wine to a simmer. Add the duck livers and cook them gently for 10 minutes until the slices are firm but still pink in the center. Drain and set them aside.

Heat 3 tablespoons [45 ml.] of the butter in a large omelet pan over high heat, season the eggs with salt and pepper, and add them to the butter. When they have begun to set, arrange the duck-liver slices over the eggs.

While the omelet finishes cooking (in approximately two minutes), bring the rest of the wine to a boil with the remaining butter. Fold the omelet over the duck livers and sprinkle the wine-and-butter mixture over it.

MARIE BISSON
LA CUISINE NORMANDE

Duck-Egg Omelet with Coconut

Telur Dadar Padang

If duck eggs are not available, substitute the same number of jumbo-sized chicken eggs. Unsweetened or natural coconut can be found in block form in the frozen-food section of Oriental grocery stores. American baking coconut is sweetened, and not suitable for this recipe.

This savory omelet is thick and satisfying, and can be eaten either as a main dish with rice and vegetables or as a snack with salad.

	To serve 4	
3	duck eggs	3
1 or 2 tbsp.	grated fresh or dried, unsweetened coconut	15 or 30 ml.
2	shallots	2
1	garlic clove	1
1	dried red chili, stemmed and seeded, or ½ tsp. [2 ml.] cayenne pepper	1
1 tbsp.	cold water	15 ml.
	salt	
2 tbsp.	vegetable oil	30 ml.

Either chop the shallots, garlic and chili fine or, better still, pound them together. Mix them with the coconut and water, and add a little salt to taste. Then beat the mixture thoroughly with the eggs. It needs more beating than an ordinary plain omelet, and should become quite fluffy.

Heat the oil in a wok or a large skillet, and spoon it over the sides or tilt and turn the wok so that the sides are well coated with oil. Pour the omelet mixture into the hot wok; swirl it around so that the omelet is not too thick in the center. Let it cook for two or three minutes.

Turn it over carefully (it should be perfectly circular) and cook slowly for another three or four minutes until the middle, which of course is still the thickest part, is firm and the whole omelet is lightly browned. The edges should be delicately crisp. Serve hot or cold, cut up into wedges like a cake.

PETITS PROPOS CULINAIRES

Spanish Omelet

Tortilla Murciana

This omelet is usually accompanied by a salad made with whatever vegetables are seasonally available.

To serve 4

6 to 8	eggs	6 to 8
7 tbsp.	olive oil	100 ml.
1 cup	chopped cooked ham	¼ liter
1	onion, diced	1
1	green pepper, stemmed, seeded, deribbed and diced	1
1	eggplant, peeled and diced	1
1	small zucchini, diced	1
2	ripe tomatoes, peeled and chopped	2
	salt	

Heat the oil in a large skillet and gently cook the ham, onion and green pepper for about 10 minutes. Add the eggplant and zucchini to the skillet, and cook gently until all of the vegetables are tender. Add the tomatoes and allow their juice to evaporate. When the tomatoes, too, are soft, season with a little salt, bearing in mind that the ham may be salty.

Beat the eggs lightly with a little salt and pour them over the vegetables. Cook over medium heat for about two minutes. When the underside is lightly browned, turn the omelet to brown the other side. Serve cut into wedges.

MARÍA DOLORES COMAS
THE BEST OF SPANISH COOKING

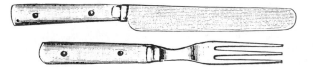

Catalan Omelet

Tortilla a la Catalana

The original version of this recipe calls for botifarra, a pork sausage produced in Catalonia and the Balearics. Black botifarra is a kind of blood sausage, but pine nuts, cumin seeds, almonds and ground cinnamon give it a distinctive flavor. White botifarra is a mild fresh sausage.

To serve 4

8	eggs, beaten	8
¼ cup	olive oil, or 2 tbsp. [30 ml.] lard	50 ml.
¼ lb.	blood sausage or mild fresh sausage, sliced ½ inch [1 cm.] thick	125 g.
½ cup	dried kidney beans, soaked in water overnight, drained, boiled in fresh water for 2 hours or until tender, drained again	125 ml.
	salt	

Heat the oil in a large skillet and fry the sausage slices until lightly browned. Remove them from the pan, add the beans and fry them lightly. Salt the eggs lightly, and add the sausage and beans. If necessary, put a little more oil or lard into the skillet, pour in the egg mixture and cook until browned on the bottom. Turn to brown the other side.

VICTORIA SERRA, TRANSLATED BY ELIZABETH GILI
TIA VICTORIA'S SPANISH KITCHEN

Omelet with Liver

Omelette de Foye de Lapin ou de Levrau

The original version of this recipe calls for the liver of a rabbit or a leveret—a young European hare.

To serve 2

4	eggs, beaten	4
2	chicken livers, coarsely chopped and pounded	2
1 tbsp.	fines herbes	15 ml.
	salt and white pepper	
2 tbsp.	lard, melted	30 ml.
2 tbsp.	lamb roasting juices	30 ml.
2 tbsp.	fresh lemon juice	30 ml.

Beat the liver and herbs into the eggs, and season with salt and pepper. Add half of the melted lard. Heat the remaining lard in a medium-sized omelet pan, pour in the egg mixture and cook until the omelet is almost set. Roll it as you slide it out of the pan onto a warmed serving dish. Sprinkle it with the lamb juices or stock and with the lemon juice, and serve.

PIERRE DE LUNE
LE NOUVEAU CUISINIER

Veal Kidney Omelet

Frittata colla Pietra di Vitella di Latte

	To serve 4	
6	eggs, beaten	6
1	veal kidney, encased in its fat	1
	oil	
	salt and pepper	
1 tbsp.	chopped fresh parsley	15 ml.
1 tbsp.	freshly grated Parmesan cheese	15 ml.
2 tbsp.	butter	30 ml.

Halve the kidney lengthwise; leave on all of its fat. Brush the kidney with oil, season it with salt and pepper, and broil it for four minutes on each side, or until it is cooked through. Cut it crosswise into small, thin slices. Season the eggs with salt and pepper and mix in the parsley and cheese. Add the kidney slices and mix well.

Melt the butter in a large omelet pan and, when it stops foaming, pour in the egg mixture. When the omelet is almost set, fold it in half and slide it onto a warmed serving dish.

PELLEGRINO ARTUSI
LA SCIENZA IN CUCINA E L'ARTE DI MANGIAR BENE

Parsley and Anchovy Omelet

Omelette aux Fines Herbes

	To serve 2	
4	eggs, beaten	4
2 tbsp.	chopped fresh parsley	30 ml.
1	salt anchovy, filleted, soaked in water for 30 minutes, drained, patted dry and chopped	1
	salt and pepper	
1 tbsp.	butter	15 ml.
2 tbsp.	oil	30 ml.

Season the eggs with salt and pepper, and mix in the parsley and the anchovy.

Heat the butter and oil in a medium-sized omelet pan and, when hot, pour in the eggs. When the eggs are set, tilt the pan and fold the omelet by letting it roll forward. It should still be creamy in the center.

CHARLES DURAND
LE CUISINIER DURAND

Scots Omelet

Milt is the reproductive gland of male fish, and is sometimes called soft roe because it is softer than the egg-filled roe of female fish. If herring milt is not available, substitute 2 pairs of female herring roe.

	To serve 4	
6	eggs, beaten	6
4	fresh herring milts (soft roe)	4
	salt	
	cayenne pepper	
1 tbsp.	finely cut fresh chives	15 ml.
1 tbsp.	finely chopped fresh parsley	15 ml.
1 tbsp.	finely chopped fresh chervil	15 ml.
4	thin slices smoked salmon	4
4 tbsp.	butter	60 ml.
2 tbsp.	fines herbes	30 ml.

Sprinkle the milt with salt, cayenne, chives, parsley and chervil. Wrap each milt in a slice of the smoked salmon and cook over gentle heat in 2 tablespoons [30 ml.] of the butter for five minutes.

While the milt is cooking, season the eggs and beat into them the fines herbes. Then heat the remaining butter in a medium-sized omelet pan. Pour in the eggs and cook the omelet for about two minutes, or until it is almost set. Set the wrapped milt aslant in the center of the omelet, roll it up and serve it immediately.

F. MARIAN MC NEILL
THE BOOK OF BREAKFASTS

Carp Roe Omelet

Aumelette Farcie en Maigre

Shad or herring may be substituted for carp roe.

Variations on this omelet may be made by using ¼ pound [125 g.] of chicken breast or veal kidney instead of the carp roe. Slice or dice the meat fine and half-cook it in butter.

Season it well, adding, if you like, 1 teaspoon [5 ml.] of chopped candied lemon peel. Alternatively, you may use ⅔ cup [150 ml.] of sliced fresh mushrooms, stewed with ¼ pound of finely sliced rabbit liver and seasoned with 2 teaspoons [10 ml.] of fines herbes.

To serve 4 to 6		
12	eggs, beaten	12
½ lb.	fresh carp roe, sliced	¼ kg.
5 tbsp.	butter	75 ml.
¼ lb.	fresh mushrooms, thinly sliced	125 g.
	salt and white pepper	
2 tbsp.	fines herbes	30 ml.

Melt 2 tablespoons [30 ml.] of the butter and sauté the mushrooms—seasoned with the salt, pepper and fines herbes—over high heat for a minute or two. Reduce the heat, add the roe, cover and stew them gently until firm, about five minutes. Cool. Season the eggs and add the roe mixture to them.

Heat the remaining butter in a large omelet pan. When the butter is foamy and beginning to brown, pour in the egg mixture. Stir once, and allow the omelet to set, lifting the edges so that the liquid egg runs underneath. When the bottom of the omelet is set and golden, but the top is still soft, turn the omelet out of the pan onto a warmed serving plate, inverting it so that the golden surface is uppermost.

L'ESCOLE PARFAITE DES OFFICIERS DE BOUCHE

Egg Foo Yong

To serve 3		
6	eggs	6
2 cups	bean sprouts, washed and drained	½ liter
2 tbsp.	finely chopped onion	30 ml.
1 tsp.	salt	5 ml.
	pepper	
1 cup	crab meat, cooked shrimp or other fish	¼ liter
	salad oil	

Soy-flavored sauce

3 tbsp.	light Chinese soy sauce or Japanese soy sauce	45 ml.
1 tbsp.	sugar	15 ml.
1 tbsp.	cornstarch	15 ml.
1½ cups	water	375 ml.

The batter can be made ahead. Beat the eggs. Add the bean sprouts, onion, salt, pepper to taste, and the crab meat, shrimp or fish. Refrigerate, if desired. To serve, beat to mix

again. Grease a skillet with a little salad oil. Cook six separate pancakes on both sides until golden brown. Keep them warm as they are done.

Make a sauce as follows, preparing the mixture ahead of time: Mix the sugar and cornstarch; add the soy sauce and water. When ready to serve, cook the mixture until thickened, stirring occasionally. Serve hot with hot pancakes.

MARIAN BURROS
PURE & SIMPLE

Hangtown Fry

According to some Californians, Hangtown Fry was created in 1849. A miner from Shirttail Bend hailed into Hangtown with a poke full of nuggets, plonked his fortune down on the counter of Cary House, and said he wanted the finest, most expensive meal they had. When he was told that oysters and eggs were the most expensive items on the menu (in those days whisky was $1,500 a barrel, turnips a dollar each), he told the cook to put them together and serve up the food. The dish was made, originally, with the small Pacific Coast Olympic oysters.

To serve 4		
9	eggs	9
12	live oysters, shucked and drained on absorbent paper	12
2 tbsp.	flour	30 ml.
	salt and pepper	
1 cup	cracker crumbs	¼ liter
3 tbsp.	butter	45 ml.

Beat one egg well. Season the flour with salt and pepper. Dip each oyster in the flour, then in the beaten egg, last of all in the cracker crumbs. Heat the butter and fry the oysters in it over medium heat for about five minutes, or until nicely browned on both sides.

Beat the remaining eight eggs with salt and pepper. Pour them over the oysters and cook for about five minutes, or until the mixture is firm on the bottom. Turn the omelet with a large spatula and cook the second side for a minute or two longer, or until set.

THE EDITORS OF AMERICAN HERITAGE
THE AMERICAN HERITAGE COOKBOOK

Oyster Omelet

Omelette aux Huitres

If you prefer to buy the oysters already shucked, be sure to ask the fish store to reserve their liquor for you.

It is essential to drain the oysters thoroughly before they are cooked, otherwise the liquor they contain will keep the oysters from mixing properly with the eggs once the omelet has set, and the appearance of the dish will be spoiled.

To serve 6

12	eggs	12
36	live oysters in their shells	36
¼ cup	chopped fresh parsley	50 ml.
2 tbsp.	heavy cream	30 ml.
	pepper	
2	thick slices dry bread, cut into ½-inch [1-cm.] cubes	2
2 tbsp.	butter	30 ml.

Open the oysters over a saucepan in order to catch all of their liquor. Remove and discard their shells and put the oysters in the pan with the liquor. Place the pan over low heat until the oysters begin to whiten. Drain the oysters; strain and reserve the liquor.

Break the eggs into a large bowl. Add the parsley, cream and 2 tablespoons [30 ml.] of the reserved oyster liquor. Season with pepper and beat rapidly for about one minute.

For the croutons, dry and lightly toast the cubes of bread in a preheated 350° F. [180° C.] oven for about 20 minutes. Melt half of the butter in a large omelet pan and, when it is quite hot, pour in half of the beaten eggs. When the eggs begin to set, add half of the oysters and half of the croutons. Continue cooking, fold the finished omelet and keep it hot. Make a second omelet in the same way and serve both omelets very hot.

CÉLINE VENCE AND ROBERT COURTINE
THE GRAND MASTERS OF FRENCH CUISINE

Cold Omelet Loaf

Gâteau de Crespèus

This *gâteau* is a loaf of multitiered omelets. Be organized when you make it. Prepare the five basic flavorings plus the sorrel purée and line them up in bowls near the stove. Before cooking the omelets, line up five plates or a couple of large

platters so as to be able to stack omelets of different flavors separately. Keep a flexible spatula at hand just in case an omelet should stick to the pan (should this happen—even though the omelet has been successfully turned out and the pan appears to be clean—rub the pan with salt before continuing to the next omelet).

Count about 1 tablespoon [15 ml.] of olive oil for the cooking of each omelet and reheat the pan for a few seconds each time before beginning another. The omelets should be from ¼ to ½ inch [6 mm. to 1 cm.] thick, depending on the material (the zucchini and spinach omelets will be thicker than the olive and mushroom omelets; the tomato mixture is more flexible).

A salad of cucumbers in a dill-flavored lemon-and-cream sauce is an exquisite accompaniment.

To serve 12 to 15

about 20	eggs, lightly beaten	about 20
4 or 5	small firm zucchini (about 1 lb. [½ kg.]), trimmed and coarsely grated or cut into julienne	4 or 5
	salt	
10 tbsp.	olive oil	150 ml.
1 tsp.	finely chopped fresh marjoram flowers (or ½ tsp. [2 ml.] dried marjoram or crumbled fresh oregano)	5 ml.
1	onion, halved and thinly sliced	1
3½ to 4 oz.	green pepper (the frying variety, if possible), halved lengthwise, seeded and sliced thin crosswise	100 to 125 g.
2	ripe firm tomatoes, peeled, seeded and coarsely chopped	2
1	large garlic clove, crushed slightly, peeled and sliced thin	1
½ tsp.	sugar	2 ml.
	cayenne pepper	
1 lb.	spinach, stems removed	½ kg.
¼ lb.	firm fresh mushrooms, very thinly sliced	125 g.
2 tbsp.	butter	30 ml.
	pepper	
10 oz.	sorrel, stems removed	300 g.
1 cup	natural black olives (no vinegar), pitted or with flesh removed and coarsely chopped	¼ liter
⅔ cup	heavy cream	150 ml.

First, prepare the various flavorings as follows.

Arrange the zucchini in layers in a mixing bowl, each layer sprinkled with salt. Leave to stand for about 30 minutes and press the mass together, squeezing to release the water. Pour the contents of the bowl into a sieve and, taking the mass in both hands, squeeze tightly and repeatedly to rid the zucchini of all the liquid possible. Sauté in 2 tablespoons [30 ml.] of olive oil over relatively high heat, tossing regularly, for six to seven minutes. Add the marjoram or oregano after removing from the heat.

Stew the onion and pepper gently in 3 tablespoons [45 ml.] of olive oil until soft, stirring regularly—10 to 15 minutes. Add the tomatoes, garlic, sugar, salt and a small pinch of cayenne pepper. Toss the mixture for about a minute over high heat, then cook gently at a simmer, tossing occasionally, for about 15 minutes. Toss for another couple of minutes over high heat until all of the liquid has evaporated.

Parboil the spinach in a large quantity of generously salted, rapidly boiling water—two or three minutes only. Drain, rinse in cold water, squeeze tightly and repeatedly with both hands, and chop. If you like, you can sauté the chopped spinach briefly in butter for extra flavor.

Sauté the mushrooms in 1 tablespoon [15 ml.] of butter, seasoned with salt and pepper, over high heat, tossing repeatedly, until their liquid is completely reabsorbed (three or four minutes—or more, depending on the size of the pan).

Cut the sorrel into a fine chiffonade and put it directly to stew, salted, in 1 tablespoon of butter over low heat, stirring from time to time, for about 20 to 30 minutes, until all liquid is evaporated and the sorrel is reduced to a purée. Season the eggs with pepper (no salt—or very little). Make two omelets each from the zucchini, tomatoes, spinach, mushrooms and olives—first putting half of each of these preparations into a soup plate and stirring in enough egg to bind well: The zucchini will take little—the equivalent of something less than one egg for each omelet; the tomato mixture will require about double that of the zucchini, etc. Salt each to taste, bearing in mind the amount of seasoning in the original preparations—it is possible that only the spinach will require additional salt. Use a 7-inch [18-cm.] omelet pan. The remaining olive oil should suffice for cooking the omelets.

Cut two rounds of kitchen parchment paper to the dimensions of the top and bottom of a 2-quart [2-liter] charlotte mold or round enameled ironware casserole about 7 inches in diameter. Butter the mold liberally, butter both sides of one round of paper for the bottom, and press it carefully into the bottom of the mold, leaving no air spaces or unstuck edges where the egg might run beneath.

Whisk together the sorrel purée, the cream and the remainder of the beaten eggs, adding more eggs if necessary—there should be the equivalent of about five eggs in the mixture. Salt and pepper to taste.

Pour a small ladle of sorrel cream into the bottom of the mold and stack the omelets in alternating colors and flavors, pressing each gently into place and pouring a small bit of sorrel cream over each before placing another. Pour in enough sorrel cream to barely submerge the omelets, tap the bottom of the mold smartly against a muffled tabletop (a couple of folded towels on it to soften the blow) to settle the contents and chase out any trapped air bubbles, and add more of the sorrel cream if necessary for the top omelet to be just covered (if there is any left over, it can be poached in a

small buttered mold apart). Butter the other round of paper and place it, buttered side down, on the surface.

Place the mold in a water bath so that it is immersed to about two thirds its height in boiling water, and cook in a preheated 375° F. [190° C.] oven for about 45 minutes, making certain that the center of the loaf is firm and elastic to slight pressure before removing it from the oven.

Let the loaf cool for about one hour until only just tepid. Lift the paper off the surface, run a knife all around the sides, and unmold onto a serving dish (placing the dish upside down over the mold and turning it and the mold over together). If not to be served immediately, press plastic wrap over the entire surface to protect it from contact with the air, and refrigerate.

Just before serving, decorate it simply (a ribbon of chopped parsley or fines herbes strung around the edge and a rosette of finely sliced tomato in the center, for instance; pitted black olives sliced into rings or chopped hard-boiled egg yolks are also good decorative elements). To serve, cut into approximately ½-inch [1-cm.] slices, using a spatula to transfer them to individual plates.

RICHARD OLNEY
SIMPLE FRENCH FOOD

Custards, Puddings and Soufflés

Cheese Custard

To serve 4

1 cup	shredded Cheddar cheese	¼ liter
2 cups	milk	½ liter
2	eggs, lightly beaten	2
	salt and pepper	
	cayenne pepper	
1 tsp.	prepared mustard	5 ml.

Stir the cheese and milk over low heat until the cheese has melted; the milk must not boil. Remove the pan from the heat, add the eggs and season with salt, pepper, a pinch of cayenne and the mustard. Pour the mixture into a buttered 1-quart [1-liter] ovenproof dish, or into four individual casseroles or ramekins, and bake in a preheated 350° F. [180° C.] oven until set, about 20 minutes for a large dish and 10 minutes for small ones.

MARY MAC KIRDY
RECIPES FOR YOU

Chinese Savory Custard

To serve 4

4	eggs	4
½ tsp.	salt	2 ml.
¼ tsp.	pepper	1 ml.
2 tsp.	soy sauce	10 ml.
2 cups	hot chicken stock (recipe, page 164)	½ liter
4	chopped scallions	4

Beat the eggs; add the salt, pepper and soy sauce; gradually stir the mixture into the stock; blend; pour into a heatproof dish; sprinkle with scallions; cover and cook on a trivet in a bain-marie until the custard sets. Serve with rice.

NINA FROUD
THE WORLD BOOK OF EGG AND CHEESE DISHES

Steamed Egg Custard with Bean Curd

Kōya Mushi

The original version of this recipe calls for yurine, or lily root, a Japanese root vegetable with a slightly sweet taste. It is not available in the United States. Yuri, a dried lily flower, can be substituted. Mitsuba, or trefoil, is a pungent herb used in salads and soups. Dashi is a Japanese soup stock that can be made by dissolving 3 tablespoons [45 ml.] of dried dashi in 1½ quarts [1½ liters] of boiling water. Yuri, mitsuba, dried dashi and tofu (bean curd) are available from Oriental grocers. Sake (rice wine) is sold at liquor stores.

To serve 6

6	eggs, lightly beaten	6
1 lb.	fresh *tofu*, drained under a weight for 20 to 30 minutes, and cut into 2-inch [5-cm.] squares	½ kg.
12	fresh sea scallops	12
	salt	
2 tbsp.	*sake* (optional)	30 ml.
6	large fresh mushrooms, stems trimmed	6
1	*yuri*, separated into segments, soaked in warm water for one hour (optional)	1
1½ quarts	*dashi* or chicken stock (recipe, page 164)	1½ liters
2 oz.	*mitsuba* or fresh spinach or watercress, coarsely chopped	60 g.

Arrange the *tofu* in the bottoms of six individual buttered casseroles. Season the scallops with a little salt and, if de-

sired, a sprinkling of *sake*. Arrange the scallops, mushrooms and *yuri* segments on top of the *tofu*.

Heat the stock to tepid and gradually add it to the eggs, mixing well. Strain this custard and pour it carefully into the casseroles. Put the casseroles in a baking pan and pour boiling water into the pan until it comes halfway up their sides. Bake in a preheated 350° F. [180° C.] oven for 15 minutes. Add the greens to the casseroles, gently pushing them down into the custard. Return to the oven and continue to bake until set, about 20 minutes more. Serve hot.

PETER AND JOAN MARTIN
JAPANESE COOKING

Farmer's Wife Egg Loaf

Pain d'Oeuf à la Fermière

To serve 6 to 8

8	eggs, beaten	8
¾ cup	thinly sliced carrot	175 ml.
¾ cup	thinly sliced turnip	175 ml.
¾ cup	freshly shelled peas	175 ml.
1 cup	thinly sliced green beans	¼ liter
¾ cup	thinly sliced peeled potato	175 ml.
2 tbsp.	butter	30 ml.
	salt and pepper	
1 tsp.	sugar	5 ml.
	grated nutmeg	
⅔ cup	white sauce (recipe, page 165)	150 ml.
1¼ cups	heavy cream	300 ml.

Cook all the vegetables for 15 minutes with the butter, salt and sugar in a saucepan with a tightly fitting lid, adding a very little water if the vegetables are not young and fresh.

Meanwhile, add salt, pepper and nutmeg to the eggs, then add the white sauce and half of the cream. Butter a deep 2-quart [2-liter] timbale or charlotte mold, pour in the mixture, and cook in a baking dish of water in an oven preheated to 375° F. [190° C.] for 15 to 18 minutes, or until the eggs are just set. Turn the egg mold onto a round serving dish and cover it with the remaining cream, lightly salted. Arrange the vegetable garnish around the edges.

LE CORDON BLEU

Spinach Timbales with Ripe Olive Sauce

To serve 6

2	eggs, beaten	2
2 lb.	spinach, parboiled for 2 minutes, drained, squeezed dry and finely chopped	1 kg.
½	garlic clove	½
½ tsp.	salt	2 ml.
1 cup	milk	¼ liter
1 tsp.	fresh lemon juice	5 ml.
3 tbsp.	butter	45 ml.
	pepper	
6	toast rounds	6

Ripe olive sauce

½ cup	chopped ripe pitted olives	125 ml.
1 cup	white sauce (recipe, page 165)	¼ liter
	fresh lemon juice	
	salt and pepper	

Pound the garlic and salt to a paste in a mortar. Add the garlic paste to the chopped spinach. Mix in the milk, beaten eggs, lemon juice, melted butter and a little fresh pepper, with more salt if necessary. Pour the mixture into six buttered custard cups. Place the custard cups in a bain-marie and bake in a preheated 325° F. [160° C.] oven for about 30 minutes, or until the timbales are firm.

Meanwhile, heat the white sauce in a saucepan. Add the ripe olives, fresh lemon juice, and salt and pepper to taste.

Turn the timbales out onto the toast rounds and pour the ripe olive sauce over them.

HELEN BROWN
HELEN BROWN'S WEST COAST COOK BOOK

Cheese and Egg Custard

Pain d'Oeufs à la Villageoise

The technique for preparing this custard demonstrates an alternative way to use the salt-pork dice: sprinkled into the bottom of the mold rather than incorporated into the egg-and-cheese mixture.

If the cheese used is very soft, drain off its excess liquid before using it. To do this, wrap the cheese in muslin or a double thickness of cheesecloth, then tie the corners of the cloth to form a bag and suspend the bag —on a wooden spoon set over a deep pot or bowl —for 30 minutes or so.

To serve 8 to 10

1 lb.	farmer or pot cheese	½ kg.
10	eggs, beaten	10
	salt and pepper	
	grated nutmeg	
7 tbsp.	butter, beaten until soft (optional)	100 ml.
2 cups	tepid milk	½ liter
¼ lb.	salt pork with the rind removed, diced, blanched in boiling water for 5 minutes, and drained	100 g.
¾ cup	heavy cream, warmed	175 ml.

Fry the salt-pork dice for two to three minutes, or until they start to crisp. Drain them. In a bowl, mix the cheese with the salt and pepper and a pinch of nutmeg. Add the butter, unless the cheese is very rich and creamy. Stir the eggs and then the milk into the cheese. Add the pork dice.

Pour the cheese mixture into one buttered 2-quart [2-liter] charlotte mold, or two buttered 1-quart [1-liter] molds. Place the mold, or molds, in a bain-marie, and bake in a preheated 325° F. [170° C.] oven until the custard has set, about 40 minutes for two smaller molds, at least one hour for the large mold. Remove the custard from the bain-marie and let it settle for 10 minutes.

To serve, unmold the custard and pour the cream over it. Serve it hot.

PHILÉAS GILBERT
LA CUISINE DE TOUS LES MOIS

Cheese and Bacon Cream

Crème au Lard

To serve 2 to 4

1 cup	shredded cheese (preferably Gruyère)	¼ liter
1 cup	heavy cream	¼ liter
1	egg, beaten	1
2	thin slices bacon, fried until crisp, drained and broken into small pieces	2

Mix the cheese, cream and egg together well; add the crisp bacon pieces. Fill four buttered, individual soufflé dishes (one for each person) with the mixture and bake the creams in a preheated 350° F. [180° C.] oven for about 20 minutes, until the mixture is set and slightly browned.

X. MARCEL BOULESTIN
A SECOND HELPING OR MORE DISHES FOR ENGLISH HOMES

Mother Poustiquet's Timbales

La Timbale de la Mère Poustiquet

To serve 6

6	eggs, 3 hard-boiled and finely diced, 3 beaten	6
2 cups	finely diced cooked ham	½ liter
1 cup	heavy cream	¼ liter
¼ cup	shredded Gruyère cheese	50 ml.
	salt and pepper	

Mix the diced hard-boiled eggs with the ham; add the cream and then the cheese. Add the beaten eggs to the mixture. Season lightly, remembering that the ham may be salty.

Butter six individual ovenproof dishes and fill them with the mixture. Bake the timbales in a bain-marie in a preheated 375° F. [190° C.] oven for 20 minutes. Serve hot in the individual dishes.

CAROLINE MIQUEL
LES BONNES RECETTES DE TANTE CAROLINE

Parmesan Egg Timbales

Oeufs à la Parmesane

Meat glaze is dark, strong meat stock reduced by boiling to a syrup. It is added to gravy and sauces to improve the taste.

Gruyère cheese may be substituted for the Parmesan that is sprinkled over the finished dish.

To serve 3

7	eggs, 6 eggs beaten	7
2 tbsp.	butter	30 ml.
	salt and pepper	
2 tbsp.	heavy cream or white sauce (recipe, page 165)	30 ml.
¾ cup	freshly grated Parmesan cheese	175 ml.
1 cup	tomato sauce (recipe, page 166)	¼ liter
2 tbsp.	meat glaze, or ¼ cup [50 ml.] beef stock (recipe, page 164) boiled to reduce it by half, and cooled	30 ml.

Place the beaten eggs in a saucepan with the butter, season with salt and pepper, and add the cream or white sauce.

Scramble the eggs over low heat, or over hot water, stirring with a whisk until they form a thick cream but are not yet set. Remove from the heat and add ⅔ cup [150 ml.] of the cheese, then stir in the remaining egg.

Fill individual buttered timbale molds with this mixture, place them in a roasting pan of hot water, and bake in a preheated 400° F. [200° C.] oven for three to four minutes, or until the eggs are set like a custard.

Unmold the eggs onto a warmed round serving dish. Mix the tomato sauce with the meat glaze and pour it over the eggs. Sprinkle with the remaining cheese, and serve.

LE CORDON BLEU

Ham and Cheese Pudding

Nelle Savoyarde

To serve 4

6	eggs, beaten	6
10 to 12	slices cooked ham	10 to 12
½ cup	shredded Gruyère cheese	125 ml.
⅔ cup	freshly grated Parmesan cheese	150 ml.
4 tbsp.	butter	60 ml.
3 tbsp.	flour	45 ml.
2 cups	milk	½ liter
	salt and pepper	
	nutmeg	
	tomato sauce (recipe, page 166)	

Line a buttered charlotte mold with the ham slices. Melt the butter and blend in the flour. Gradually add the milk and cook, stirring, until this sauce is thick and smooth. Season to taste with salt, pepper and a little nutmeg; stir in the cheese. Remove the sauce from the heat and stir in the eggs.

Pour the sauce into the ham-lined mold and place foil on the mold, tying it down firmly. Place the mold on a rack over boiling water in a deep kettle, cover the kettle and steam the pudding for one and a quarter hours, replenishing the water when it evaporates too much.

Remove the mold from the steamer and take off the foil. Bake it in a preheated 350° F. [180° C.] oven for 15 to 20 minutes, or until it is completely set. Unmold it and serve with the tomato sauce.

JAMES BEARD
HOW TO EAT BETTER FOR LESS MONEY

Anchovy and Egg Custard

Anjovismunahyydyke

This dish may be made with canned Scandinavian sprat fillets, smoked herring or kipper fillets.

To serve 4		
6	eggs	6
12	oil-packed flat anchovy fillets, rinsed and patted dry	12
2 cups	milk	½ liter
	salt and pepper	

Bring the milk almost to a boil, then remove it from the heat and let it cool a little. Meanwhile, fork the eggs lightly together, with a little seasoning, and combine them with the milk. Stir a little, but do not beat.

Dispose the anchovy fillets in the bottom of a buttered 2-to 4-cup [½- to 1-liter] ovenproof dish, pour the mixture over them and set the dish to cook in a bain-marie in an oven preheated to 400° F. [200° C.].

It will be ready in 40 minutes, when the custard is set.

ALAN DAVIDSON
NORTH ATLANTIC SEAFOOD

Mystery Eggs

Oeufs à l'Intrigue

To serve 8 to 10		
24	eggs, 18 beaten, 6 poached	24
1¼ cups	heavy cream	300 ml.
	salt and pepper	
¾ cup	finely chopped scallions	175 ml.
½ cup	fines herbes	125 ml.
4 tbsp.	butter	60 ml.
1 cup	diced Gruyère cheese	¼ liter
4	salt anchovies, filleted, soaked in water for 30 minutes, drained, patted dry and diced	4
¼ cup	freshly grated Parmesan cheese	50 ml.
2 tbsp.	fresh lemon juice	30 ml.

Mix the beaten eggs with the cream, salt and pepper, scallions and fines herbes. Heat half of the butter in a wide shallow fireproof casserole, and pour in a third of the beaten egg mixture. Allow it to set over medium heat. Cover this layer with half of the Gruyère and half of the anchovies, and arrange three poached eggs on top.

Pour in another third of the beaten egg mixture, cover the casserole and cook until the beaten eggs are almost set.

Cover with the remaining Gruyère, anchovies and poached eggs. Pour in the rest of the beaten eggs. When the last layer of beaten eggs is almost set, dot the top with butter, sprinkle it with Parmesan and place the dish in a preheated 400° F. [200° C.] oven for about 10 minutes, or until the top is set and golden. Sprinkle with lemon juice and serve.

PIERRE DE LUNE
LE NOUVEAU CUISINIER

Bread Pudding with Sliced Cheese

Ramequin mit Kasescheiben

To serve 4		
8	slices Gruyère cheese (about ½ lb. [¼ kg.])	8
8	slices bread	8
2½ cups	milk	625 ml.
2	eggs, lightly beaten	2
	salt	
	grated nutmeg	

Place alternate layers of bread and cheese in a buttered, deep pie dish or shallow 1-quart [1-liter] casserole, with the slices overlapping in each layer. Finish with a layer of cheese. Mix together the milk, eggs, salt and nutmeg to taste, and pour the mixture over the bread and cheese. Stand the pie dish in a bain-marie and bake for 30 minutes in a preheated 425° F. [220° C.] oven. The top should be golden and the egg-and-milk mixture set.

EVA MARIA BORER
TANTE HEIDI'S SWISS KITCHEN

Cheese Pudding

To serve 2		
1 cup	shredded Cheshire cheese	¼ liter
1¼ cups	milk	300 ml.
1½ cups	fresh bread crumbs	375 ml.
2	eggs, the yolks separated from the whites, and the whites stiffly beaten	2
	salt and pepper	
1 tsp.	English prepared mustard	5 ml.

Boil the milk, stir in the crumbs, take the pan from the heat and add the cheese, egg yolks and seasoning. Fold in the whites, and pour the mixture into a buttered 1-quart [1-liter] ovenproof dish. Bake the pudding in an oven preheated to 375° F. [190° C.] for 20 to 25 minutes, or until it is brown and set. Serve hot.

MARY MAC KIRDY
RECIPES FOR YOU

Cheddar Cheese Pudding

The original version of this recipe specifies farmhouse Cheddar, an English white Cheddar that may range in flavor from mild to sharp.

To serve 2

½ cup	shredded Cheddar cheese	125 ml.
1¼ cups	milk	300 ml.
1 cup	fresh white bread crumbs	¼ liter
	salt and pepper	
½ tsp.	prepared mustard	2 ml.
1	egg, lightly beaten	1

Boil the milk, pour it over the bread crumbs, add the cheese, seasonings and mustard, and stir in the egg. Pour the mixture into a buttered 2½-cup [625-ml.] deep-dish pie dish or casserole, and bake in a preheated 375° F. [190° C.] oven for about 30 minutes, or until golden brown and well risen.

AUDREY PARKER
COTTAGE AND COUNTRY RECIPES

Swiss Cheese Ramekin
Waadtländer Käseauflauf

There are almost as many recipes for this dish as there are Swiss cantons. One alternative version is to arrange thick slices of bread and cheese in layers in the dish, and pour on the well-seasoned egg and milk mixture.

To serve 4

1¼ to 1¾ cups	grated Emmentaler cheese	300 to 425 ml.
4	eggs, the yolks separated from the whites, and the whites stiffly beaten	4
	salt	
	grated nutmeg	
2 cups	milk, or 1 cup [¼ liter] milk and 1 cup cream	½ liter
8	thick slices firm-textured white bread	8
7 tbsp.	butter	105 ml.
2 tbsp.	kirsch	30 ml.

Whisk the egg yolks with salt, nutmeg to taste and the cheese. Gradually add the milk, or milk and cream, and finally fold in the egg whites. Fry the bread in the butter until it is golden brown on both sides.

Arrange the bread slices in layers in a buttered 2½-quart [2½-liter] soufflé dish, add the kirsch and pour in the egg mixture. Bake in a preheated 350° F. [180° C.] oven for 30 to 40 minutes or until golden. Serve immediately.

GRETE WILLINSKY
KULINARISCHE WELTREISE

Farmer's Loaf

To serve 4

1 lb.	cottage cheese	½ kg.
4 tbsp.	butter, softened	60 ml.
1 cup	diced cooked ham	¼ liter
6	eggs, well beaten	6
	salt and pepper	

Butter sauce

6 tbsp.	butter	90 ml.
1 tbsp.	flour	15 ml.
⅔ cup	salted water	150 ml.
5 tbsp.	heavy cream (optional)	75 ml.

Put the cottage cheese into a bowl and work into it the softened butter. Mix in the diced ham. Salt and pepper the eggs well, work them by degrees into the cheese and ham, and then pour the mixture into a buttered 1½- to 2-quart [1½- to 2-liter] ovenproof mold. Stand the mold in a pan of water and put it into a preheated 350° F. [180° C.] oven for one hour until it is set. Turn it out onto a dish, and serve either hot with butter sauce or cold with salad.

For the sauce, melt 4 tablespoons [60 ml.] of the butter in a saucepan, add the flour and stir until it is well blended, then add the water gradually until all of it is absorbed, stirring constantly so that no lumps can form. Let the mixture boil for a minute or two, then take the pan off the stove and stir in the remaining butter as soon as the sauce has ceased to boil. A little cream is a great improvement, added when the last of the butter has been smoothly absorbed.

MARY AYLETT
COUNTRY FARE

Steamed Bacon and Egg Pudding

To serve 4

4	eggs, slightly beaten	4
4	slices bacon, diced and fried until crisp	4
6	slices stale bread	6
	butter	
	salt and pepper	
1 quart	milk	1 liter

Cut the bread slices into fingers and use half of them to line a deep buttered dish. Sprinkle the slices with the bacon and its fat; cover with the remaining bread slices. Season the eggs to taste. Heat the milk almost to the boiling point, remove it from the heat and gradually stir it into the eggs. Pour the egg mixture over the bread and let it stand for 20 to 30 minutes. Set the dish in a pan of hot water and bake in a preheated 375° F. [190° C.] oven for 45 minutes. Serve the pudding from the same dish.

NINA FROUD
THE WORLD BOOK OF EGG AND CHEESE DISHES

Perfect Cheddar Cheese Soufflé

To serve 6

1½ cups	shredded Cheddar cheese	375 ml.
2 tbsp.	butter	30 ml.
2 tbsp.	flour	30 ml.
1¼ cups	milk	300 ml.
3	egg yolks	3
1 tsp.	salt	5 ml.
½ cup	finely cut fresh dill leaves or chives	125 ml.
5	egg whites, stiffly beaten	5

Melt the butter in a saucepan. When it has stopped foaming, add the flour and mix well. Slowly add the milk and stir until the sauce is thick. Remove the pan from the heat and beat in the egg yolks, one at a time, then all but 1 tablespoon [15 ml.] of the shredded cheese, the salt and the dill or chives. Stir about one third of the egg whites into the yolk mixture and fold in the rest. Do not overmix.

Put the soufflé in a buttered 6-cup [1½-liter] soufflé dish. Sprinkle the remaining tablespoon of cheese on top. Bake in a preheated 400° F. [200° C.] oven for 30 to 35 minutes, or until the soufflé has risen and the top is golden brown.

SONDRA GOTLIEB
THE GOURMET'S CANADA

Pizza Soufflé

To serve 6

1½ lb.	mozzarella, Bel Paese or Fontina cheese, sliced	¾ kg.
20	thin slices bread	20
2½ cups	milk	625 ml.
2½ cups	tomato sauce *(recipe, page 166)*	625 ml.
1 tbsp.	finely chopped fresh oregano	15 ml.
6	eggs	6
4 to 5 tbsp.	grated Parmesan cheese	60 to 75 ml.
3 tbsp.	butter, cut into small pieces	45 ml.

Soak the bread slices in the milk for 15 minutes, then drain off the excess liquid. Line the bottom of a buttered 2½- to 3-quart [2½- to 3-liter] casserole with bread slices. Top the slices with a layer of tomato sauce, sprinkle with a bit of oregano and add a layer of cheese.

Continue making the layers, finishing by covering the last layer of bread with just the tomato sauce and oregano. The casserole should be nearly full.

Beat the eggs with the Parmesan cheese. Pour the mixture over the bread and, with a fork, pierce through the layers in three or four places until the egg mixture is completely absorbed by the bread.

Distribute the butter pieces over the top, and bake the casserole in a preheated 350° F. [180° C.] oven for about one hour, or until the top is browned and puffed.

LES PETITS PLATS ET LES GRANDS

Cheese Soufflé

Soufflé au Fromage

To serve 4

1¼ cups	shredded Gruyère cheese	300 ml.
5 tbsp.	butter	75 ml.
3 tbsp.	flour	45 ml.
1 cup	milk, heated to boiling	¼ liter
	salt and pepper	
	grated nutmeg	
4	eggs, the yolks separated from the whites, and the whites stiffly beaten	4

In a heavy saucepan, melt 4 tablespoons [60 ml.] of the butter over medium heat. Stir in the flour and, when the mixture is smooth, gradually stir in the boiling milk. Season the sauce with salt, pepper and a little nutmeg. Cook, stirring, until the sauce thickens, about five minutes.

Off the heat, stir in the remaining butter. Then add the egg yolks, one by one, stirring vigorously with a wooden spatula after each addition. Add all but 1 tablespoon [15 ml.] of the shredded cheese, and fold in the egg whites.

Pour the mixture into a buttered 1½-quart [1½-liter] soufflé dish. It should come halfway up the sides of the dish. Sprinkle the top with the remaining cheese. Bake the soufflé in a preheated 350° F. [180° C.] oven for 30 to 40 minutes, or until the soufflé is well risen and the top is browned. Serve immediately from the baking dish.

EUGÉNIE BRAZIER
LES SECRETS DE LA MÈRE BRAZIER

Swiss Soufflés

Soufflés à la Suissesse

The technique of preparing Swiss soufflés is demonstrated on pages 78-79.

The composition of these soufflés differs from that of an ordinary cheese soufflé only in that the latter contains one more beaten egg white. The final result in no way resembles a classic soufflé, but more nearly brings to mind quenelles.

	To serve 6	
about 1 cup	freshly grated Parmesan cheese	about ¼ liter
1 cup	milk	¼ liter
about ⅓ cup	flour	about 75 ml.
	salt	
	freshly ground white pepper	
	freshly grated nutmeg	
2 tbsp.	butter	30 ml.
3	egg yolks	3
2	egg whites, stiffly beaten	2
1½ cups	heavy cream	375 ml.

Bring the milk to a boil, leave until lukewarm and pour it slowly into the flour, stirring to avoid lumping. Season with salt, pepper and nutmeg and, stirring constantly with a wooden spoon, cook over medium heat until thickened. Leave to cool for several minutes. Add the butter, something over half of the grated cheese, and the egg yolks, and mix thoroughly. Fold the egg whites in gently but thoroughly.

Butter six individual molds or porcelain ramekins, spoon them about two thirds full of the mixture, place them in a large pan, and pour enough hot but not boiling water into the pan to immerse them by two thirds. Poach in a preheated 350° F. [180° C.] oven for 15 or 20 minutes, or until the soufflés are firm and spongy to the touch. Unmold them carefully so as not to damage them, one by one, first running the blade of a knife around the edges to loosen them. This first cooking process may be carried out in advance.

Butter a shallow baking or gratin dish of the right size to hold the little soufflés, placed side by side but not—or barely—touching. Sprinkle the bottom of the dish with half of the remaining cheese, place the soufflés on top, and pour over enough cream to immerse them by half. Sprinkle the rest of the cheese over the surface. Return the soufflés to the oven for another 15 or 20 minutes—or until the cream is nearly all absorbed and a light, golden gratin has formed.

RICHARD OLNEY
THE FRENCH MENU COOKBOOK

Ramekins

This is a recipe from the beginning of the 19th Century.

The batter for ramekins is equally good over macaroni when boiled tender; or on stewed broccoli, celery or cauliflower, a little of the stewing gravy being put in the dish with them, but not enough to make the vegetable swim.

	To serve 6	
1 cup	shredded Cheshire cheese	¼ liter
1 cup	shredded Cheddar cheese	¼ liter
1	dinner roll with the crusts removed, crumbled	1
½ cup	light cream	125 ml.
8 tbsp.	butter	120 ml.
4	eggs, the yolks separated from the whites, and the whites stiffly beaten	4
½ cup	dry white wine (optional)	125 ml.

Boil the crumbs of the roll in the cream for about five minutes or until soft. Beat the cheeses and the butter in a large mortar with the egg yolks and the cream mixture. Add the wine, if using it, and fold in the egg whites.

Divide the mixture among six individual buttered ramekins, and bake them in a preheated 350° F. [180° C.] oven until they are a fine brown, about 20 minutes. They should be eaten quite hot.

MRS. RUNDELL
MODERN DOMESTIC COOKERY

Savory Egg Cream on Toast

Crème aux Oeufs sur Croûtes

	To serve 4	
4	eggs, the yolks separated from the whites, and the whites stiffly beaten	4
2 tbsp.	butter	30 ml.
2 tbsp.	flour	30 ml.
½ cup	heavy cream	125 ml.
⅓ cup	milk	75 ml.
	salt and pepper	
	cayenne pepper	
1 tsp.	chopped mixed fresh parsley, tarragon and chervil	5 ml.
4	slices bread, toasted	4

Melt the butter in a saucepan, add the flour and let it cook a little. Stir in the cream and milk, and simmer, stirring constantly, until the mixture thickens—taking care that it does not burn or curdle.

Off the heat, mix the egg yolks with the sauce, and season it with salt, pepper and cayenne. Fold in the egg whites with the herbs. Put the mixture onto the slices of toast, heaping it up; smooth over with the blade of a knife. Put into a preheated 425° F. [220° C.] oven until a golden color—about 10 minutes—dish up, and serve quickly.

C. HERMANN SENN
HOW TO COOK EGGS AND OMELETS IN 300 DIFFERENT WAYS

Semolina Soufflé with Cheese

Griessschaum-Auflauf mit Käse

Semolina is milled from the heart of durum-wheat berries. It is ground to different degrees of fineness, ranging from flour to coarse granules. Farina may be substituted for semolina.

To serve 4

⅔ cup	freshly grated Parmesan cheese	150 ml.
½ cup	shredded Emmentaler cheese	125 ml.
¾ cup	coarse semolina	175 ml.
2 cups	milk	½ liter
4 tbsp.	butter	60 ml.
5	eggs, the yolks separated from the whites, and the whites stiffly beaten	5
	salt	
	paprika	

Place the milk and butter in a saucepan and bring them gently to a boil. Sprinkle in the semolina and cook over low heat for a few minutes, stirring continuously, until the mixture thickens. Remove the pan from the heat and allow the mixture to cool slightly.

Meanwhile, butter a 1-quart [1-liter] soufflé dish or four individual molds.

Stir the egg yolks and the cheeses into the semolina mixture, season with a pinch each of salt and paprika, and fold in the egg whites. Pour the mixture into the soufflé dish or molds and place the dish in a roasting pan containing enough hot water to come halfway up the sides of the dish. Bake in a preheated 425° F. [220° C.] oven until the top of the soufflé is crusty and brown. This will take about 30 minutes for one large soufflé and 15 to 20 minutes for individual ones. Serve in the baking dish or molds.

HERMINE KIEHNLE AND MARIA HÄDECKE
DAS NEUE KIEHNLE-KOCHBUCH

Tomato Cheese Soufflé

To serve 4

1¼ cups	shredded Cheddar or Gruyère cheese	300 ml.
2 tbsp.	butter	30 ml.
3 tbsp.	flour	45 ml.
¾ cup	milk	175 ml.
1	bay leaf	1
1	whole clove	1
4	sprigs parsley	4
4	thin onion slices	4
¼ tsp.	dill	1 ml.
½ cup	puréed tomato	125 ml.
	salt and pepper	
4	eggs, the yolks separated from the whites, the whites stiffly beaten with ⅓ tsp. [1½ ml.] salt	4
¼ tsp.	dry mustard	1 ml.

Melt the butter, stir in the flour, and cook until this roux mixture is frothy and bubbling, but not brown. Heat the milk to the boiling point with the bay leaf, clove, parsley, onion and dill. Strain the milk into the roux. Add the puréed tomato, stirring constantly, then add the cheese. Season to taste with salt and pepper. Remove from the heat and let the cheese sauce cool slightly. Beat the egg yolks lightly, add the mustard and beat again until well blended. Gradually stir the egg-yolk mixture into the cheese sauce, beating briskly after each addition. Lastly fold in the beaten egg whites. Pour into a buttered soufflé dish, and bake in a preheated 400° F. [200° C.] oven for 20 to 25 minutes until the soufflé is well puffed up and nicely browned on top. Serve at once.

LOUIS P. DE GOUY
THE GOLD COOK BOOK

Cheese Roll, Four Ways

The technique of filling and shaping a cheese roll is demonstrated on pages 80-81. The roll may be served either warm or cold, and filled with either the mushroom duxelles below, or with 12 tablespoons [180 ml.] of butter creamed with ⅔ cup [150 ml.] of chopped walnuts. If it is to be served warm, the roll may be covered with tomato sauce, or it may be sprinkled with 2 tablespoons [30 ml.] of melted butter and ⅓ cup [75 ml.] of grated Parmesan cheese, then placed in an oven preheated to 350° F. [180° C.] for 10 to 12 minutes, or until a light crust has formed and the roll is heated through.

To serve 8

⅔ cup	freshly grated Parmesan cheese	150 ml.
2 tbsp.	butter	30 ml.
2 tbsp.	flour	30 ml.
1 cup	milk	¼ liter
5	eggs, the yolks separated from the whites, and the whites stiffly beaten	5
	chopped fresh parsley or a bunch of fresh watercress (optional)	
2 cups	tomato sauce *(recipe, page 166)*, heated	½ liter

Mushroom duxelles

¼ lb.	fresh mushrooms, very finely chopped	125 g.
4 tbsp.	butter	60 ml.
3 tbsp.	finely chopped shallots	45 ml.
1 tbsp.	fresh lemon juice	15 ml.
½ tsp.	salt	2 ml.
¼ tsp.	freshly ground black pepper	1 ml.

Butter or oil a jelly-roll pan, 17 by 11 inches [42 by 27 cm.]. Line it with wax paper, and butter or oil the paper. Melt the butter over a medium-high heat and stir in the flour. Cook, stirring with a wooden spatula, for two minutes—do not let it brown. Remove the pan from the heat and add the milk, whisking vigorously. Return the pan to the heat and cook, stirring, until the mixture thickens and boils. Remove the mixture from the heat and cool for five to 10 minutes. Beat the egg yolks and beat them into the sauce, mixing thoroughly. Stir in a third of the egg whites, then fold in the remainder. Lightly fold in the grated Parmesan cheese. Spread this egg-sponge mixture in the prepared pan and bake it in a preheated 350° F. [180° C.] oven for 15 minutes.

Meanwhile, for the *duxelles* filling, cook the shallots in the butter over high heat until transparent. Then add the mushrooms, lemon juice and seasoning. Cook over medium heat, stirring constantly, until the vegetables are soft and all excess liquid has evaporated.

Remove the baked sponge from the oven and turn it out onto two sheets of wax paper that overlap lengthwise.

Spread the sponge with the *duxelles* and roll it up, jelly-roll fashion. Serve it garnished with chopped parsley sprinkled over the roll or with a large bunch of watercress at one end of the platter. Pour the hot tomato sauce over the roll.

JULIE DANNENBAUM
MENUS FOR ALL OCCASIONS

Egg Soufflé with or without Ham

Oeufs Frais Soufflés avec ou sans Jambon

To serve 6

6	eggs, 3 hard-boiled, the yolks of 3 separated from the whites, and the whites stiffly beaten	6
¼ cup	dry bread crumbs	50 ml.
1 cup	milk, warmed	¼ liter
	salt and pepper	
	grated nutmeg	
4 tbsp.	butter, or ⅓ cup [75 ml.] heavy cream plus 2 tbsp. [30 ml.] butter	60 ml.
½ cup	finely chopped cooked ham (optional)	125 ml.

Stir the bread crumbs into the milk, and let them soak until the mixture forms a thick paste.

Quarter the hard-boiled eggs lengthwise, remove the yolks, and arrange the whites in a star shape in a buttered 1-quart [1-liter] soufflé dish. Mash the hard-boiled yolks with the bread-crumb mixture and the raw yolks. Season with salt, pepper and nutmeg. Melt 2 tablespoons [30 ml.] of the butter and add it—or the heavy cream—to the yolk mixture with the ham, if you are including it. Fold in the beaten egg whites, and pour the mixture over the hard-boiled egg whites in the dish. Dot the top with the remaining 2 tablespoons butter, and bake the soufflé in a preheated 425° F. [220° C.] oven for 15 to 20 minutes. Serve at once when the soufflé has risen well.

ÉDOUARD M. NIGNON
LE LIVRE DE CUISINE DE L'OUEST-ÉCLAIR

Pies and Quiches

Cheese Pie

To serve 4

½ cup	shredded Cheddar cheese	125 ml.
4 tbsp.	butter	60 ml.
⅔ cup	rolled oatmeal, coarsely ground in a blender or food processor	150 ml.
	salt	
½ tsp.	dry mustard	2 ml.
1	egg, beaten	1
	short-crust pastry (recipe, page 166)	

Roll out the dough and use it to line an 8-inch [20-cm.] pie-pan. Melt the butter in a saucepan. Take the pan from the heat and stir in the cheese, oats, a pinch of salt, the mustard and the egg. Mix well. Put the mixture into the lined pan and bake the pie in a preheated 350° F. [180° C.] oven for 30 minutes, or until golden brown. Serve with salad.

SHIRLEY M. HANSON (EDITOR)
FOOD FOR THOUGHT

Country Cheese Pie

To serve 4

1 lb.	farmer cheese (about 2 cups [½ liter])	½ kg.
6 tbsp.	plain yogurt	90 ml.
½ tsp.	ground coriander	2 ml.
¼ tsp.	grated nutmeg	1 ml.
1 tbsp.	finely cut fresh chives or chopped scallion	15 ml.
1 tsp.	sugar	5 ml.
	salt and pepper	
3	eggs, beaten	3
¼ cup	freshly grated Parmesan cheese	50 ml.
	short-crust pastry (recipe, page 166)	

Preheat the oven to 400° F. [200° C.]. Roll out the pastry and line a 9-inch [22-cm.] piepan with it. Prick the bottom of the pastry shell and bake it blind for 10 minutes.

Meanwhile, mix together in a bowl the farmer cheese, yogurt, coriander, nutmeg, chives or scallion, sugar and pep-per to taste. Taste for salt before adding any. Beat the cheese mixture with a wooden spoon until it is smooth. Add the eggs gradually and beat the mixture thoroughly again.

Pour the batter into the baked pie shell and smooth the top with a spatula. Sprinkle the pie with the Parmesan cheese. Reduce the oven temperature to 375° F. [190° C.] and bake the pie for 45 minutes, or until the top is nicely browned and puffy. Serve immediately.

CAROL CUTLER
THE SIX-MINUTE SOUFFLÉ AND OTHER CULINARY DELIGHTS

Brie Tart

Tarte de Bry

This cheese tart should be eaten immediately, while it is still hot, as it puffs up rather dramatically. Like a soufflé, it is delicious cold as well, but not quite so impressive to look at. It could be made with any of the soft cheeses of Northern France. It makes a delicious savory ending to a meal—and a novel way of eating the cheese.

To serve 4 to 6

½ lb.	very ripe Brie cheese, scraped from its crust	¼ kg.
1 to 2 tbsp.	light cream (optional)	15 to 30 ml.
2	eggs, beaten	2
1½ tsp.	superfine sugar	7 ml.
1 tsp.	ground ginger	5 ml.
¼ tsp.	ground saffron	1 ml.
	salt	
	short-crust pastry (recipe, page 166, but double the quantities called for)	

Line an 8-inch [20-cm.] piepan with the pastry and bake it blind for 10 to 15 minutes in an oven preheated to 425° F. [220° C.]. Allow the pastry shell to cool.

Melt the cheese very slowly in the top of a double boiler, adding a little cream if it seems lumpy. Add the remaining ingredients, mixing thoroughly. Pour the mixture into the pastry shell and bake it in a preheated 375° F. [190° C.] oven for about 30 minutes, or until the tart is lightly browned and puffy. Serve immediately.

MICHÈLE BROWN
FOOD BY APPOINTMENT

Cheese Tart from Obwalden

Gâteau au Fromage d'Obwald

The original version of this recipe calls for sbrinz cheese, a Swiss cheese, not obtainable in the United States, that is similar to aged Gruyère, although higher in fat content.

To serve 6

2 oz.	aged Gruyère cheese, shredded (about ½ cup [125 ml.])	60 g.
1¾ cups	flour	425 ml.
7 tbsp.	butter, softened	105 ml.
1 tbsp.	distilled white vinegar, diluted with 7 tbsp. [105 ml.] water	15 ml.
¼ tsp.	salt	1 ml.

Two-cheese filling

5 oz.	aged Gruyère cheese, shredded (about 1¼ cups [300 ml.])	150 g.
5 oz.	Emmentaler cheese, shredded (about 1½ cups [375 ml.])	150 g.
1 cup	milk	¼ liter
1 cup	heavy cream	¼ liter
2	eggs, the yolks separated from the whites, and the whites stiffly beaten	2
	salt and pepper	

Heap the flour on a pastry board and make a well in the center. Into this, put the Gruyère cheese, butter, diluted vinegar and salt. Mix the ingredients together with your finger tips to make a smooth dough. Roll it into a ball, wrap it in a floured cloth and let it rest for 30 minutes in a cool place.

For the filling, mix the milk, cream and egg yolks. Fold in the whites. Season to taste with salt and pepper.

Roll out the pastry ⅛ to ¼ inch [3 to 6 mm.] thick. Butter an 8-inch [20-cm.] pie plate, line it with the pastry and prick the pastry all over with a fork. Dust it with flour, sprinkle on the shredded cheeses and pour in the egg mixture. Place the tart on a baking sheet and put it into a preheated 400° F. [200° C.] oven. Bake for 30 to 35 minutes, or until the filling is set and the top is golden.

PIERRE ANDROUET
LA CUISINE AU FROMAGE

Roquefort Quiche

Tarte Aveyronnaise

There is a good case for the use of two 6-inch [16-cm.] quiche pans for this quiche rather than one large one. It is a question of synchronization. In small pans the yeast pastry and the fillings are ready at precisely the same moment, whereas in one big pan the filling tends to cook more quickly than the dough. To a certain extent this depends upon your oven. It is in any case a wise precaution to use the buttered wax paper covering as directed.

Roquefort varies a good deal in quality. If it is very strong use a little less, and compensate for the difference with extra cream or milk.

To make one 10-inch [25-cm.] quiche or two 6-inch [16-cm.] quiches

Yeast pastry

1 cup	unbleached flour	¼ liter
¼ oz.	cake yeast or ½ tsp. [2 ml.] dried yeast creamed with 2 tbsp. [30 ml.] tepid water	7 g.
1 tsp.	salt	5 ml.
1	egg	1
3 tbsp.	heavy cream, or softened unsalted butter	45 ml.

Roquefort filling

3½ to 4 oz.	Roquefort cheese	100 to 125 g.
3 tbsp.	heavy cream	45 ml.
2	eggs	2
4 tbsp.	milk	60 ml.
	freshly grated nutmeg	
	freshly ground pepper	
	salt	

To make the pastry: Warm the flour very slightly by putting it in its bowl in a slow oven for a few minutes, add the salt, then the egg and the creamed yeast. Mix all of the ingredients into a light dough. Add the cream or softened butter and, with your hands, beat the dough into a soft batter. Dry this by sprinkling it with a little flour, form it into a bun, and cover the bowl with a plate or cloth.

Leave in a warm place for approximately two hours, until the dough has doubled in volume and is light and spongy. Break it down, sprinkle again with flour, reshape into a bun. Unless you are going to use the dough at once, cover the bowl again, and this time leave it in a cold place—not the refrigerator—until the next day.

To mix the filling: Mash the cheese to a paste. Add the cream. Stir rather gently until the two are amalgamated. Beat the eggs and the milk—the blender can be used for this operation but *not* for mixing the cheese and cream—and amalgamate the two mixtures. Season with nutmeg, pepper and salt to taste. Gentle stirring with a fork or spoon is necessary now, and there is no cause for worry if there are a few recalcitrant lumps of cheese in the filling. They will smooth themselves out during the cooking. On the other hand, overvigorous whisking can curdle the cream and the cheese, a minor disaster which does not affect the flavor but results in a rather flat filling when the quiche is cooked.

When the time comes to cook the quiche, butter and flour a 10-inch [25-cm.] quiche pan with a removable base. Work the dough into a ball, and put this into the center of the pan. Sprinkling the dough with flour from time to time, press it out gently with your knuckles until it covers the base of the pan. Leave it, covered with a sheet of plastic wrap or wax paper, and in a warm place, for about 25 minutes, until it has again become very pliable and has sufficiently risen to be gently pressed out again to line the sides of the pan.

To bake the quiche: Have the oven preheated to 425° F. [220° C.]. Spoon the filling into the dough-lined pan, and put this quickly onto a baking sheet on the center shelf of the oven. Bake for 15 minutes before reducing the oven heat to 375° F. [190° C.], covering the filling with buttered wax paper and cooking the quiche for another 10 minutes. Serve quickly, before the filling sinks.

ELIZABETH DAVID
ENGLISH BREAD AND YEAST COOKERY

Cheese and Herb Tart

Tartre Bourbonoise

The technique of baking a tart shell blind, or empty, is demonstrated on pages 74-75. If Swiss chard is not available, 1 pound [½ kg.] of spinach may be substituted.

	To serve 6 to 8	
1½ lb.	farmer cheese or ricotta	¾ kg.
5	eggs	5
1½ lb.	Swiss chard, the ribs removed and the leaves chopped	¾ kg.
½ cup	chopped fresh parsley	125 ml.
1 tbsp.	chopped fresh marjoram flowers and leaves	15 ml.
	salt and freshly ground pepper	
¼ tsp.	ground saffron, dissolved in 1 tbsp. [15 ml.] boiling water	1 ml.
7 tbsp.	lard or butter, softened	105 ml.
1	12-inch [30-cm.] baked tart shell made from short-crust pastry (recipe, page 166, but double the quantities called for)	1

Mash the cheese in a bowl and beat in four of the eggs. Add the chopped chard leaves, the parsley, marjoram, salt and pepper, half of the dissolved saffron, and the lard or butter. Mix with your hands until thoroughly blended.

Fill the tart shell with the cheese mixture. Bake the tart in a preheated 400° F. [200° C.] oven. After about 15 minutes, when the tart is half-cooked, beat the remaining egg with the remaining saffron liquid and pour the mixture evenly over the surface of the tart. Continue to bake until the surface is golden and slightly puffed at the center— about 15 minutes more.

BAPTISTE PLATINE DE CRÉMONNE
LE LIVRE DE L'HONNESTE VOLUPTÉ

Spinach and Feta Pie

The techniques of shaping a pastry shell and blind baking it partially are demonstrated on pages 74-75.

	To serve 6	
½ cup	crumbled feta cheese	125 ml.
2 lb.	spinach, chopped, cooked and drained	1 kg.
2	eggs	2
2	egg yolks	2
½ cup	plain yogurt	125 ml.
½ cup	milk	125 ml.
1 tbsp.	chopped fresh parsley	15 ml.
½ tsp.	each salt and crumbled dried tarragon	2 ml.
	grated nutmeg	
1 tbsp.	butter, melted	15 ml.
	9-inch [23-cm.] short-crust pastry shell (recipe, page 166), baked partially	

First prepare the pastry-lined pan and spread with a thin coating of mustard. Beat eggs and egg yolks until blended and mix in yogurt, milk, parsley, salt, tarragon, nutmeg, spinach and feta. Spoon the mixture into the pastry-lined pan and drizzle the top with melted butter. Bake in a preheated 400° F. [200° C.] oven for 10 minutes; reduce the heat to 350° F. [180° C.] and bake 25 minutes longer or until set. Let the pie cool five minutes before cutting it.

LOU SEIBERT PAPPAS
EGG COOKERY

Asparagus Quiche

The techniques of shaping a pastry shell and blind baking it partially are demonstrated on page pages 74-75.

	To serve 4 to 6	
½ to ¾ lb.	asparagus	¼ to ⅓ kg.
¼ cup	chopped scallions, white parts only	50 ml.
1 tbsp.	butter	15 ml.
1 cup	half-and-half cream	¼ liter
2	eggs, beaten	2
½ tsp.	salt	2 ml.
¼ tsp.	white pepper	1 ml.
¼ tsp.	savory	1 ml.
½ cup	shredded Gruyère cheese	125 ml.
	paprika	
	8-inch [20-cm.] short-crust pastry shell *(recipe, page 166)*, partially baked	

Slice the asparagus on the diagonal, parboil for three to five minutes and drain. Sauté the scallions in the butter until soft and combine them with the asparagus. Arrange in the pastry shell. Beat together the cream, eggs and seasonings, strain the mixture over the asparagus, and sprinkle with the cheese and paprika. Bake in a preheated 375° F. [190° C.] oven for 25 to 30 minutes, or until a toothpick inserted in the center comes out clean.

CORALIE CASTLE AND BARBARA LAWRENCE
HORS D'OEUVRE ETC.

Cheese and Tomato Flan

The techniques of shaping a pastry shell and blind baking it partially are demonstrated on pages 74-75.

	To serve 4	
1½ cups	shredded Cheddar cheese	375 ml.
2	medium-sized tomatoes, peeled and sliced	2
2	eggs, beaten	2
1 tbsp.	flour	15 ml.
1 to 1¼ cups	milk	250 to 300 ml.
	salt and pepper	
	butter	
8	flat oil-packed anchovy fillets, drained	8
	8-inch [20-cm.] short-crust pastry shell *(recipe, page 166)*, partially baked	

Mix the cheese, eggs, flour and sufficient milk to make a soft paste, spread the cheese mixture inside the pastry shell, and season with the salt and pepper. Place the sliced tomatoes over the cheese mixture. Dot the top with butter and seasoning, and bake in a preheated 350° F. [180° C.] oven for 20 to 30 minutes, or until the filling is set. Garnish the flan with the anchovy fillets.

IRISH RECIPES TRADITIONAL AND MODERN

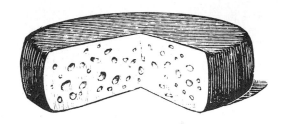

Open-faced Cheese Pie

Quiche au Fromage

The techniques for baking cheese pie appear on pages 74-75.

	To make an 8- to 9-inch [20- to 23-cm.] pie	
¾ cup	shredded Gruyère cheese, or shredded Gruyère and freshly grated Parmesan cheese combined	175 ml.
1 tsp.	butter	5 ml.
6	slices lean bacon, cut in ¼-inch [6-mm.] pieces	6
2	eggs, plus 2 egg yolks	2
1½ cups	heavy cream	375 ml.
½ tsp.	salt	2 ml.
	white pepper	
2 tbsp.	butter, cut in tiny pieces	30 ml.
	8- to 9-inch [20- to 23-cm.] partially baked short-crust pastry shell *(recipe, page 166)*	

In a heavy 8- to 10-inch [20- to 25-cm.] skillet, melt the butter over medium heat. When the foam subsides, cook the bacon until it is lightly browned and crisp. Remove it from the skillet with a slotted spoon and drain it on paper towels. Beat the eggs, egg yolks, cream and seasonings together in a large mixing bowl. Stir in the cheese.

Place the cooled pastry shell on a baking sheet. Scatter the bacon over the bottom of the shell and gently ladle the egg-cheese custard over it. To prevent spilling and allow for expansion, leave a clearance of at least ⅛ inch [3 mm.] between the top of the custard and the rim of the shell. Sprinkle the top with dots of butter and bake in the upper third of a preheated 375° F. [190° C.] oven for 25 minutes, or until the custard has puffed and browned and a knife inserted in the center comes out clean. Serve hot or warm.

FOODS OF THE WORLD/THE COOKING OF PROVINCIAL FRANCE

Italian Cheese Pie

Pizza Rustica

This pie may be made on a baking sheet, by simply pinching the edges of the pastry together.

Pizza has a much wider meaning in Italy than it does in the United States or Britain. In its wider sense it means pie, and to call the following recipe a pizza would be misleading to anyone other than Italians.

In winter, two Italian pork sausages are added to the pie. They are first fried until brown, then skinned, and the meat crumbled and spread over the bottom of the pastry before the rest of the filling is added.

To serve 6

1¼ cups	ricotta or good-quality cottage cheese	300 ml.
5 oz.	smoked provolone cheese, diced	150 g.
7 oz.	mozzarella cheese, diced	200 g.
1⅔ cups	freshly grated Parmesan cheese	400 ml.
5	eggs, lightly beaten	5
4 oz.	prosciutto or salami, diced	125 g.
2 to 3	sprigs fresh parsley, finely chopped	2 to 3
	salt and pepper	

Rich short-crust pastry

3 cups	flour	¾ liter
12 tbsp.	butter	180 ml.
2	small eggs, lightly beaten	2
	salt	

For the pastry, sift the flour onto a pastry board and make a well in the center. Work in the butter with your finger tips. Add the two beaten eggs and a pinch of salt. Working quickly, mix the ingredients into a dough. Put it aside in a floured bowl, cover and let it stand for 30 minutes.

To make the filling, mix the cheeses in a bowl and add four of the beaten eggs, the ham or salami, the parsley and a pinch each of salt and pepper. Put the mixture aside.

Divide the dough into two pieces, one slightly larger than the other. Roll out both pieces into round sheets—sufficient to cover a 12-inch [30-cm.] flan or quiche pan. Line the pan with the larger sheet of pastry. Trim the edges. Spread the pastry shell with the filling and cover it with the remaining sheet of pastry. Press down the edges firmly. Gather together the scraps of the pastry and roll them into a long strip, like a thin cord. Press the cord lightly around the edges. Prick the top of the pie all over with a fork. Brush the pastry with the remaining beaten egg.

Bake the pie in a preheated 375° F. [190° C.] oven for one hour, or until the top is golden brown. Serve warm or cold.

ADA BONI
ITALIAN REGIONAL COOKING

Shabra Chipple and Bacon Pie

Shabra is an old Welsh word —probably spelled sgabrwbh — that means quick. Chipple translates as scallion.

To serve 4 to 6

6	scallions, sliced lengthwise	6
4	slices bacon, chopped	4
1 tbsp.	lard or rendered bacon fat	15 ml.
4	eggs	4
3 oz.	cream cheese	90 g.
2 tbsp.	finely chopped fresh parsley	30 ml.
	salt and freshly ground black pepper	
	short-crust pastry (recipe, page 166)	

Roll out the short-crust pastry and use it to line a 9-inch [23-cm.] buttered quiche or flan pan. Press well-buttered foil over the pastry and bake it in a preheated 400° F. [200° C.] oven for 10 minutes, or until the pastry is firm. Reduce the heat to 350° F. [180° C.], remove the foil, and bake the pastry case for a further 10 minutes so that it is crisp but not colored. Take it out of the oven and cool. Heat the lard or bacon fat in a frying pan, add the bacon pieces and cook over medium heat for five minutes. Lift out the bacon with a slotted spoon and drain. Arrange the bacon in the pastry shell.

Add the scallions to the juices in the frying pan and cook over low heat until they are soft and transparent. Drain off the excess fat and arrange the scallions over the bacon.

Beat the eggs with the cream cheese (a rotary beater is best for this) until the mixture is smooth. Mix in the parsley and season fairly generously with salt and pepper.

Pour the egg mixture over the bacon and scallions, put the pie into a preheated 350° F. [180° C.] oven and bake it for 20 to 30 minutes, or until the eggs are just set. Cover the pie with foil if the edges of the pastry tend to get too brown.

MARIKA TENISON HANBURY
RECIPES FROM A COUNTRY KITCHEN

Quiche Piperade Biscayne

The techniques of shaping a pastry shell and blind baking it partially are demonstrated on pages 74-75.

	To serve 4 to 6	
3	eggs, beaten	3
2 tbsp.	olive oil	30 ml.
1	small onion, sliced	1
1	green pepper, seeded, deribbed and diced	1
2 cups	peeled, seeded and diced tomatoes	½ liter
1	clove garlic, finely chopped	1
1 tbsp.	diced pimiento	15 ml.
½ cup	diced smoked Virginia ham	125 ml.
	salt and pepper	
1 tbsp.	chopped fresh parsley	15 ml.
	9-inch [23-cm.] short-crust pastry shell (recipe, page 166), partially baked	

In a saucepan, heat the oil and add the onion and green pepper. Sauté for two minutes. Add the tomatoes, garlic, pimiento, ham, and salt and pepper to taste. Cook for 10 minutes. Cool and add the eggs and parsley.

Pour the mixture into the pie shell and bake for 25 minutes in a preheated 350° F. [180° C.] oven.

RENÉ VERDON
THE WHITE HOUSE CHEF COOKBOOK

Aunt Carla's Tart

Torta della Zia Carla

The techniques of shaping and blind baking a pastry shell are demonstrated on pages 74-75.

	To serve 6 to 8	
1⅓ cups	freshly grated Parmesan cheese	325 ml.
3	eggs, 1 egg lightly beaten	3
5 oz.	prosciutto or other raw cured ham, diced (about 1 cup [¼ liter])	150 g.
1 cup	white sauce (recipe, page 165)	¼ liter
	short-crust pastry (recipe, page 166, but double the quantities called for and add 1 egg to the dough)	

Line a buttered 10-inch [25-cm.] piepan with the pastry. Brush the pastry with the beaten egg, line it with a piece of wax paper, fill the lining with dried beans and bake the pastry shell blind for 15 minutes in a preheated 375° F. [190° C.] oven. Remove the paper and beans.

Stir the grated cheese, the two remaining eggs and the ham into the white sauce. Fill the pastry shell with the cheese mixture. Reduce the oven temperature to 325° F. [170° C.] and bake for 20 minutes, or until the filling is set.

FERRUCCIO BOTTI
GASTRONOMIA PARMENSE OSSIA PARMA CAPITALE DEI BUONGUSTAI

Sausage and Egg Pie

Torta di Salsiccia

Serve the pie for lunch with salad, or cut it into small wedges and serve as an appetizer.

	To serve 6 to 10	
12	eggs, beaten	12
2 lb.	fresh Italian pork sausage	1 kg.
2 tbsp.	finely chopped fresh parsley	30 ml.
3 tbsp.	freshly grated Parmesan or Romano cheese	45 ml.
	salt and pepper	
	short-crust pastry (recipe, page 166, but double the quantities called for)	

Remove the casing from the sausage, and brown the meat in a large skillet over medium heat. Then remove the sausage from the heat.

Add to the eggs the parsley, cheese, and salt and pepper to taste. Add the sausage and mix well. Set aside.

Roll out half of the pastry to line a baking pan 8 by 8 by 2 inches [20 by 20 by 5 cm.]. Pour the sausage-and-egg mixture into the pie shell. Roll out the remaining pastry and use it to cover the pie.

Bake the pie in a preheated 350° F. [180° C.] oven for one hour, or until the top crust is golden. Remove the pie from the oven and let it cool before slicing.

JOE FAMULARO AND LOUISE IMPERIALE
THE FESTIVE FAMULARO KITCHEN

Crab Quiche

The techniques of shaping a pastry shell and blind baking it partially are demonstrated on pages 74-75.

	To serve 4 to 6	
2½ cups	flaked crab meat	625 ml.
½ cup	finely chopped scallions, white parts only	125 ml.
¼ cup	finely chopped celery	50 ml.
2 tbsp.	finely chopped shallots	30 ml.
½ tsp.	finely chopped garlic	2 ml.
2 tbsp.	butter	30 ml.
2 tbsp.	finely chopped fresh parsley	30 ml.
1½ cups	half-and-half cream	375 ml.
3	eggs, beaten	3
¼ tsp.	salt	1 ml.
¼ tsp.	white pepper	1 ml.
¼ tsp.	grated nutmeg	1 ml.
⅛ tsp.	cayenne pepper	½ ml.
1 cup	shredded Gruyère or Emmentaler cheese	¼ liter
½ tsp.	paprika	2 ml.
	10-inch [25-cm.] short-crust pastry shell *(recipe, page 166)*, partially baked	

Sauté the scallions, celery, shallots and garlic in the butter until soft. Cool. With a fork, stir in the crab meat and parsley. Place the mixture in the pastry shell. Beat the half-and-half cream with the eggs and seasonings. Strain the cream mixture over the crab-meat mixture and sprinkle the top with the cheese and paprika. Bake in a preheated 375° F. [190° C.] oven for 30 to 40 minutes, or until a toothpick inserted in the center of the filling comes out clean.

CORALIE CASTLE AND BARBARA LAWRENCE
HORS D'OEUVRE ETC.

Crab Meat Quiche

Quiche au Crabe

The techniques of shaping a pastry shell and blind baking it partially are demonstrated on pages 74-75.

This quiche of crab is a rich combination of eggs and cream. It is versatile enough to be used as a hot hors d'oeuvre, baked in an oblong baking pan and cut into bite-sized squares, or as a main-course supper or luncheon dish. I find it rather too substantial as a first course. It may be cooked in advance and reheated. If used in this way, do not refrigerate unless you plan to keep it for several days.

	To serve 6 to 8	
6	eggs	6
1 cup	shredded crab meat	¼ liter
¾ cup	heavy cream	175 ml.
½ tsp.	salt	2 ml.
	cayenne pepper	
	freshly grated pepper	
1 tsp.	Worcestershire sauce	5 ml.
¼ cup	freshly grated Parmesan cheese	50 ml.
	9-inch [23-cm.] short-crust pastry shell *(recipe, page 166)*, partially baked	

Break the eggs into a mixing bowl, pour in the cream and beat with a whisk until thoroughly blended. Add the salt, cayenne, two twists of black pepper, and the Worcestershire sauce. Stir in the crab meat and mix until it is evenly distributed. Pour the mixture into the pie shell, sprinkle the surface with Parmesan cheese and bake in a preheated 350° F. [180° C.] oven for 30 minutes, or until golden brown and set.

MAURICE MOORE-BETTY
COOKING FOR OCCASIONS

Cheese Tricorns

Corniottes

	To make 12 tricorns	
½ lb.	farmer or pot cheese	¼ kg.
½ lb.	Gruyère cheese, shredded (2 cups [½ liter])	¼ kg.
4	eggs, beaten	4
	salt and pepper	
3 tbsp.	crème fraîche or substitute heavy cream	45 ml.
	short-crust pastry (recipe, page 166, but double the quantities called for)	

Mix the two cheeses into three of the beaten eggs, season with salt and pepper, and add the *crème fraîche*. Roll out the pastry very thin and cut it into 6-inch [15-cm.] rounds, using the rim of a bowl as a guide. Place 2 or 3 tablespoons [30 or 45 ml.] of the cheese mixture on each round. Fold up the edges of the dough toward the center in three segments to create triangular pastries; pinch the edges of the dough together to seal them. Brush the pastries with the remaining beaten egg. Bake in a preheated 350° F. [180° C.] oven for 25 minutes, or until lightly browned.

JEHANNE JEAN-CHARLES
LE LEXIQUE DES BONS PETITS PLATS

Cheese Custard Tarts

Flans Suisses au Fromage

Scraps of puff pastry may be used in this recipe instead of the short crust. An alternative method is to bake the pastry cases blind at 350° F. [180° C.] for 10 to 15 minutes, or until they are three quarters cooked. They are then filled with the mixture and baked for about 15 minutes at 400° F. [200° C.].

To make 24 tarts

4 tbsp.	freshly grated Parmesan cheese	60 ml.
1 tbsp.	flour	15 ml.
4	eggs, the yolks separated from the whites, and the whites stiffly beaten	4
2	egg yolks	2
1 cup	light cream	¼ liter
2 tbsp.	butter, cut into small pieces	30 ml.
	grated nutmeg	
	sugar	
	pepper	
	salt	
	short-crust pastry (recipe, page 166, but double the quantities called for)	

Lightly oil 24 small oval tart pans. Roll out the pastry thinly and line the pans with it.

Put the cheese in a bowl with the flour, egg yolks and cream. Mix them together and press the mixture through a fine sieve into a saucepan. Add the butter, a pinch each of nutmeg, sugar and pepper, and very little salt. Place the pan over medium heat and stir until the butter melts. Remove the cheese mixture from the heat and fold in the egg whites.

Divide the cheese mixture equally among the pastry shells. Place them on baking sheets and bake them in a preheated 350° F. [180° C.] oven for about 20 minutes, or until the filling is set and the pastry golden brown.

URBAN DUBOIS AND ÉMILE BERNARD
LA CUISINE CLASSIQUE

Pastry Boats with Blue-Cheese Cream

Blauwschuitjes

The original version of this recipe calls for saingorlon, a mild French blue cheese, made to imitate Gorgonzola, but not ob-

tainable in the United States. The techniques of shaping and blind baking a pastry shell are shown on pages 74-75.

To serve 6

5 oz.	Gorgonzola or other mild blue cheese, crumbled (about 1¼ cups [300 ml.])	150 g.
1	shallot, finely chopped	1
½ cup	dry white wine	125 ml.
6	eggs, lightly beaten	6
8 tbsp.	butter, flaked	120 ml.
	salt and pepper	
	ground allspice	
	rough puff pastry (recipe, page 166, but double the quantities called for)	

Roll out the dough and use it to line 16 small oval *barquette*, or boat, molds. Bake the pastry boats blind, then keep them warm while you make the cream.

In a saucepan simmer the shallot in the wine over gentle heat, until the wine is reduced by half. Rub the mixture through a fine sieve and cool.

In a second saucepan or fondue pan, combine the eggs with the blue cheese, butter, salt, pepper and a pinch of allspice. Stir in the wine with a wooden spoon and continue to stir over very low heat until the mixture is smooth.

Fill the pastry boats with the warm cheese cream and serve immediately.

HUGH JANS
VRIJ NEDERLANDS KOOKBOEK

Chester Cakes

These little cakes are also excellent without the filling, and they keep well in an airtight container.

To make about 12 filled cakes

6 oz.	Cheshire cheese, shredded (about 1½ cups [375 ml.])	175 g.
12 tbsp.	butter, softened	180 ml.
1½ cups	flour	375 ml.
	salt	
	cayenne pepper	
2 tbsp.	heavy cream	30 ml.
Cheshire filling		
2 oz.	Cheshire cheese, shredded (about ½ cup [125 ml.])	60 g.
4 tbsp.	butter, softened	60 ml.

Cream the butter on a marble slab; then, with your hand, work in the flour, cheese, salt, cayenne pepper and cream.

Handle the dough as lightly as possible. When it is blended, flour your hands and roll the dough into a ball. Let it rest in a cool place or in the refrigerator for about one hour.

Roll the dough about ¼ inch [6 mm.] thick; stamp out 1-inch [2½-cm.] rounds. Bake the rounds in an oven preheated to 350° F. [180° C.] for 20 minutes, or until they are golden brown. Meanwhile, make the filling by creaming the cheese and butter together.

Cool the cakes a little on the baking sheet. Use the filling to stick the cakes together in pairs. Reheat the filled cakes slightly, and serve them on a hot dish.

ANDRÉ L. SIMON
CHEESES OF THE WORLD

Farm Cheese Patties

Kirkcudbright is a town in Scotland.

This Kirkcudbright recipe is at least 155 years old. Any type of pastry may be used. As an alternative method, you may put the pastry and filling in an 8-inch [20-cm.] piepan and bake the pie for about 25 minutes.

	To make 18 to 24 tarts	
½ lb.	mild Cheddar cheese, shredded (about 2 cups [½ liter])	¼ kg.
2	eggs, beaten	2
1 tbsp.	butter, melted	15 ml.
1 tbsp.	dry bread crumbs	15 ml.
½ cup	heavy cream	125 ml.
	salt and pepper	
	cayenne pepper	
¼	garlic clove, crushed, or 1 tsp. [5 ml.] grated onion (optional)	¼
	rough puff or short-crust pastry (recipe, page 166, but double the quantities called for)	

Roll the pastry out thin and line small buttered patty or tart pans with it. Mix the remaining ingredients together and put a little into each lined pan. Bake the tarts in a preheated 400° F. [200° C.] oven for 15 minutes, or until the tops are beginning to color.

BEE NILSON (EDITOR)
THE WI DIAMOND JUBILEE COOKBOOK

Fondues and Rabbits

Mother Tant Pis' Fondue

Fondue de la Mère Tant Pis

Potato flour is made by grinding dehydrated potatoes to a flourlike consistency. If not obtainable, 1 teaspoon [5 ml.] of all-purpose flour may be substituted.

To prepare the fondue, I use a small earthenware dish—with a handle—measuring about 6 inches [15 cm.] across. In Geneva this is called a *câclon*.

	To serve 4	
14 oz.	Gruyère cheese, cut into small pieces	360 g.
1	garlic clove, halved	1
1¼ cups	very dry white wine	300 ml.
	freshly ground white pepper	
	grated nutmeg	
4 tbsp.	kirsch	60 ml.
½ tsp.	potato flour, mixed with 2 tbsp. [30 ml.] white wine	2 ml.
	dry French bread, cubed	

Rub the inside of a suitable earthenware pot with the cut sides of the garlic clove. Pour in the wine, season it with pepper and nutmeg, add the cheese and bring the mixture to a boil. Whisk over medium heat for eight to 10 minutes: Gradually the cheese melts and the wine begins to turn milky. The cheese forms a mass in the middle of the *câclon* and the wine remains obstinately separate. This is the moment to use the potato flour.

Pour in the dissolved flour little by little, beating all the time. Gradually the mixture thickens and the wine mixes with the cheese. Then add the kirsch and continue to beat. The fondue is reaching its final texture. Boil for one minute. If the flavor of alcohol is too strong, boil for three or four minutes longer. Taste it again—delicious. Set the pot on a hot plate or over an alcohol burner adjusted to keep the fondue just bubbling.

Serve each guest about 20 pieces of dry bread, each fairly thick, but small enough to be eaten in one mouthful. The bread is speared on a fork and dipped into the fondue pot.

ÉDOUARD DE POMIANE
COOKING WITH POMIANE

Geneva Fondue
Fondue Genfer

This is a creamy cheese mixture that can be served with toast, but is also delicious with pasta, or potatoes boiled in their jackets.

To serve 4 to 6

1 lb.	Emmentaler or Gruyère cheese, shredded (about 4 cups [1 liter])	½ kg.
5 tbsp.	heavy cream	75 ml.
3 or 4	egg yolks	3 or 4
⅓ cup	dry white wine	75 ml.
	pepper	
	grated nutmeg	

Mix all of the ingredients in a fireproof fondue dish. Stir over the lowest possible heat until the mixture melts and begins to thicken. It must not be allowed to boil, or it will curdle. Serve the fondue in the fireproof dish, keeping it warm.

EVA MARIA BORER
TANTE HEIDI'S SWISS KITCHEN

Cheese Fondue with Truffles
Fondue aux Truffes

To serve 4 to 6

14 oz.	Fontina cheese, cut into small cubes	400 g.
2 cups	milk	½ liter
7 tbsp.	butter	105 ml.
8	egg yolks	8
	white pepper	
1	fresh white truffle, very finely sliced	1

Place the cheese in a bowl, cover with the milk and let it soak for several hours.

To prepare the fondue, use either a double boiler or a saucepan set in a pan of hot water. Place half of the butter in the top pan together with the egg yolks, cheese and milk. Melt over low heat, mixing continuously with a whisk. The cheese will turn into a thick cream; add a little white pepper at this point. Cut the remaining butter into small pieces and add them to the cheese mixture. Stir for a few moments and serve at once, sprinkled with the slices of truffle. This fondue is eaten with a fork, like scrambled eggs.

F. AND T. RARIS
LES CHAMPIGNONS, CONNAISSANCE ET GASTRONOMIE

Baked Rarebit

To serve 4

6 oz.	Cheddar cheese, thinly sliced	175 g.
2 cups	fresh bread crumbs	½ liter
2	eggs, lightly beaten	2
1¼ cups	milk	300 ml.
	salt and pepper	

Butter a fairly deep 1-quart [1-liter] ovenproof dish and put in some of the cheese slices, then a layer of crumbs. Repeat the layers until the dish is about three quarters full. Mix the eggs with the milk and the seasoning, and pour the mixture over the cheese and crumbs. Bake uncovered in a preheated 350° F. [180° C.] oven for about 30 minutes, or until the mixture is set and golden brown on top.

MARY MAC KIRDY
RECIPES FOR YOU

A Scotch Rabbit

The original version of this recipe calls for porter, a rich, dark, sweet ale with a heavy foam. Porter is not obtainable in the United States, but stout—although somewhat lighter—may be used instead. To replace the old-fashioned cheese toaster, you may substitute a fondue pot or other heatproof serving dish.

Some gourmands use red wine for this dish instead of porter; but the latter liquor is much better adapted to the flavor of cheese. Others use a proportion of soft ripened cheese, or the whole of it in that state.

To serve 4

6 oz.	Stilton, Gouda or Cheshire cheese, crumbled or shredded (about 1½ cups [375 ml.])	175 g.
4 tbsp.	butter (optional)	60 ml.
⅔ cup	stout	150 ml.
1 tsp.	prepared English mustard	5 ml.
	pepper	
	hot toast, buttered if desired	

Put the cheese into a cheese toaster, with the butter if you wish. Add the stout and mustard, and pepper to taste. Stir over low heat until the mixture is completely dissolved, then put it under a hot broiler for two minutes to brown the top.

Serve the cheese, keeping it warm if possible over a pan of boiling water or over an alcohol burner. Serve dry or buttered hot toast on a separate dish. The cheese mixture is ladled onto the toast.

MISTRESS MARGARET DODS
THE COOK AND HOUSEWIFE'S MANUAL

Cheese Soup

Glarus

Despite its title, this recipe produces a dish more akin to a fluid Welsh rabbit than to a soup.

Another method of making this dish is not to stir the bread and cheese in the pan, but to make a pancake of it, turning it to cook it on both sides. In this case, double the amount of butter.

To serve 3 or 4		
1 cup	shredded Gruyère cheese	¼ liter
8	thin slices bread, toasted in a 350° F. [180° C.] oven	8
2½ cups	boiling water	625 ml.
2 tbsp.	butter	30 ml.

Lay the cheese in a bowl in alternating layers with the bread. Pour the water over them and leave for 10 minutes. Press the bread and cheese down firmly and pour off the superfluous water.

Melt the butter in a frying pan on medium heat and put in the bread and cheese. Cook, stirring all the time, till the cheese has melted and the whole becomes shiny (about two minutes). Serve very hot.

HELEN GUGGENBÜHL (EDITOR)
THE SWISS COOKERY BOOK

Welsh Rabbit (Rarebit)

The addition of a little Worcestershire sauce and mustard will give extra flavor to this traditional British dish. The author suggests that the bread may be fried in bacon fat instead of being toasted and buttered.

To serve 1		
½ cup	shredded Cheddar cheese	125 ml.
1 tbsp.	butter	15 ml.
2 tbsp.	ale	30 ml.
	salt and pepper	
1	slice bread, toasted and buttered	1

Put the butter into a saucepan and melt it. Add the ale, a pinch of salt and two pinches of pepper. When just about to boil, stir in the cheese (stir only just lightly enough to dissolve the cheese). On no account let the mixture boil after the cheese is in—and cook it only just long enough to blend it.

Put the toast on a heatproof plate, pour the rabbit quickly over it, and place it under the broiler for a few seconds until the top browns.

DOROTHY HARTLEY
FOOD IN ENGLAND

Eggs with Cheese, Minorcan-Style

Huevos con Queso

In Spain, which has few native cheeses, any grating cheese of the hard Gruyère type would be used for this dish.

To serve 6		
1 cup	freshly grated cheese	¼ liter
6	eggs	6
4 tbsp.	butter	60 ml.
1	onion, chopped	1
1 tbsp.	chopped fresh parsley	15 ml.
½ cup	dry white wine	125 ml.

Heat the butter in a saucepan. Add the onion to the pan and cook gently for five minutes without browning. Add the grated cheese, parsley and wine, and simmer until the cheese has melted—about five minutes. Break the eggs into this mixture and poach them slowly in the cheese-and-wine sauce until just set.

LUIS RIPOLL
NUESTRA COCINA: 600 RECETAS DE MALLORCA, MENORCA, IBIZA Y FORMENTERA

Way Down South Rarebit

To serve 4 to 6		
4 cups	shredded cheese	1 liter
1½ tbsp.	butter	22 ml.
1	onion, shredded	1
2 lb.	tomatoes, cooked (3 cups [¾ liter])	1 kg.
1½ tbsp.	sugar	22 ml.
2	eggs, lightly beaten	2
¼ tsp.	salt	1 ml.
½ tsp.	pepper	2 ml.

Get a good thick frying pan and fry the onion in your butter, and then add the tomatoes and sugar. Never letting this mixture boil, add the cheese a little at a time, stirring so that it melts. Then stir in the eggs and season with salt and pepper. Serve the rarebit piping hot on fried bread.

T. A. LAYTON
THE WINE AND FOOD SOCIETY'S GUIDE TO CHEESE AND CHEESE COOKERY

Rum Tum Tiddy, Rink Tum Ditty, etc. (Old Boston Style)

Rum Tum Tiddy is the name used for many early American versions of Welsh rabbit, or rarebit.

	To serve 2	
¾ lb.	Cheddar cheese, shredded (about 3 cups [¾ liter])	350 g.
1	onion, finely chopped	1
1 tbsp.	butter	15 ml.
1 tsp.	salt	5 ml.
	pepper	
2	medium-sized tomatoes, peeled, seeded, chopped and cooked until soft	2
1 tbsp.	sugar	15 ml.
1	egg, lightly beaten	1

Slowly fry the onion bright golden in the butter; season and add the tomatoes with the sugar. Heat to just under the bubbling point. Don't let the mixture boil. Add the cheese, little by little, shaking the pan until all of the cheese melts. Then stir in the egg gently and serve very hot.

BOB BROWN
THE COMPLETE BOOK OF CHEESE

Tiri Mezedes

This flavorful melted-cheese dish is eaten, like a fondue, by dipping chunks of crusty bread into it.

In Greece one eats the most delicious *mezedes* (appetizers)—they are so good and so varied one is often tempted to make a meal of them. One of my favorites is simply made with cheese—usually from fresh white feta.

	To serve 2 to 4	
1 lb.	feta cheese, cut into ½-inch [1-cm.] slices	½ kg.
3 tbsp.	unsalted butter	45 ml.
3 tbsp.	strained fresh lemon juice	45 ml.
	freshly ground pepper	

Melt the butter in a shallow fireproof dish; arrange the feta slices in layers in the dish, seasoning them with a little pepper. Warm over low heat until the cheese softens and begins to bubble slightly. Add the lemon juice and serve at once, garnishing with coarsely chopped celery leaves or uncurled parsley, or with a sprinkling of poppy seeds. Serve very hot—if this dish cools, much of the flavor is lost.

T. A. LAYTON
THE WINE AND FOOD SOCIETY'S GUIDE TO CHEESE
AND CHEESE COOKERY

Roasted Cheese

Raclette

Johanna Spyri described the prototype of all Swiss national dishes made from melted cheese in *Heidi*, in a famous scene where the old grandfather cooks the cheese at an open fire. Basically, *raclette* is just that—cheese fried in the fire; and in Canton Wallis, and many restaurants all over Switzerland, this specialty is prepared at an open wood fire. A mature Gomser raclette cheese is halved and the cut side held in the flames till the surface begins to melt. The melting cheese is scraped onto a warm plate—*racler* means to scrape—and eaten with small potatoes, salt cucumbers and onions pickled in vinegar. *Raclette* can easily be made at an open fire in the sitting room. In Switzerland there are electric stoves to put on the dining table, not as romantic as an open fire, but not as hot and messy either.

	To serve 4	
about ¾ lb.	raclette or Gruyère cheese, in 1 piece	about ⅓ kg.
1	egg yolk, beaten (optional)	1

Fix the piece of cheese on the end of a toasting fork, hold the piece in front of the flames of an open fire, or over glowing coals, and scrape the melting cheese off into a warmed dish.

To make an easy and equally tasty, if not quite so genuine *raclette*, butter the inside of a fireproof dish, remove the rind from the cheese, and place the cheese in the dish. Brush it very thinly with the egg yolk, and allow the cheese to melt in a preheated 450° F. [230° C.] oven for about 15 minutes.

EVA MARIA BORER
TANTE HEIDI'S SWISS KITCHEN

Toasted Cheese

This is a good version of a favorite Victorian dish. Quantities seem tiny, but they are enough for eight for a first course.

	To serve 4	
½ lb.	aged Cheddar cheese, grated (2 cups [½ liter])	¼ kg.
6 tbsp.	butter	90 ml.
½ cup	heavy cream	125 ml.
3	egg yolks	3
	salt and pepper	
	cayenne pepper	

Melt the butter in a pan over low heat; add the remaining ingredients, stirring them vigorously together. Heat slowly until you have a thick cream. Keep under the boiling point, but give the whole thing time to thicken. Divide among four or eight small pots, and brown lightly under the grill. Serve with plenty of toast fingers, or pieces of baked bread.

JANE GRIGSON
FOOD WITH THE FAMOUS

Special Cheese Presentations

Cheese Cutlets

Cotolette di Scamorza

The original version of this recipe calls for scamorza—a soft, white, mild-flavored cheese that is made in Italy, but not exported to the United States.

	To serve 6	
1¾ lb.	mozzarella cheese, cut into 12 slices, ½ inch [1 cm.] thick	850 g.
½ cup	flour	125 ml.
2 or 3	eggs, beaten	2 or 3
1 cup	dry bread crumbs	¼ liter
	vegetable oil for deep frying	

Dip the slices of cheese in flour, coat them with beaten egg and then roll them in the bread crumbs, being careful to cover the edges and corners. Heat the oil in a deep frying pan to 375° F. [190° C.] and fry the cheese cutlets one or two at a time, over very high heat, until they are browned, about five to 10 minutes. Keep the prepared cutlets warm. When all are ready, serve immediately.

JEANNE CARÒLA FRANCESCONI
LA CUCINA NAPOLETANA

Fried Cheese Squares

Fondue Bruxelloise

	To serve 6	
1 cup	shredded Gruyère cheese	¼ liter
1 cup	freshly grated Parmesan cheese	¼ liter
⅛ tsp.	cayenne pepper	½ ml.
¼ tsp.	grated nutmeg	1 ml.
5	egg yolks	5
	salt and pepper	
2 cups	white sauce (recipe, page 165, but double the quantities called for)	½ liter
2 tsp.	water	10 ml.
1 tbsp.	peanut oil	15 ml.
3	eggs, lightly beaten	3
¼ cup	flour	50 ml.
3 cups	fresh bread crumbs	¾ liter
	oil or fat for deep frying	
12	sprigs fresh parsley, washed and thoroughly dried	12

Stir the Gruyère, Parmesan, cayenne pepper, nutmeg, egg yolks, and salt and pepper to taste into the white sauce. Put the sauce on low heat and cook, stirring constantly, until it thickens. Do not boil the sauce. Remove it from the heat.

Butter a 13-by-9-inch [32-by-23-cm.] or a 9-inch [23-cm.] square baking pan generously and pour the sauce into it. Spread the sauce smooth with a spatula. Cover it with buttered wax paper and refrigerate it overnight or longer. It will become quite firm. Cut the firm mixture into squares, rectangles, rounds or diamond shapes.

Beat the water, peanut oil, and salt and pepper to taste into the eggs. Coat the croquettes on all sides with the flour, dip them into the egg mixture and shake off the excess. Finally, coat the croquettes on all sides with the bread crumbs, tapping them lightly with the flat side of a knife so that the crumbs will adhere better.

Fry the croquettes in oil or fat, preheated to 375° F. [180° C.], until golden; drain on kitchen toweling. Deep fry the parsley and use it to garnish the croquettes.

NIKA HAZELTON
THE BELGIAN COOK BOOK

Geneva Cheese Fritters

Genfer Käsebeignets

This can be served as a rich, hot starter for eight people or, with a salad or vegetables, as a main course for four.

To serve 4 to 8		
1 lb.	Emmentaler or Gruyère cheese, cut into 8 slices ½ inch [1 cm.] thick by 3 inches [8 cm.] square	½ kg.
1 cup	flour	¼ liter
	salt and pepper	
1	egg	1
1¼ cups	dry white wine, warmed	300 ml.
2	egg whites, stiffly beaten	2
	prepared mustard	
	fat for deep frying	

Sift the flour into a bowl and season with a pinch each of salt and pepper. Make a well in the center and break the egg into it. Gradually work the egg into the flour, then slowly stir in about half of the wine. Beat well, then stir in the remaining wine and fold in the egg whites.

Spread the cheese slices thinly with mustard and dip them into the fritter batter. Fry them in very hot deep fat until they are golden on both sides. Serve hot.

GRETE WILLINSKY
KULINARISCHE WELTREISE

Parmesan Bavarian Cream

Parmesan Bavarois

Essentially this is a Bavarian cream, but it is not sweetened and it is not a dessert but rather a cold entrée. In France it might be spooned directly from its own glass bowl or terrine. Others may prefer to mold it, in a ring perhaps, and garnish it with hearts of lettuce or romaine.

To serve 4		
¼ cup	freshly grated Parmesan cheese	50 ml.
1¼ cups	milk	300 ml.
4	egg yolks, beaten	4
1 tsp.	unflavored powdered gelatin	5 ml.
⅓ cup	heavy cream, whipped	75 ml.

Put 1 cup [¼ liter] of the milk in a saucepan over medium heat. When it is about to boil, pour the milk over the egg yolks and stir well. Return the mixture to the saucepan, place it over low heat and stir without boiling until the mixture coats the spoon. Remove the custard from the heat and allow it to cool, stirring from time to time to prevent a skin from forming.

Soften the gelatin in the remaining milk, heat the mixture, stirring constantly, and add it to the custard. Stir to dissolve the gelatin thoroughly. Add the cheese, and allow the mixture to cool completely. Fold in the whipped cream, and pour the mixture into a serving dish or a 1-quart [1-liter] mold. Place the dish in the refrigerator for at least one hour, or until the cream is set. Unmold, if desired, to serve.

ALICE B. TOKLAS
AROMAS AND FLAVORS OF PAST AND PRESENT

Cottage-Cheese Dumplings, Moravian-Style

Hanácké Noky

Quark is a German fresh cheese with a tangy flavor. It can be made by hanging yogurt in a cloth to drain. A suitable substitute is the farmer cheese demonstrated on pages 10-11.

To serve 8 to 10		
14 oz.	quark or farmer cheese, drained (about 1¾ cups [425 ml.])	400 g.
12 tbsp.	butter, 5 tbsp. [75 ml.] softened, the rest melted	180 ml.
3	eggs, lightly beaten	3
	salt	
1½ cups	milk	375 ml.
	flour	
¼ cup	grated dry pumpernickel	50 ml.

Place the cheese in a bowl and gradually beat in the softened butter, eggs and a pinch of salt. Add the milk, alternately with additions of flour, until you have a soft dough. The quantity of flour depends on the consistency of the cheese.

Bring a large saucepan of water to a boil and, when the dough is thoroughly mixed, form small dumplings, using a spoon dipped in cold water so that the dough doesn't stick to it. For each dumpling, scoop out a little dough and drop it into the boiling water. Boil for 10 minutes. When the dumplings rise to the surface, remove one and cut it in half to make sure it is cooked through.

When they are cooked, drain the dumplings, sprinkle them with the grated pumpernickel and pour the melted butter over them.

JOZA BŘÍZOVÁ AND MARYNA KLIMENTOVÁ
TSCHECHISCHE KÜCHE

Malakoffs

	To serve 8	
8	slices Swiss cheese (⅛ inch [3 mm.] thick)	8
1 cup	flour	¼ liter
	salt	
¼ cup	warm water	50 ml.
1 tbsp.	olive oil	15 ml.
3	eggs, beaten until foamy	3
2 tbsp.	butter	30 ml.
	Hungarian paprika	

Mix the flour, a pinch of salt, the water and olive oil to a smooth paste with a wooden spoon. Fold the eggs into the paste. Coat the slices of cheese with this batter and fry them in the melted butter until they are brown. Sprinkle with a little paprika and serve immediately.

SIGRID SCHULTZ (EDITOR)
OVERSEAS PRESS CLUB COOKBOOK

Parmesan Balls

These delicate balls should be mixed and rolled quickly, then deep fried immediately—before the egg whites collapse.

	To make 10 to 12 small balls	
¾ cup	freshly grated Parmesan cheese	175 ml.
2	egg whites, stiffly beaten	2
	cayenne pepper	
	vegetable oil for deep frying	

Heat oil to 375° F. [190° C.]. Mix ⅔ cup [150 ml.] of the cheese with the egg whites and cayenne. Roll the mixture

into small balls, using the remaining cheese instead of flour to dust your hands. Deep fry the balls in the oil, about six at a time, until they are light brown. Drain; pile them up on a hot dish and serve at once.

MARY MAC KIRDY
RECIPES FOR YOU

An Old-fashioned Cheese Pastry

Flamiche à l'Ancienne

The original recipe calls for mariolles cheese—a pungent, semisoft French cheese not available in the United States. Port-Salut makes a satisfactory substitute. Cut into strips or wedges, this pastry may be served as a first course, a light luncheon dish or an accompaniment to drinks.

	To serve 4	
3½ oz.	Port-Salut cheese, shredded and mashed to a paste (about ¾ cup [175 ml.])	100 g.
1¼ cups	flour	300 ml.
2	eggs, beaten	2
¼ cup	water	50 ml.
	salt	
7 tbsp.	butter, softened	100 ml.

Put the flour on a board and make a well in the center. Add the eggs, water and salt, and incorporate them into the flour with your fingers. Knead the dough for about 10 minutes, until it is springy, then allow it to rest in a cool place for 30 minutes. Roll out the dough on a floured board to a thickness of ½ inch [1 cm.].

Work together the cheese and butter, form the mixture into a ball, and place it in the center of the pastry. Fold the pastry over the cheese mixture and seal the edges to enclose it. Roll the pastry to a thickness of ½ inch [1 cm.] and fold it in half. Turn the dough 90 degrees and roll it out again. This is the first turn. Let the pastry rest for 15 minutes in the refrigerator, then repeat the folding and rolling process twice more, chilling the dough after each one and turning the pastry 90 degrees in the same direction each time.

Butter an 8-inch [20-cm.] pie plate and lay the pastry in it. Bake it in a preheated 400° F. [200° C.] oven for 35 minutes, or until it is golden brown.

PIERRE ANDROUET
LA CUISINE AU FROMAGE

Farmhouse Macaroni and Cheese

To serve 4

1 lb.	sharp Cheddar cheese, coarsely shredded (about 4 cups [1 liter])	½ kg.
½ lb.	elbow macaroni, boiled in salted water for 8 to 10 minutes, or until barely tender, and drained	¼ kg.
1 tbsp.	butter	15 ml.
1 cup	milk	¼ liter
2	eggs, beaten	2
1 tsp.	salt	5 ml.
⅛ tsp.	pepper	½ ml.

Turn the macaroni into a buttered 5- to 6-cup [1½-liter] baking dish, and toss it with the butter until the butter is melted. Add 3 to 3½ cups [750 to 875 ml.] of the cheese and toss it with the macaroni. Mix the milk, eggs, salt and pepper. Pour this mixture over the macaroni. Sprinkle the remaining cheese over the macaroni.

Bake in a preheated 325° F. [160° C.] oven for 30 minutes or until the milk is absorbed and the cheese on top is melted into a golden mass.

JEANNE A. VOLTZ
THE FLAVOR OF THE SOUTH

Cottage-Cheese Pancakes

Blintzes

To serve 4 to 6

1½ lb.	dry cottage cheese	¾ kg.
	salt	
2	egg yolks, beaten	2
1 tbsp.	melted butter	15 ml.
1 tbsp.	sugar	15 ml.

Pancakes

1 cup	milk	¼ liter
4	eggs, beaten	4
1 cup	flour	¼ liter
1 tsp.	salt	5 ml.
	butter	

Press the cheese through a strainer; stir in salt to taste, and add the egg yolks, melted butter and sugar.

To make the pancakes, first add the milk to the eggs; gradually stir in the flour, add the salt and mix until smooth. Heat a heavy 6-inch [15-cm.] skillet; butter it lightly. Pour in only enough batter to make a very thin pancake, tipping the pan from side to side until the batter covers the bottom of the pan. Bake the pancake on one side only until it blisters; toss it onto a board fried side up. Proceed in this manner until all of the batter has been used.

Place a rounded tablespoon [20 ml.] of the cheese filling in the center of each pancake. Fold over both sides and roll into an envelope shape. Fry the envelopes on both sides or bake them until golden brown. Serve hot with sugar or with sour cream and jam.

THE SETTLEMENT COOKBOOK

Fried Stuffed Peppers with Cheese

Pulneni Chushki sus Sirene

The sweet peppers in this recipe should be the long, single-tipped variety without grooves. Choose ones that are thin-fleshed so that they take more stuffing.

To serve 2

4	long green frying peppers	4
½ lb.	feta cheese, crumbled	¼ kg.
1 tsp.	finely chopped flat-leafed parsley	5 ml.
	freshly ground black pepper	
2	egg yolks	2
	flour	
1	egg, lightly beaten	1
about 1¼ cups	oil	about 300 ml.

Broil the peppers over charcoal or under a broiler, turning them frequently, until the skins puff and scorch evenly all over, and the flesh becomes soft. Put the peppers into a small saucepan and cover with a well-fitting lid. When they are quite cold, peel off the scorched skins and carefully remove the cores and seeds, leaving the shells intact.

Combine the crumbled cheese with the parsley, a little pepper and the egg yolks, and stuff the peppers with this mixture. Flatten the peppers slightly, flour them thoroughly, patting a little flour onto the opening over the filling. Then roll the peppers in the beaten egg.

Select a deep frying pan that will accommodate the peppers easily. Pour in oil to a depth of about ½ inch [1 cm.] and place the pan over medium heat. You can test the oil by dipping in a pepper stem; when the oil froths on contact with the stem, put in the peppers. Turning them occasionally, fry the peppers for about 10 minutes, reducing the heat if they are browning too quickly. Drain the peppers. Serve the peppers cold, with bread and a tomato salad.

SONYA CHORTANOVA
NASHA KUCHNIYA

Cheese and Dandelion Roll

To serve 4

1 cup	shredded Cheddar cheese	¼ liter
1 lb.	dandelion leaves or other greens (spinach, beet or turnip greens, sorrel), parboiled for 2 minutes, drained and chopped	½ kg.
1 tbsp.	butter	15 ml.
2 tbsp.	tomato ketchup	30 ml.
1 tbsp.	grated horseradish	15 ml.
1 cup	cooked hominy grits or rice	¼ liter
2	eggs, hard-boiled and sliced	2
1¼ cups	tomato sauce *(recipe, page 166)*	300 ml.

Combine the cheese, greens, butter, ketchup, horseradish and grits or rice. Form the mixture into a cylindrical roll. Place it on a buttered baking sheet and bake it in a preheated 350° F. [180° C.] oven for 25 minutes.

Place the roll on a warmed serving dish and garnish with the egg slices. Serve with tomato sauce.

ANDRÉ L. SIMON
CHEESES OF THE WORLD

Chilies Stuffed with Cheese

Chiles Rellenos con Queso

To make 8 stuffed chilies

¼ lb.	Monterey Jack cheese	125 g.
4	canned peeled green chilies, drained and halved lengthwise	4
	flour	
2	eggs, the yolks separated from the whites	2
	oil for deep frying	

Tomato sauce

½	medium-sized onion, chopped	½
1	small clove garlic, crushed to a paste	1
1 tbsp.	oil	15 ml.
1 cup	drained canned tomatoes	¼ liter
2 cups	chicken broth *(recipe, page 164)*	½ liter
	salt and pepper	
	oregano	

Cut the cheese in eight rectangles, each about ½ inch [1 cm.] thick and 1 inch [2½ cm.] long. Wrap a strip of chili around each piece of cheese. Roll the stuffed chilies in flour. Make a batter by beating the egg whites until stiff and beating the yolks lightly. Fold the yolks into the whites, then fold in 2 tablespoons [30 ml.] flour.

Drop the stuffed and floured chilies into the batter one at a time. Pick up each chili with a spoon and transfer it to a saucer; then slide it from the saucer into about 1½ inches [4 cm.] of moderately hot oil. This technique keeps the chilies neater and holds more of the batter on them. Basting with hot oil, fry them until golden brown on each side, but work quickly. Drain them well on absorbent paper and let stand. Don't worry if the nice puffy coating deflates. It will puff up again when heated in the thin sauce before serving.

To make the sauce, first cook the onion and garlic in the oil until wilted. Add the tomatoes, pressing them through a strainer. Put in a pot with the stock and bring to a boil, then season to taste with salt, pepper, and oregano rubbed between the palms of the hands. At serving time, heat the chilies in the boiling sauce for about five minutes.

ELENA ZELAYETA
ELENA'S SECRETS OF MEXICAN COOKING

Scalloped Potatoes with Reblochon

Gratin de Pommes de Terre au Reblochon

Serve this hot, as an accompaniment to white meats or to poultry. The baking dish should be only half-full; otherwise the cheese sauce will overflow.

To serve 4 to 6

1¼ lb.	reblochon cheese, crust removed, mashed to a paste	⅔ kg.
6	medium-sized potatoes, peeled and thinly sliced into rounds ⅛ inch [3 mm.] thick	6
½ cup	heavy cream	100 ml.
¾ cup	milk	200 ml.
	salt and white pepper	
	grated nutmeg	
1	garlic clove, halved	1
2 tbsp.	butter	30 ml.

Plunge the potatoes into boiling water for three minutes. Drain them, run cold water over them and drain again. In a saucepan, melt the reblochon cheese in the cream and milk over very low heat. Add salt, pepper and nutmeg to taste.

Rub the cut sides of the garlic over the inside of a shallow casserole, then butter the dish well. Arrange the potatoes in the casserole and pour the cheese mixture over them.

Bake the potatoes in a preheated 400° F. [200° C.] oven for 30 minutes. Reduce the heat to 325° F. [170° C.] and bake for a further hour, or until the top is well browned and the potatoes are completely soft.

PIERRE ANDROUET
LA CUISINE AU FROMAGE

Baked Eggplant, Mozzarella, Eggs and Tomatoes

Tortino di Melanzane e Mozzarella

To serve 3 or 4

½ to ¾ lb.	mozzarella cheese, cut into ¼-inch [6-mm.] slices	¼ to ⅓ kg.
4	eggplants, each about 6 inches [15 cm.] long, trimmed, peeled and cut into ¼-inch [6-mm.] slices	4
3	eggs, hard-boiled and sliced	3
2	large ripe tomatoes, peeled and cut into ¼-inch [6-mm.] slices	2
	salt and freshly ground pepper	
4	oil-packed flat anchovy fillets, drained and finely chopped	4
1 cup	chopped fresh flat-leafed parsley	¼ liter
¼ cup	chopped fresh basil leaves or 2 tbsp. [30 ml.] dried basil	50 ml.
2	garlic cloves	2
¼ cup	olive oil	50 ml.

Put the slices of eggplant on a large platter and sprinkle each slice with about ⅛ teaspoon [½ ml.] of salt. Let the slices stand at room temperature to draw out their excess moisture. Drain the eggplant slices and dry them between sheets of paper towels. Spread a little of the chopped anchovies on each tomato slice.

In a buttered shallow ovenproof dish, which can go to the table, or a pie plate (10 inches [25 cm.]), make overlapping rows of the slices of eggplant, hard-boiled egg, tomato and mozzarella, in that order. Sprinkle with very little salt (the eggplant slices and the anchovies are salty) and pepper.

Chop the parsley, basil and garlic together until they are finely minced. Sprinkle the mixture over the vegetables and cheese, and sprinkle everything with olive oil. Cover the dish with foil. Bake in a preheated 350° F. [180° C.] oven for 30 minutes. Remove the foil and bake for about 10 minutes longer, to let any excess moisture in the dish evaporate. The cheese should begin to brown. Serve hot, lukewarm or cold, but not chilled.

NIKA HAZELTON
THE REGIONAL ITALIAN KITCHEN

Baked Cheese, Shopski-Style

Pecheno Sirene po Shopski

Before use, the feta cheese should be rinsed and—for those who prefer less salty cheese—can be soaked in cold water for up to one hour. This recipe may be varied by the addition of

frankfurters, salami or broiled and peeled green peppers, diced and added to the bowls with the tomatoes.

To serve 4

¾ lb.	feta cheese, coarsely crumbled	⅓ kg.
2	medium-sized tomatoes, peeled and chopped	2
4 tbsp.	butter, sliced	60 ml.
8	eggs	8
	salt	
4	fresh hot chilies, green or red, stemmed and seeded	4
	paprika	

Butter four small earthenware ovenproof bowls and distribute the cheese among them. Put the chopped tomatoes over the cheese, then add half of the butter.

Bake the mixture on the top shelf of a preheated 400° F. [200° C.] oven for 10 to 12 minutes.

Whisk the eggs lightly with a pinch of salt and pour them over the tomato-and-cheese mixture. Into each bowl put a whole fresh chili. Add the remaining butter and sprinkle each bowl with a pinch of paprika. Bake for a further 10 to 15 minutes, or until the tops are a deep copper brown. Serve hot.

BULGARIAN CUISINE

Deep-fried Cheese Balls

Any cheese firm enough to grate, such as aged Cheddar or Gruyère, may be used for this dish. As an alternative to oil, the author suggests frying the cheese balls in ghee—the Indian version of clarified butter.

To serve 4 to 6

1 cup	grated cheese	¼ liter
1 cup	milk	¼ liter
1 cup	flour	¼ liter
6 tbsp.	butter	90 ml.
	salt	
1 tsp.	cayenne pepper	5 ml.
3	eggs, beaten	3
	oil for deep frying	
	tomato sauce (recipe, page 166, but double the quantities called for)	

In a large saucepan, warm the milk and gradually add the flour, stirring constantly so that no lumps are formed. Add the butter and, when the mixture thickens, remove it from the heat and add the cheese. Blend well. Add salt to taste, the cayenne pepper and the beaten eggs. When cool, the mixture should be thick enough to shape into balls.

Heat the oil to 350° F. [180° C.]. Make approximately 24 balls the size of a lemon from the mixture and drop a few of them at a time into the hot oil. Deep fry until the balls are a golden brown on all sides (about two minutes). Drain. Serve immediately with tomato sauce.

PREMILA LAL
THE EGG & CHEESE COOK-BOOK

Neapolitan Crepes

To serve 6

6 oz.	mozzarella cheese, thinly sliced	175 g.
⅔ cup	freshly grated Parmesan cheese	150 ml.
6	eggs, beaten	6
2 tbsp.	flour	30 ml.
⅓ cup	milk	75 ml.
	salt	
about 4 tbsp.	vegetable oil	about 60 ml.
	tomato sauce *(recipe, page 166)*	

In a bowl, mix the eggs with half of the milk. Mix the flour to a paste with the remaining milk, and stir the paste into the egg mixture. Add a pinch of salt.

Heat 1 tablespoon [15 ml.] of the oil in a crepe pan, and use the batter to make 12 thin crepes, cooking them on both sides until lightly browned. They must be wafer-thin, practically transparent. As they are fried, lay them on absorbent paper to drain. Add more oil to the pan as necessary.

Place a slice of cheese on each crepe. Roll it up. Arrange the rolls in a baking dish, packing them very tightly. Cover the rolls with the tomato sauce, sprinkle them with the grated Parmesan and bake in a preheated 350° F. [180° C.] oven for 30 minutes. Serve very hot.

SOPHIA LOREN
IN THE KITCHEN WITH LOVE

Cheese in Vine Leaves

The author does not specify what sort of cheese to use, but you will find any fairly firm well-flavored type suitable —Cheddar, Gouda, Swiss or goat's-milk cheese among them.

A recipe from the cave village of Trôo in the Bas Vendomois region of western France. This recipe can be used for any old end of cheese —it was a way of using up the last dried pieces —and in winter, pickled vine leaves make a good substitute for fresh. Buy them in jars or from the brine tub. Canned leaves are too tender. The fresh, slightly lemony taste of the vine leaves has a revivifying effect on the cheese.

In the old days, the packages went into the oven when the bread came out, to cook in the dying heat, and then to be eaten with the still-warm bread.

To serve 4

12	¾-inch [2-cm.] cheese cubes	12
12	vine leaves, fresh or pickled	12
12	slices bread, fresh or toasted in a 400° F. [200° C.] oven for 5 minutes	12

If using fresh leaves, just wash them and wrap them around the pieces of cheese. Place the little packages, seam side down, close together in an ovenproof dish. Put them in a preheated 450° F. [230° C.] oven for about 15 minutes, or until the leaves darken and stick slightly, and the whole thing feels soft when you press it. Serve on slices of bread.

For pickled leaves, pour boiling water over them, separate them carefully with a wooden spoon, and leave them for 20 to 30 minutes. Drain and cover them generously with cold water. Now taste a corner—if the leaves are not too sharply salty, they can be used. If they are still very strong, repeat the boiling water procedure. Wrap the leaves around the pieces of cheese and complete as above.

JANE GRIGSON
OBSERVER MAGAZINE

Gratin of Ricotta
Ricotta Gratinata

To serve 6

½ lb.	ricotta cheese (1 cup [¼ liter])	¼ kg.
1 cup	flour	¼ liter
1	egg	1
6 tbsp.	milk	90 ml.
	salt	
1 cup	finely chopped fresh parsley	¼ liter
2 oz.	prosciutto, diced (about ½ cup [125 ml.])	60 g.
1 oz.	salami, diced (about ¼ cup [50 ml.])	30 g.
2 tbsp.	butter, cut into small pieces	30 ml.
¼ cup	freshly grated Parmesan cheese	50 ml.

Mix the flour and the egg in a small earthenware bowl. Add the ricotta and dilute it with the milk, beating the mixture until it resembles a thick cream. Season it with a pinch of salt, and add the parsley, prosciutto and salami. Butter an 8-inch [20-cm.] gratin dish and pour in the ricotta mixture. Dot the top with the butter and sprinkle with the Parmesan. Bake the gratin in a preheated 375° F. [190° C.] oven for 20 minutes, or until it is firm and browned. Serve hot.

LUIGI VOLPICELLI AND SECONDINO FREDA
L'ANTIARTUSI: 1000 RICETTE

Cheese, Ham and Almond Croquettes

Delicias de Queso, Jamón y Almendras

To roast almonds, place blanched almonds on a baking sheet in a preheated 400° F. [200° C.] oven for 10 minutes, or until lightly browned.

To serve 4 to 6

2 cups	freshly grated Parmesan cheese	½ liter
3 oz.	ham, finely chopped (¾ cup [175 ml.])	100 g.
12	roasted blanched almonds, very thinly sliced	12
6	egg whites	6
	salt and pepper	
2 cups	fresh bread crumbs	½ liter
2	eggs, beaten (optional)	2
	butter	

Beat the egg whites until stiff. Fold the cheese, ham and almonds into the egg whites and season to taste. The mixture will be a very thick paste that can be easily shaped. Form the paste into small, round croquettes. Roll these in the bread crumbs, then the eggs, and again in the crumbs. (The egg coating may be omitted if desired.) Melt 2 tablespoons [30 ml.] of butter in a skillet and sauté the croquettes a few at a time until evenly browned. Drain the croquettes on paper towels. Serve at once, while they are hot and fresh.

NURI FONSECA
RECETAS DE AMERICA LATINA

Basic Cheeses

A recipe for basic farmer or pot cheese appears in Standard Preparations, page 166.

Curd or Cottage Cheese

If you wish to make this cheese with pasteurized milk, sour it by adding to it 1 cup [¼ liter] of distilled white vinegar or strained fresh lemon juice. The technique of draining curd cheese is demonstrated on pages 10-11.

Some cooks mash and rub the cheese thoroughly with the cream; others dress it with sugar, cream and a little nutmeg, omitting the salt and pepper. Another way is to chop fine,

add salt to taste, work in a very little cream or butter, and mold into round balls.

To make about 2 pounds [1 kg.] cheese

1 gallon	raw milk, soured	4 liters
	salt and pepper	
2½ cups	heavy cream	625 ml.

Set the milk over the lowest possible heat or in an oven at its lowest setting, leaving the door open.

As the curd begins to separate from the whey, cut it into squares with a knife. Stir gently now and then until it is about as warm as the finger will bear and the whey shows all around the curd.

Pour all into a coarse bag, and hang to drain in a cool place for three or four hours, or overnight if made in the evening. When wanted, turn from the bag, chop the cheese rather coarse with a knife, and dress it with salt, pepper and the cream.

THE BUCKEYE COOKBOOK

A Strong Potted Cheese

Foudjou

This recipe is from the lower Ardèche. Traditionally the cheese pot is never emptied, and a great connoisseur, native to the region, describes knowing a house where the bottom of such a *brêch* —or pot—had not been seen for 15 years. Eat this cheese with hot potatoes, boiled in their jackets and peeled as you eat them.

To make 2 pounds [1 kg.] cheese

1 lb.	fresh goat cheese, mashed to a paste	½ kg.
1 lb.	dried goat cheese with the rind removed, grated, and forced through a sieve or the fine disk of a food mill	½ kg.
3 tbsp.	brandy	50 ml.
3 tbsp.	olive oil	50 ml.
	pepper	
2 or 3	garlic cloves, crushed to a paste and sieved	2 or 3
	salt	
2 tbsp.	mixed dried herbs, pulverized (thyme, marjoram, oregano, savory)	30 ml.

Put the fresh and dried cheeses in a bowl and sprinkle the brandy and olive oil over them. Season the mixture well with pepper and add the garlic. Add the salt and herbs, and knead the mixture until it is well blended. Put it in a pot with a lid, cover it and let it mature for two to three months in a cool place before opening it.

PIERRE ANDROUET
LA CUISINE AU FROMAGE

Cream Cheese

Heavy cream that is not ultrapasteurized is available at health-food stores. Rennet tablets are sold at health-food stores and some supermarkets.

To make about 1 ½ cups [375 ml.] cheese

1 quart	whole milk	1 liter
1 cup	heavy cream (not ultrapasteurized)	¼ liter
¼ cup	buttermilk	50 ml.
1	rennet tablet	1
1 tbsp.	water	15 ml.
¼ tsp.	salt	1 ml.

Combine the milk, cream and buttermilk in a stainless-steel, enameled or flameproof-glass saucepan. Warm the mixture over low heat, stirring, until its temperature registers 100° F. [38° C.] on an instant-response thermometer, or until a few drops on the inside of your wrist feel neither cool nor warm. Remove from the heat.

Dissolve the rennet tablet in the water. Add the rennet to the milk mixture, stirring for one minute. Cover the pot and let it rest undisturbed at room temperature for 16 to 24 hours, or until a firm curd has formed. At this stage there will be an ample amount of clear, faintly yellowish liquid (whey) over and around a solid-appearing cake of curd.

Line a fine-meshed sieve with two layers of dampened cheesecloth (or, better yet, fine-meshed nylon curtain netting) cut large enough to be tied into a bag later. Set the sieve over a bowl and ladle into it first the whey, then the curd. Let the mixture drain until only an occasional drop of whey falls into the bowl. The curd will still be quite soft.

Tie the corners of the cloth to make a bag and hang it over a bowl or the sink to drain for a few hours (contrive a way to hang it in the refrigerator if the weather is hot). Work in a little salt, then refrigerate the cheese in a covered bowl; it will be fairly soft. Alternatively, if you want a firmer consistency, fold the ends of the cloth over the cheese in the sieve, then cover the cheese with a saucer or small plate. Set the sieve over a bowl that will fit in the refrigerator and weight the plate with an object weighing about a pound [½ kg.]. Refrigerate. Double the weight after a few hours and let the cheese drain overnight, or until it is as firm as you like.

Remove the cheese from the cloth and work in a little more salt. Either pack it into a bowl and cover it with plastic wrap, or mold it as follows: Line a small wicker basket, a bowl, a large, flat-bottomed cup or a small *coeur à la crème* mold with cheesecloth. Pack in the cheese and fold the cloth over it. Set the basket or *coeur* mold upright on a small plate, or invert the bowl or cup on a plate covered with folded paper towels (this will facilitate a little further draining). Wrap the mold and plate in plastic wrap and refrigerate.

To unmold, lift the cheese by the wrapping, peel back the cloth and invert the cheese onto a serving dish. The cheese will be at its best for three days, though it will keep longer.

HELEN WITTY AND ELIZABETH SCHNEIDER COLCHIE
BETTER THAN STORE-BOUGHT

Lancaster County Egg Cheese

To serve 8

6	eggs, beaten	6
2 cups	buttermilk	½ liter
1 tsp.	salt	5 ml.
2 tsp.	sugar	10 ml.
2 quarts	milk, warmed	2 liters

Add to the beaten eggs the buttermilk, salt and sugar. Beat lightly and pour the mixture into the warmed milk. Cover the pan and let it stand for several minutes over medium-low heat, stirring only occasionally.

Remove the lid and watch for the curds (the cheese) and the whey to separate. Immediately spoon the curds gently into a pierced mold, using a slotted spoon. Balance the mold on a bowl into which the liquid can drip and let the curds cool and drain. It is the gentle spooning into the mold that prevents the cheese from getting solid and heavy. If you drop the curds into a sieve, the cheese will get as heavy as lead. The curds should be removed very delicately from the pan and just laid in the mold.

When cold and drained, unmold the cheese onto a dish and serve it with bread and molasses.

JOSÉ WILSON AND BETTY GROFF
GOOD EARTH & COUNTRY COOKING

Farmer or Pot Cheese with Herbs

Cervelle de Canut

To serve 6 to 8

1 lb.	farmer or pot cheese, well beaten	½ kg.
2 cups	fines herbes	½ liter
2	shallots, very finely chopped	2
1	garlic clove, crushed to a paste	1
	salt and pepper	
¼ cup	heavy cream (optional)	50 ml.
2 tbsp.	dry white wine (optional)	30 ml.
2 tbsp.	oil (optional)	30 ml.
1 tsp.	vinegar (optional)	5 ml.

Beat the herbs, shallots, garlic, salt and pepper to taste into the cheese. If desired, beat in the cream, wine, oil and/or vinegar. To serve, form the cheese into a round on a plate. Tightly covered and refrigerated, it will keep for several days, becoming more strongly flavored the longer it stands.

FÉLIX BENOIT AND HENRY CLOS JOUVE
LA CUISINE LYONNAISE

Ricotta

Although ricotta is traditionally made with whey or a mixture of whey and milk, this whole-milk version is more practical for the modern cook.

Unlike most fresh cheeses—cottage and cream cheese, for example—the curd of this bland, light cheese is formed by the addition of acid to the milk, not by fermentation. For that reason, the time required to make it is generally short. Try this Italian favorite in place of cottage cheese, as well as in Italian recipes for such dishes as lasagne and manicotti. You'll find it is a bit creamier than most cottage cheeses, with a much finer curd.

For a pleasant light milk dessert, sweeten this ricotta slightly and sprinkle with grated chocolate or cinnamon.

To make about 1 pound [½ kg.] cheese

2 quarts	milk	2 liters
3 tbsp.	distilled white vinegar or ¼ cup [50 ml.] strained fresh lemon juice	45 ml.
	salt (optional)	

Pour the milk into a heavy stainless-steel or enameled saucepan and stir in the white vinegar or lemon juice. Set the pan over very low heat and bring the milk very slowly to the simmer (a reading of 200° F. [95° C.] on a thermometer). There will be fine beads around the edge of the milk, which will look foamy but will not appear to be boiling.

Remove the pan from the heat and set it, covered, in a spot where it can remain undisturbed and where the temperature will remain between 80° and 100° F. [25° and 40° C.]. (An unheated oven, without a pilot light, is a good spot.) Let the milk stand for about six hours, or until a solid curd floats above the liquid (the whey). More or less time may be required, depending on the temperature of the environment and the characteristics of the milk.

Line a fine sieve with doubled, dampened cheesecloth (or, better yet, two layers of very fine-meshed nylon curtain netting, dampened) and set it over a bowl. Ladle the curds and whey into the sieve and allow the whey to drain off until the ricotta is as thick as yogurt. If you want firmer cheese, tie the corners of the cloth to form a bag and hang it up to drain further. (In warm weather, the draining might well be completed in the refrigerator.)

When the texture of the ricotta is to your liking, add a little salt (from ¼ to ½ teaspoon [1 to 2 ml.]) if you wish. Store the cheese, covered, in the refrigerator. It will be at its best after it has been chilled for at least 24 hours, and it will keep well for four to five days.

HELEN WITTY AND ELIZABETH SCHNEIDER COLCHIE
BETTER THAN STORE-BOUGHT

Standard Preparations

Court Bouillon

To make 1 ½ quarts [1 ½ liters] court bouillon

1½ quarts	water	1½ liters
2	onions, thinly sliced	2
2	carrots, thinly sliced	2
1	bouquet garni	1
1 tbsp.	salt	15 ml.
1 cup	dry white wine (optional)	¼ liter

In a large saucepan, boil the water with the onions, carrots and bouquet garni for 10 to 15 minutes. Add the salt, and the wine if desired, and continue to cook for another 15 minutes. Before using the court bouillon, strain it through a sieve set into a bowl or clean pan.

Basic Meat Stock

This stock may be made, according to your taste and recipe needs, from beef, veal, pork or chicken—or a combination of these meats. For the beef, use such cuts as shank, short ribs, chuck and oxtail; for the veal, use neck, shank and rib tips; for the pork, use hocks, Boston shoulder and back ribs; for the chicken, use backs, necks, wings and carcasses. Adding gelatinous elements such as calf's feet, pig's feet or pork rind will make the finished stock set to a clear, firm jelly that can serve as an aspic if prepared carefully enough.

To make about 2 quarts [2 liters] stock

4 to 5 lb.	meat, bones and trimmings of beef, veal, pork or chicken	2 to 2½ kg.
1 lb.	pig's, calf's or chicken feet, pig's ears or fresh pork rind (optional)	½ kg.
3 to 4 quarts	water	3 to 4 liters
4	carrots	4
2	large onions, 1 stuck with 2 or 3 whole cloves	2
1	rib celery	1
1	leek, split and washed	1
1	large bouquet garni	1

Put the pieces of bone on a rack in the bottom of a heavy stockpot, and place the meat and trimmings on top of them.

Add cold water to cover by 2 inches [5 cm.]. Bring to a boil over low heat, starting to skim before the liquid comes to a boil—this may take one hour. Keep skimming, occasionally adding a glass of cold water, until no scum rises—this may take up to 30 minutes. Do not stir, lest you cloud the stock.

Add the vegetables and bouquet garni to the pot, pushing them down into the liquid so that everything is submerged. Continue skimming until the liquid again reaches a boil. Reduce the heat to very low, partially cover the pan, and cook undisturbed at a bare simmer for two hours if you are using only chicken trimmings, otherwise for five hours.

Skim off the surface fat. Then strain the stock by pouring the contents of the pot through a colander into a large bowl or clean pot. Discard the bones and meat trimmings, vegetables and bouquet garni. Cool the strained stock and remove the last traces of fat from the surface with a folded piece of paper towel. If there is any residue at the bottom of the container after the stock cools, pour the clear liquid slowly into another container and discard the sediment.

Refrigerate the stock if you do not plan to use it immediately; it will keep safely for three to four days. To preserve the stock longer, refrigerate it for only 12 hours—or until the last bits of fat solidify on the top—then scrape off the fat and warm the stock enough so that it may be poured into four or five pint-sized freezer containers. Be sure to leave room in the containers to allow for expansion, and cover the containers tightly. The freezer stock will keep for six months while you draw on the supply as necessary.

Basic White Sauce

Use this recipe whenever béchamel sauce is required.

To make about 1 ½ cups [375 ml.] sauce

2 tbsp.	butter	30 ml.
2 tbsp.	flour	30 ml.
2 cups	milk	½ liter
	salt	
	white pepper	
	grated nutmeg (optional)	
	heavy cream (optional)	

Melt the butter in a heavy saucepan. Stir in the flour and cook, stirring, over low heat for two to five minutes. Pour in all of the milk at once, whisking constantly to blend the mixture smoothly. Raise the heat and continue whisking while the sauce comes to a boil. Season with very little salt. Reduce the heat to very low and simmer for about 40 minutes, stirring every so often to prevent the sauce from sticking to the bottom of the pan.

When the sauce thickens to the desired consistency, add white pepper and a pinch of nutmeg if desired; taste for seasoning. Whisk again until the sauce is perfectly smooth, then add cream if you prefer a richer and whiter sauce.

Velouté Sauce

To make 1 ½ to 2 quarts [1 ½ to 2 liters] sauce

4 tbsp.	butter	60 ml.
¼ cup	flour	50 ml.
2 quarts	veal or chicken stock	2 liters

Melt the butter in a heavy saucepan over low heat and stir in the flour until this roux mixture is smooth. Cook, stirring constantly, for two to three minutes. When the roux stops foaming and is a light golden color, pour in the stock and whisk continuously until the mixture reaches a boil. Move the saucepan half off the heat, so that the liquid on one side of the pan maintains a steady, but very light, boil. Skim off fat and impurities that form on the surface of the other, calm side of the liquid. From time to time spoon off the skin. Cook for 30 minutes, or until the sauce is the desired consistency.

Hollandaise Sauce

This sauce can be turned into a mousseline sauce by the addition of cream. Whip ¾ cup [175 ml.] heavy cream until foamy but not stiff, and stir it into the prepared hollandaise sauce, off the heat.

To make about 1 cup [¼ liter] sauce

3	egg yolks	3
1 tbsp.	cold water	15 ml.
16 tbsp.	cold unsalted butter (½ lb. [¼ kg.]), finely diced	240 ml.
	salt and white pepper	
	cayenne pepper	
1 tsp.	strained fresh lemon juice	5 ml.

Pour water to a depth of about 1 inch [2½ cm.] into the bottom of a double boiler, or a large saucepan or fireproof casserole if you are making a bain-marie. Heat the water until it simmers, then reduce the heat to low. Place the top of the double boiler over the bottom; or set a rack or trivet into the water bath and place the saucepan on the rack or trivet. Put the egg yolks and the cold water in the upper pan and beat the yolks until smooth. Whisk a handful of the butter into the yolks and beat until the butter has been absorbed; continue adding diced butter in this way until all of it has been used. Beat until the sauce becomes thick and creamy. Season the sauce to taste with salt, white pepper and cayenne pepper. Then add the lemon juice.

Tomato Sauce

When fresh ripe tomatoes are not available, use 3 cups [¾ liter] of drained, canned Italian plum tomatoes.

To make about 1 cup [¼ liter] sauce

6	medium-sized ripe tomatoes, chopped	6
1	onion, diced	1
1 tbsp.	olive oil	15 ml.
1	garlic clove (optional)	1
1 tsp.	chopped fresh parsley	5 ml.
1 tsp.	mixed dried basil, marjoram and thyme	5 ml.
1 to 2 tbsp.	sugar (optional)	15 to 30 ml.
	salt and freshly ground pepper	

In a large enameled or stainless-steel saucepan, gently fry the diced onion in the oil until soft, but not brown. Add the other ingredients and simmer for 20 to 30 minutes, or until the tomatoes have been reduced to a thick pulp. Sieve the mixture, using a wooden pestle or spoon. Reduce the sauce further, if necessary, to reach the required consistency. Adjust the seasoning.

Olive and Anchovy Sauce

Tapenade

This highly flavored mixture has many variations. If you wish, you can pound in thyme or powdered bay leaf, garlic cloves or tuna, or stir in a small amount of Cognac. If desired, the mixture may be prepared in a food processor.

To make about 1 cup [¼ liter] sauce

½ cup	pitted ripe oil-packed olives, coarsely chopped	125 ml.
2	salt anchovies, filleted, soaked in water for 30 minutes, patted dry and coarsely chopped	2
¼ cup	capers, rinsed and drained	50 ml.
about ¼ cup	olive oil	about 50 ml.
2 to 3 tsp.	fresh lemon juice	10 to 15 ml.
	freshly ground pepper	
1 tsp.	dry mustard (optional)	5 ml.

In a large mortar, pound together the olives, anchovies and capers until they form a paste. Little by little, stir in enough oil to make a sauce of rather firm consistency. Then season the mixture with the lemon juice, pepper to taste, and dry mustard if you are using it.

Creamed Spinach

This preparation may be used as the basis for a gratin of hard-boiled eggs or as a filling for layered omelets. To make a similar dish of creamed sorrel, the sorrel should be coarsely chopped and then sautéed in the butter—parboiling is not necessary if tender young leaves are used.

To serve 4 to 6

2 lb.	spinach, stemmed	1 kg.
2 tbsp.	butter	30 ml.
½ cup	heavy cream	125 ml.
	salt and pepper	
	grated nutmeg	

Bring a large pot of water to a boil, plunge in the spinach and parboil it for two minutes. Drain the spinach in a colander, running cold water over it to stop the cooking. With your hands, squeeze out the excess moisture. Chop the spinach. Over medium heat, melt the butter and stir in the chopped spinach. Stir until any excess moisture has evaporated. Reduce the heat. Stir in the cream, being careful not to let the mixture boil. Season with salt, pepper and a little nutmeg.

Basic Farmer or Pot Cheese

The demonstration on pages 10-11 shows how to gauge the temperature of milk for cheese making with a dairy thermometer. The quantities given in this recipe may be halved or quartered, and finished cheese may be flavored in a variety of ways. You can add chopped garlic and mixed fresh herbs, or grated lemon peel or crushed green peppercorns. A small cheese shaped into a cake or cylinder may be rolled in paprika or cracked black pepper, or wrapped in vine leaves. Small cheeses may be shaped in perforated cheese molds:

Spoon the drained curd into the molds, salt the surface and drain the cheese until it is firm enough to be unmolded. The cheeses then may be flavored or wrapped, or left to ripen on layers of straw—turned and salted every day—for several days, or until the desired degree of ripeness is achieved.

The unflavored cheese may, of course, be used in any of the Anthology recipes calling for cottage cheese. If the mixture is beaten until smooth, it may be used in any recipe calling for farmer or pot cheese.

To make 2 to 2½ pounds [1 to 1¼ kg.] cheese

4½ quarts	milk	4½ liters
2 tbsp.	buttermilk	30 ml.
	salt	

In a saucepan set in a larger pan of hot water, slowly heat the milk to a temperature of 80° F. [27° C.], then add the buttermilk. Stir thoroughly, cover the milk and let it stand for up to 24 hours at a room temperature of 65° to 70° F. [18° to 21° C.]. If the curd has not set, put the milk pan in a larger pan of tepid water and let it stand, covered, for two hours.

When the curd forms a mass that can be seen to be separate from the surrounding clear whey, line a large colander with dry cheesecloth. Pour in the curd and drain it for five hours. Then pull up the corners of the cloth, tie them tightly and hang up the resulting bag to allow the curd to drain thoroughly. After six to eight hours, or longer depending on the degree of firmness you want, salt the curd to taste, and flavor it if you wish. Beating will make the curd creamier.

Croutons

You can substitute olive oil or clarified butter for the combination of butter and oil specified in this recipe.

To make about 1 cup [¼ liter] croutons

2	bread slices, ½ inch [1 cm.] thick, cut from a day-old, firm-textured white loaf	2
4 tbsp.	butter	60 ml.
¼ to ½ cup	oil	50 to 125 ml.

Remove the crusts from the bread and cut the slices into cubes. Combine the butter and ¼ cup [50 ml.] of the oil in a large skillet. Melt the butter over medium heat and, as soon as the butter-and-oil mixture is hot, add the bread cubes and increase the heat to high. Turn the cubes frequently on all sides, and add more oil as necessary to keep the cubes from burning. The croutons will be done in about two or three minutes. Before serving, drain the croutons on paper towels.

Short-Crust and Rough Puff Pastry

One simple formula produces dough for both plain short-crust pastry and for rough puff pastry. The difference is in how you roll it out.

To make enough pastry for an 8- to 10-inch [20- to 25-cm.] pie shell or about twelve 3-inch [8-cm.] tart shells

1½ cups	flour	375 ml.
¼ tsp.	salt	1 ml.
12 tbsp.	cold unsalted butter, cut into small pieces	180 ml.
4 to 6 tbsp.	cold water	60 to 90 ml.

Mix the flour and salt in a mixing bowl. Add the butter and cut it into the flour rapidly, using two table knives, until the butter is in tiny pieces. Do not work for more than a few minutes. Add half the water and, with a fork, quickly blend it into the flour-and-butter mixture. Add just enough of the rest of the water to allow you to gather the dough together with your hands into a firm ball. Wrap the dough in plastic wrap or wax paper and refrigerate it for two to three hours, or put it in the freezer for 20 minutes until the outside surface is slightly frozen.

To roll out short-crust pastry: Remove the ball of pastry dough from the refrigerator or freezer and put it on a cool, floured surface (a marble slab is ideal). Press the dough out partially with your hand, then give it a few gentle smacks with the rolling pin to flatten it and render it more supple. Roll out the dough from the center until the pastry forms a circle about ½ inch [1 cm.] thick. Turn the pastry over so that both sides are floured and continue rolling until the circle is about ⅛ inch [3 mm.] thick.

To roll out rough puff pastry: Place the dough on a cool, floured surface and smack it flat with the rolling pin. Turn the dough over to make sure that both sides are well floured. Roll out the pastry rapidly into a rectangle about 1 foot [30 cm.] long and 5 to 6 inches [13 to 15 cm.] wide. Fold the two short ends to meet each other in the center, then fold again to align the folded edges with each other. Following the direction of the fold lines, roll the pastry into a rectangle again, fold again in the same way and refrigerate for at least 30 minutes. Repeat this process two or three more times before rolling the pastry into a circle about ⅛ inch thick as described above for short-crust pastry. Always let the pastry dough rest in the refrigerator between rollings.

Recipe Index

All recipes in the index that follows are listed by English titles except in cases where a dish of foreign origin, such as blintzes, is universally recognized by its source name. Entries are organized in separate categories for eggs and cheese and also by major ingredients specified in recipe titles. Fillings and sauces are listed separately. Foreign recipes are listed under the country or region of origin. Recipe credits appear on pages 174-176.

General Index/ Glossary

Included in this index to the cooking demonstrations are definitions, in italics, of special culinary terms not explained elsewhere in this volume. The Recipe Index begins on page 168.

Recipe Credits

The sources for the recipes in this volume are shown below. Page references in parentheses indicate where the recipes appear in the anthology.

Allen, Ida Bailey, *Best Loved Recipes of the American People.* Copyright © 1973 by Ruth Allen Castelli. Reprinted by permission of Doubleday & Company, Inc.(99).

Allen, Jana and Margaret Gin, *Offal.* © Jana Allen and Margaret Gin, 1974. © Pitman Publishing 1976. Published in Great Britain 1976. First published in the United States 1974 by 101 Productions as *Innards and Other Variety Meats.* By permission of 101 Productions(119).

American Heritage, the editors of, *The American Heritage Cookbook.* © 1964 American Heritage Publishing Co., Inc., New York. Published by American Heritage Publishing Co., Inc. By permission of American Heritage Publishing Co., Inc.(131).

Anderson, Beth, *Wild Rice for All Seasons Cookbook.* © 1977 Minnehaha Publishing. Published by Minnehaha Publishing, 1977. By permission of Beth Anderson and Minnehaha Publishing, Minnesota(118).

Androuët, Pierre, *La Cuisine au Fromage.* © 1978, Éditions Stock. Published by Editions Stock, Paris. By permission of Éditions Stock(144, 157, 159, 162).

Artusi, Pellegrino, *La Scienza in Cucina e l'Arte di Mangiar Bene.* Copyright © 1970 Giulio Einaudi Editore S.p.A., Torino. Published by Giulio Einaudi Editore S.p.A., Torino(107, 122, 130).

Aylett, Mary, *Country Fare.* © Mary Aylett, 1956. Published by Odhams Press Limited, London 1956. By permission of David Higham Associates Ltd., London, for the author(138).

Beard, James, *How to Eat Better for Less Money.* Copyright © 1954, 1970 by James A. Beard and Sam Aaron. Reprinted by permission of Simon & Schuster, a division of Gulf & Western Corporation(136).

Beebe, Ruth Anne, *Sallets, Humbles, & Shrewsberry Cakes: An Elizabethan Cookbook.* Copyright © 1976 by permission of David R. Godine, Inc.(92).

Benoit, Félix and Henry Clos Jouve, *La Cuisine Lyonnaise.* © Solar, 1975. Published by Solar, Paris. Translated by permission of Solar(124, 163).

Bisson, Marie, *La Cuisine Normande.* © Solar, 1978. Published by Solar, Paris. Translated by permission of Solar(108, 114, 128).

Boni, Ada, *Italian Regional Cooking.* Copyright © 1969 s.c. Arnoldo Mondadori. English translation copyright © 1969 s.c. by Thomas Nelson & Sons Ltd., and E. P. Dutton and Co., Inc. Published by Bonanza Books, a division of Crown Publishers, Inc., New York. By permission of Arnoldo Mondadori Editore, Milan(147).

Borer, Eva Maria, *Tante Heidi's Swiss Kitchen.* English text copyright © 1965 by Nicholas Kaye Ltd. Published by Kaye & Ward Ltd., London. Originally published as *Die Echte Schweizer Küche* by Mary Hahns Kochbuchverlag, Berlin W., 1963. By permission of Kaye & Ward Ltd.(137, 152, 154).

Botti, Ferruccio (Mastro Prosciutto), *Gastronomia Parmense ossia Parma Capitale dei Buongustai.* Fourth Edition. Published by Scuola Tipografica Benedettina, Parma, 1963. Translated by permission of Scuola Tipografica Benedettina(111, 148).

Bouillard, Paul, *La Cuisine au Coin du Feu.* Copyright 1928 by Albin Michel. Published by Éditions Albin Michel, Paris. Translated by permission of Éditions Albin Michel(107). *La Gourmandise à Bon Marché.* Copyright 1925 by Albin Michel. Published by Éditions Albin Michel, Paris. Translated by permission of Éditions Albin Michel(107).

Boulestin, Marcel and Robin Adair, *One Hundred and Twenty Ways of Cooking Eggs.* Published by William Heinemann Ltd., London 1956. By permission of William Heinemann Ltd.(115).

Boulestin, X. M. and A. H. Adair, *Savouries and Hors-d'Oeuvre.* Published by William Heinemann Ltd., London 1932. By permission of William Heinemann Ltd.(117).

Boulestin, X. Marcel, *A Second Helping or More Dishes for English Homes.* Published by William Heinemann Ltd., London 1928. By permission of A. D. Peters & Co. Ltd., London(135). *Simple French Cooking for English Homes.* Published by William Heinemann Ltd., London 1923. By permission of A. D. Peters & Co. Ltd., London(126).

Brazier, Eugénie, *Les Secrets de la Mère Brazier.* © Solar, 1977. Published by Solar Éditeur, Paris. Translated by permission of Solar(108, 120, 139).

Breteuil, Jules, *Le Cuisinier Européen.* Published by Garnier Frères Libraires-Éditeurs c. 1860(102).

Břízová, Joza and Maryna Klimentová, *Tschechische Küche.* Published by Verlag Práce, Prague and Verlag für die Frau, Leipzig. Translated by permission of Práce, Prague(156).

Brown, Bob, *The Complete Book of Cheese.* © Copyright 1955 by Robert Carlton Brown. Published by Random House, Inc., New York. By permission of Random House, Inc.(154).

Brown, Helen, *Helen Brown's West Coast Cook Book.* Copyright 1952 by Helen Evans Brown. Published by Little, Brown and Company, Boston. By permission of Little, Brown and Company(127, 135).

Brown, Michèle, *Food by Appointment.* Copyright © 1977 by Michèle Brown. Published by Elm Tree Books, London. By permission of Hamish Hamilton Ltd., London(143).

Buckeye Cookbook, The: Traditional American Recipes. As published by the Buckeye Publishing Co., 1883. Published by Dover Publications, Inc., New York 1975(162).

Bugialli, Giuliano, *The Fine Art of Italian Cooking.* Copyright © 1977 by Giuliano Bugialli. Published by Times Books, a division of Quadrangle/The New York Times Book Co., Inc., New York. By permission of Times Books, a division of Quadrangle/The New York Times Book Co., Inc.(97, 127).

Bulgarian Cuisine. Published by the Tourist Publicity Centre, Sofia. By permission of the Balkan Tourist Publicity Centre, Sofia, c/o Jusautor, Sofia(160).

Burros, Marian, *Pure and Simple.* Copyright © 1978 by Marian Fox Burros. By permission of William Morrow & Company(131).

Calera, Ana-Maria, *365 Recetas de Cocina Vasca.* © Ana-Maria Calera. © Editorial Everest. Published by Editorial Everest, S.A., Leon. Translated by permission of Editorial Everest(112, 118).

Castle, Coralie & Barbara Lawrence, *Hors D'Oeuvre etc.* Copyright 1973. Published by 101 Productions. By permission of 101 Productions, San Francisco(146, 149).

Cavalcanti, Ippolito, Duca di Buonvincino, *Cucina Teorico-Pratica.* Second Edition 1839. Fifth Edition 1847. Naples(94).

Chamberlain, Narcissa, *The Omelette Book.* Published by The Cookery Book Club, London 1967. Originally published by Sidgwick & Jackson Limited, London 1956. By permission of Sidgwick & Jackson Ltd.(122, 128).

Chanot-Bullier, C., *Vieilles Recettes de Cuisine Provençale.* Published by Tacussel, Éditeur, Marseille. Translated by permission of Tacussel, Éditeur(126).

Chortanova, Sonya, *Nasha Kuchniya.* Published by Nauki I Izkustvo, Sofia 1955. Translated by permission of Jusautor Copyright Agency, Bulgaria(158).

Comas, Maria Dolores, *The Best of Spanish Cooking.* © Geocolor S.A., 1979. Published by Geocolor S.A. Barcelona. By permission of Geocolor S.A.(129).

Conrad-Bateman, Ruth, *I Love to Cook Book.* Copyright © 1962. Published by the Ward Ritchie Press, Los Angeles(109).

Cordon Bleu, Le. Published by Le Cordon Bleu de Paris, 1932. Translated by permission of Le Cordon Bleu de Paris(92, 134, 136).

Corrado, Vincenzo, *Il Cuoco Galante.* Published in Naples 1820(96, 122).

Courtine, Robert, *Mes Repas les Plus Étonnants.* © 1973 Éditions Robert Laffont, S.A. Published by Éditions Robert Laffont, Paris. Translated by permission of Robert Courtine, Bois-Colombes(119).

Cuisine Lyonnaise, La. Published by Éditions Gutenberg, 1947(102).

Cuoco Piemontese Ridotto all'Ultimo Gusto, Il. Published in Milano 1828(94, 115, 123).

Cutler, Carol, *The Six-Minute Soufflé and Other Culinary Delights.* Copyright © 1976 by Carol Cutler. Published by Crown Publishers Inc., New York. By permission of Crown Publishers Inc.(143).

Dannenbaum, Julie, *Menus for All Occasions.* Copyright © 1974 by Julie Dannenbaum. Published by Saturday Review Press/E. P. Dutton & Co., Inc., New York. By permission of John Schaffner, Literary Agent, New York(142).

David, Elizabeth, *English Bread & Yeast Cookery.* Copyright © 1977 by Elizabeth David. Reprinted by permission of Viking Penguin Inc.(144). *French Country Cooking.* Copyright © Elizabeth David 1951, 1958, 1966. Published by Penguin Books Ltd., London. By permission of Penguin Books Ltd.(95).

Davidson, Alan, *North Atlantic Seafood.* Copyright © Alan Davidson, 1979. Reprinted by permission of Viking Penguin Inc.(137).

De Bourbon, Louis Auguste, *Le Cuisinier Gascon.* Published by permission of Éditions Daniel Marcrette, Luzarches, 1740. Translated by permission of Éditions Daniel Marcrette(125).

De Crémonne, Baptiste Platine, *Le Livre de l'Honneste Volupté.* Published in 1539(145).

de Bonnefons, Nicholas, *Les Délices de la Campagne.* (1655)(104).

De Gouy, Louis P., *The Gold Cook Book.* © 1948, 1964 by the author. Published by Chilton Book Company, Radnor, Pennsylvania. By permission of Chilton Book Company(141).

De la Chapelle, Vincent, *The Modern Cook.* London, 1733(93, 110).

De Lazarque, E. Auricoste, *Cuisine Messine.* Published by Sidot Frères, Libraires-Éditeurs, 1927(100).

De Lune, Pierre, *Le Nouveau Cuisinier.* Paris, 1656(129, 137).

De Périgord, A. B., *Le Trésor de la Cuisinière et de la Maîtresse de Maison.* Published by Garnier Frères, Paris, 1852(96).

De Pomiane, Édouard, *Cooking with Pomiane.* © 1976 Bruno Cassirer. Published by Bruno Cassirer (Publisher) Ltd., Oxford. By permission of Bruno Cassirer (Publisher) Ltd.(151).

Derys, Gaston, *Les Plats au Vin.* Copyright 1937 by Albin Michel. Published by Éditions Albin Michel, Paris. Translated by permission of Éditions Albin Michel(104-105).

De Zuliani, Mariu Salvatori, *La Cucina di Versilla E. Garfagnana.* Copyright © by Franco Angeli Editore, Milano. Published by Franco Angeli Editore, Milan 1969. Translated by permission of Franco Angeli Editore(95).

Dods, Mistress Margaret, *The Cook and Housewife's Manual.* Originally published in 1826 by Oliver and Boyd, Edinburgh(152).

Dubois, Urbain and Émile Bernard, *La Cuisine Classique.* Published by E. Dentu, Éditeur, Palais-Royal, Paris 1882(150).

Duff, Gail, *Gail Duff's Vegetarian Cookbook.* © Gail Duff 1978. Published by Macmillan London Limited, 1978. By permission of Macmillan, London and Basingstoke(109).

Durand, Charles, *Le Cuisinier Durand.* Privately published by the author, Nîmes, 1863(130).

Elles, Frederick and Sacha Sosno, *99 Omelettes Originales.* © Librairie Artheme Fayard, 1976. Published by Librairie Artheme Fayard, Paris. Translated by permission of Librarie Artheme Fayard(119, 123).

L'Escole Parfaite des Officiers de Bouche. Published by Jean Ribou, Paris, 1662(121, 130).

Famularo, Joe and Louise Imperiale, *The Festive Famularo Kitchen.* Copyright © 1977 by Joe Famularo and Louise Imperiale. Published by Atheneum Publishers, New York 1977. By permission of Atheneum Publishers(148).

Field, Michael, *Cooking Adventures with Michael Field.* © 1972. Published by Nelson Doubleday, Inc., Garden City,

New York. Reprinted by permission of Jonathan Rude-Field (120).

Filippini, Maria Nunzia, *La Cuisine Corse.* Published by Société d'Éditions: Serena, Ajaccio 1978. Translated by permission of Société d'Éditions: Serena(120).

Fonseca, Nuri, *Latinoamerica en su Cocina.* © 1977 Editorial Concepto, S.A. Av. Cuauhtémoc 1434, Mexico 13, D.F.(106, 121). *Recetas de America Latina.* © 1978 Editorial Concepto, S.A. Av. Cuauhtémoc 1434, Mexico 13, D.F.(92, 162).

Foods of the World/The Cooking of Provincial France. Copyright © 1968. Published by Time-Life Books, Inc. Alexandria(146).

Francesconi, Jeanne Caròla, *La Cucina Napoletana.* Copyright 1965 by Casa Editrice Fausto Fiorentino, Napoli. Published by Casa Editrice Fausto Fiorentino, Naples, 1965. Translated by permission of Jeanne Caròla Francesconi(155).

Froud, Nina, *The World Book of Egg & Cheese Dishes.* Copyright 1967 by permission of Horizon Press, New York, New York(134, 139).

Gilbert, Philéas, *La Cuisine de Tous les Mois.* Published by Abel Goubaud, Éditeur, Paris, 1893(135).

Gotlieb, Sondra, *The Gourmet's Canada.* Copyright © 1972 by Sondra Gotlieb. Published by New Press, Toronto. By permission of Sondra Gotlieb(139).

Grigson, Jane, *Food with the Famous.* © 1979 by Jane Grigson. Published by Michael Joseph, London. By permission of David Higham Associates Limited, for the author(155). *Observer Magazine,* October 1977. By permission of Jane Grigson(161).

Guggenbühl, Helen (Editor), *The Swiss Cookery Book.* Copyright by Guggenbühl & Huber Schweizer Spiegel Verlag AG, Zurich 1967. Published by Schweizer Spiegel Verlag AG. By permission of Schweizer Spiegel Verlag AG(153).

Hanson, Shirley M. (Editor), *Food for Thought.* © 1961 Shirley M. Hanson. Published by The Lincolnshire Old Churches Trust, The Subdeanery, Lincoln. By permission of The Lincolnshire Old Churches Trust(106, 143).

Hartley, Dorothy, *Food in England.* Copyright © 1954 by Dorothy Hartley. Published by Macdonald and Jane's, London, 1954. By permission of Macdonald and Jane's Publishers Limited(153).

Hazelton, Nika, *The Belgian Cook Book.* Copyright © 1970 by Nika Standen Hazelton. Published by Atheneum Publishers, Inc., New York. By permission of Curtis Brown Ltd., New York(155). *The Regional Italian Kitchen.* Copyright © 1978 by Nika Hazelton. Published by M. Evans and Company, Inc., New York. By permission of Curtis Brown Ltd., New York(160).

House and Garden, the editors of, *House and Garden's New Cook Book.* Copyright © 1967 by the Condé Nast Publications Inc. Published by the Condé Nast Publications Inc., New York. By permission of the Condé Nast Publications Inc.(99).

Irish Recipes Traditional and Modern. Published by Mount Salus Press Limited, Dublin. By permission of Mount Salus Press Limited(146).

Jans, Hugh, *Vrij Nederlands Kookboek.* © 1973 Unieboek BV/C.A.J. van Dishoeck, Bussum. Published by Unieboek BV/C.A.J. van Dishoeck. Translated by permission of Unieboek BV/C.A.J. van Dishoeck(150).

Jean-Charles, Jehanne, *Le Lexique des Bons Petits Plats.* © Presses de la Cité, 1970. Published by Presses de la Cité, Paris. Translated by permission of Presses de la Cité(149).

Jerez, Maria Pilar, *Tu Cocina.* © Maria Pilar Jerez, 1976. © de la Cubierta, Rosquellas. Published by Ediciones 29, Barcelona. Translated by permission of Ediciones 29, Barcelona(93).

Jolly, Martine, *Réussir Votre Cuisine.* © Éditions Robert Laffont, S.A., Paris 1979. Published by Éditions Robert Laffont, Paris. Translated by permission of Éditions Robert Laffont(103).

Karsenty, Irène and Lucienne, *La Cuisine Pied-noir* (*Cuisines du Terroir*). © 1974 by Éditions Denoël, Paris. Published by Éditions Denoël. Translated by permission of Éditions Denoël(125).

Kenney, A. Herbert ("Wyvern"), *Fifty Breakfasts.* First

Edition. Published by Edward Arnold, London 1894(96, 110).

Keys, John D., *Food for the Emperor.* Copyright 1963 by John D. Keys. Published by The Ward Ritchie Press, Los Angeles. By permission of The Ward Ritchie Press(105).

Kiehnle, Hermine and Maria Hädecke, *Das Neue Kiehnle-Kochbuch.* © Walter Hädecke Verlag (vorm. Sud-deutsches Verlagshaus) Weil der Stadt, 1960. Published by Walter Hädecke Verlag, Weil der Stadt. Translated by permission of Walter Hädecke Verlag(141).

Kouki, M., *Poissons Méditerranéens.* © by Mohamed Kouki. Published in collaboration with L'Office National des Pêches, Tunis, 1970. Translated by permission of Mohamed Kouki(139).

Laasri, Ahmed, *240 Recettes de Cuisine Marocaine.* © 1978, Jacques Grancher, éditeur. Published by Jacques Grancher, éditeur, Paris. Translated by permission of Jacques Grancher, éditeur(99).

Labarre, Irène and Jean Mercier, *La Cuisine du Mouton.* © Solar, 1978. Published by Solar, Paris. Translated by permission of Solar(98).

Lal, Premila, *The Egg and Cheese Cook-Book.* © Premila Lal 1978. Published by India Book House Pvt. Ltd., Bombay. By permission of India Book House Pvt. Ltd.(92, 108, 113, 161).

Lang, George, *The Cuisine of Hungary.* Copyright © 1971 by George Lang. Published by Atheneum Publishers, Inc., New York. By permission of Atheneum Publishers, Inc.(116).

Layton, T. A., *The Wine & Food Society's Guide to Cheese.* Reprinted by permission of the International Wine & Food Society, London(153, 154).

Loren, Sophia, *In the Kitchen with Love.* © Rizzdi Editore, S.P.A. Via Civitavecchia, 102. 20132 Milano, Italy(127,161).

Lucas, Dione and Marion Gorman, *The Dione Lucas Book of French Cooking.* Copyright 1947 by Dione Lucas. Copyright © 1973 by Mark Lucas and Marion F. Gorman. Published by Little, Brown and Company, Boston. By permission of Little, Brown and Company(113).

Lustig, Lillie S., Claire Sondheim and Sarah Rensel, *The Southern Cookbook of Fine Old Recipes.* Copyright © 1939. Culinary Arts Press(101).

Lyon, Ninette, *Les Oeufs.* Copyright 1979 by Ninette Lyon and Editions Arts & Voyages, Lucien De Meyer, Brussels. Published by Editions Art & Voyages, Gamma. Translated by permission of Editions Arts & Voyages(101, 102).

MacKirdy, Mary, *Recipes for You.* Published by Collins Clear-Type Press, London and Glasgow, © 1930. By permission of William Collins Sons & Co., Ltd., Glasgow(133, 137, 152, 157).

McNeill, F. Marian, *The Book of Breakfasts.* Published by Alexander Maclehose & Co., London 1932. By permission of Gordon Wright Publishing, Edinburgh(130).

Magyar, Elek, *Kochbuch für Feinschmecker.* © Dr. Magyar Bálint. © Dr. Magyar Pál. Originally published by Corvina, Budapest. Translated by permission of Artisjus, author's agents(107).

Manuel de la Friandise, Le, (*Ou les Talents de ma Cuisinière Isabeau Mis en Lumière*). Attributed to author of *Le Petit Cuisinier Econome.* Published by Janet, Libraire rue Saint-Jacques, Paris, in 1796 and 1797(115).

Margiotta, Guido, *Valtellina e Valchiavenna Riscopena al una Cucina.* Published by Bissoni Editore, Sondrio. Translated by permission of Libreria Bissoni(160).

Marin, *Les Dons de Comus.* Vol. III, Paris, 1739(97, 102,119).

Marshall, Mel, *The Delectable Egg and How to Cook It.* Copyright © 1968 by Mel Marshall. Published by Trident Press, a division of Simon & Schuster, Inc., New York. By permission of Toni Strassman, agent for the author(100).

Martin, Peter and Joan, *Japanese Cooking.* Copyright © 1970 by Peter and Joan Martin. Published by André Deutsch Limited, London. By permission of André Deutsch Limited(134).

Marty, Albin, *Fourmiguetto: Souvenirs, Contes et Recettes du Languedoc.* Published by Éditions Creer, F 63340, Nonette, 1978. Translated by permission of Éditions Creer(124).

Mascarelli, Benoit, *La Table en Provence et sur la Côte d'Azur.* Published by Jacques Haumont, Paris, 1947(128).

Massialot, *Le Cuisinier Roial et Bourgeois.* Paris, 1691(121).

Menon, *Les Soupers de la Cour.* Volume 4, 1755(98, 116, 126).

Menus Propos sur la Cuisine Comtoise. Published by Just Poisson, Éditeur, Paris 1907(116).

Miguel, Caroline, *Les Bonnes Recettes de Tante Caroline.* © Presses de la Renaissance, 1979. Published by Presses de la Renaissance, Paris. Translated by permission of Presses de la Renaissance(136).

Montagné, Prosper, *New Larousse Gastronomique.* Originally published under the title *Nouveau Larousse Gastronomique.* © Copyright Librairie Larousse, Paris 19. 1960. © Copyright English text The Hamlyn Publishing Group Limited 1977. Published by The Hamlyn Publishing Group Limited, London. By permission of The Hamlyn Publishing Group Limited(124).

Montagné, Prosper and Dr. A. Gottschalk, *Mon Menu —Guide d'Hygiène Alimentaire.* Published by Société d'Applications Scientifiques, Paris(108, 111, 127).

Moore-Betty, Maurice, *Cooking for Occasions.* Copyright 1970 by Maurice Moore-Betty. David White, Inc., New York, New York(149).

Nignon, M. Edouard (Editor), *Le Livre de Cuisine de L'Ouest-Éclair.* Published by L'Ouest-Éclair, Rennes 1941. Translated by permission of Société d'Éditions Ouest-France, Rennes(101, 103, 125, 142).

Nilson, Bee (Editor), *The WI Diamond Jubilee Cookbook.* © A. R. Nilson and National Federation of Women's Institutes 1975. Published by William Heinemann Ltd., London. By permission of William Heinemann Ltd.(151).

Norman, Barbara, *The Russian Cookbook.* Copyright © 1967 by Bantam Books, Inc. Published by Bantam Books Inc., New York. By permission of Robert P. Mills Ltd., Literary Agency, New York, and Atheneum Publishers, Inc., New York(147).

Nouveau Manuel de la Cuisinière Bourgeoise et Economique. Published by Bernardin-Bechet, Libraire, Paris, 1868(114, 116).

Olney, Judith, *Comforting Food.* Copyright © 1979 by Judith Olney. Published by Atheneum Publishers Inc., New York. By permission of Atheneum Publishers Inc.(111, 112).

Olney, Richard, *The French Menu Cookbook.* Copyright © 1970 by Richard Olney. Published by Simon & Schuster, New York. By permission of John Schaffner, Literary Agent, New York(140). *Simple French Food.* Copyright © 1974 by Richard Olney. Published by Atheneum Publishers, New York. By permission of Atheneum Publishers, Inc.(104, 117, 132).

Pappas, Lou Siebert, *Egg Cookery.* Copyright © 1976 Lou Siebert Pappas. Reprinted by permission of the publisher, 101 Productions, San Francisco(145).

Paradissis, Chrissa, *The Best Book of Greek Cookery.* Copyright © 1976 P. Efstathiadis & Sons. Published by Efstathiadis Group, Athens, 1976. By permission of P. Efstathiadis & Sons SA(122).

Parker, Audrey, *Cottage and Country Recipes.* © Audrey Parker 1975. Published by Faber and Faber Limited, London. By permission of Faber and Faber Limited(138).

Peck, Paula, *The Art of Good Cooking.* Copyright © 1961, 1966 by Paula Peck. Published by Simon & Schuster, a division of Gulf & Western Corporation, New York. By permission of John Schaffner, Literary Agent, New York(108).

Les Petits Plats et les Grands. © 1977 by Éditions Denoël, Paris. Published by Éditions Denoël Sarl, Paris. Translated by permission of Éditions Denoël Sarl(139).

Petits Propos Culinaires (Volume 6, October 1980). © Prospect Books 1980. Published by Prospect Books, London and Washington, D.C. By permission of the publisher(128).

Philippon, Henri, *Quercy Périgord.* Copyright © 1979. Éditions Denoël, Paris(95).

Price, Rebecca, *The Compleat Cook.* © Madeleine Masson 1974. Published by Routledge & Kegan Paul Ltd., London. By permission of Routledge & Kegan Paul Ltd.(106).

Raris, F. and T., *Les Champignons, Connaissance et Gastronomie.* © Librairie Larousse, 1974, for French language rights. Published by Librairie Larousse, Paris. Originally

published by Fratelli Fabbri Editori, Milan as *I Funghi, Cercarli, Conoscerli, Cucinarli.* © 1973 Fratelli Fabbri Editore, Milano. Translated by permission of Fratelli Fabbri Editori(96, 152).
Ratto, G. B. and Giovanni, *Cuciniera Genovese.* Published by Edizioni Pagano, Genova 1963. Translated by permission of Industrie Grafiche Editoriali, Fratelli Pagano S.p.A.(93).
Ripoll, Luis, *Nuestra Cocina: 600 Recetas de Mallorca, Menorca, Ibiza y Formentera.* © by Luis Ripoll. Published by Editorial H.M.B., S.A., Barcelona 1974. Translated by permission of Luis Ripoll, Mallorca(153).
Root, Waverly, *The Best of Italian Cooking.* Copyright © 1974 by Edita S.A. Published by André Deutsch Limited, London. By permission of André Deutsch Limited. © 1974 by Edita S.A. Published by Helvetica Press, Inc., New York. By permission of Helvetica Press, Inc.(123).
Rundell, Mrs., *Modern Domestic Cookery.* Published by Milner and Company, Limited, London(140).
Savarin, Mme. Jeanne (Editor), *La Cuisine des Familles* (Magazine). No. 122, October 20, 1907, No. 109, July 1907(11).
Schultz, Sigrid, *Overseas Press Club Cookbook.* Copyright © 1962 by Overseas Press Club of America, Inc. Reprinted by permission of Doubleday & Company, Inc.(157).
Senn, C. Herman, *Breakfast Dishes and Savouries.* © Ward Lock Ltd., London. Published by Ward, Lock & Co., Limited, London 1923. By permission of Ward Lock Limited Publishers, London(106). *How to Cook Eggs and Omelets in 300 Different Ways.* © Ward Lock Ltd., London. Published by Ward, Lock & Co., Limited, London. By permission of Ward Lock Limited Publishers, London(103, 140).
Serra, Victoria, *Tia Victoria's Spanish Kitchen.* English text copyright © Elizabeth Gili, 1963. Published by Kaye & Ward Ltd., London, 1963. Translated by permission of Elizabeth Gili from the original Spanish entitled "Sabores: Cocina del Hogar" by Victoria Serra Sunol. By permission of Kaye & Ward Ltd.(129).
The Settlement Cookbook. Copyright © 1965, 1976 by the Settlement Cookbook Co. Reprinted by permission

of Simon & Schuster, a division of Gulf & Western Corporation(158).
70 Médecins de France, *Le Trésor de la Cuisine du Bassin Méditerranéen.* Published by Les Laboratoires du Dr. Zizine(97).
Sherman, Margaret, *The Wine and Food Society's Guide to Eggs.* © The Wine and Food Society Publishing Company 1968. Published by Michael Joseph Ltd., London, in association with The Wine and Food Society. By permission of Michael Joseph Ltd.(118).
Simon, André L., *Cheeses of the World.* Copyright André L. Simon, 1956. Published by Faber and Faber Ltd., London. By permission of Faber and Faber Ltd.(150-151, 159).
Sing, Phia, *Traditional Recipes of Laos.* © Prospect Books 1980. Published by Prospect Books, London and Washington, D.C. By permission of the publisher(105).
Slater, Mary, *Caribbean Cooking for Pleasure.* © Copyright Mary Slater 1970. Published by The Hamlyn Publishing Group Limited, London. By permission of The Hamlyn Publishing Group Limited(100).
Stan, Anisoara, *The Romanian Cookbook.* Copyright © 1951 by Anisoara Stan. Published by Citadel Press, Inc., New York, 1969. By permission of Citadel Press, Inc. (112).
Szathmáry, Louis, *American Gastronomy.* Copyright 1974 by permission of Contemporary Books, Inc., Chicago(117).
Tendret, Lucien, *La Table au Pays de Brillat-Savarin.* Published by Librairie-Dardel, Chambery 1934. Translated by permission of Jacques Grancher, Éditeur, Paris(113).
Tenison, Marika Hanbury, *Recipes from a Country Kitchen.* © Marika Hanbury Tenison 1978. Published by Hart-Davis, MacGibbon Ltd./Granada Publishing Ltd. Hertfordshire, England(147).
Thurber, Carol Coliver (The Mad Hatter), *The Calypso Cookbook.* Published by Ashley Books Inc., New York 1974. By permission of Ashley Books Inc.(109).
Toklas, Alice B., *The Alice B. Toklas Cook Book.* Copyright 1954 by Alice B. Toklas. Published by Harper and Row Publishers, Inc., New York. By permission of Harper

and Row Publishers, Inc.(115). *Aromas and Flavors of Past and Present.* © 1958 by Alice B. Toklas and © 1955 and 1956 by the Hearst Corporation. Published by Michael Joseph Ltd., London. By permission of Michael Joseph Ltd.(156).
Tribus, Sue, *The Wonderful World of Breakfast.* Copyright © 1964 Pergamon Press Ltd. Published by Pergamon Press Ltd., Oxford. By permission of Pergamon Press Ltd.(98).
Vence, Céline and Robert Courtine, *The Grand Masters of French Cuisine.* Copyright © 1978 by G. P. Putnam's Sons, New York. Originally published in France as *Les Grands Maîtres de la Cuisine Française.* Copyright © 1972 Éditions Bordas. Published by G. P. Putnam's Sons, New York. By permission of G. P. Putnam's Sons(132).
Verdon, René, *The White House Chef Cookbook.* Copyright © 1967 by René Verdon. Reprinted by permission of Doubleday & Company Inc.(148).
Volpicelli, Luigi and Secondino Freda, *L'Antiartusi: 1000 Ricette.* © 1978 Pan Editrice, Milano. Published by Pan Editrice, Milan. Translated by permission of Pan Editrice(161).
Voltz, Jeanne A., *The Flavor of the South.* Copyright © 1977 by Jeanne A. Voltz. Published by Doubleday & Company, Inc., New York. By permission of Doubleday & Company, Inc.(158).
Willinsky, Grete, *Kulinarische Weltreise.* © 1961 by Mary Hahns Kochbuchverlag, Berlin W. Published by Büchergilde Gutenberg, Frankfurt. Translated by permission of Mary Hahns Kochbuchverlag, Munich(138, 156).
Wilson, José and Betty Grott, *Good Earth and Country Cooking.* Published by Stackpole Books, Harrisburg, Pennsylvania. By permission of Stackpole Books(163).
Witty, Helen and Elizabeth Schneider Colchie, *Better Than Store-Bought.* Copyright © 1979 by Helen Witty and Elizabeth Schneider Colchie. Published by Harper & Row, Publishers, Inc., New York. By permission of Harper & Row, Publishers, Inc.(163, 164).
Zelayeta, Elena, *Elena's Secrets of Mexican Cooking.* Copyright © 1958 by Prentice-Hall, Inc. Published by Prentice-Hall, Inc., Englewood Cliffs, New Jersey(159).

Acknowledgments

The indexes for this book were prepared by Louise W. Hedberg. The editors are particularly indebted to Pat Alburey, Hertfordshire, England; Shelley Bartholomew, Washington, D.C.; Maggie Black, London; Barbara Day, Eagle Wine and Cheese, Washington, D.C.; Roland S. Golden, Tracy Schonrock, Richard Webber, Dairy Standardization Branch, U.S. Department of Agriculture, Washington, D.C.; and Ann O'Sullivan, Majorca, Spain.

The editors also wish to thank: Sue Altman, London; Pierre Androuët, Fromagers Androuët S. A., Paris; Alison Attenborough, Essex, England; Mary Attenborough, Essex, England; Caroline Baum, York, England; The British Egg Information Service, London; Emma Codrington, Surrey, England; Beryl Downing, Warwickshire, England; English Country Cheese Council, London; Mimi Errington, London; Susan Foresman, Arlington, Virginia; Henrietta Green, London; Fayal Greene, London; Harrods Cheese Department, London; Maggie Heinz, London; Brenda Jayes, London; Maria Johnson, Hertfordshire, England;

Dr. Norman Knowles, The Eggs Authority, Kent, England; Édouard Longue, Paris; Ninette Lyon, Paris; Carol Mason, Washington, D.C.; Pippa Millard, London; Sonya Mills, Kent, England; Wendy Morris, London; Dilys Naylor, Surrey, England; Paxton & Whitfield Ltd., London; Michael Schwab, London; Anne Stephenson, London; Stonegate Farmers Ltd., London; Fiona Tillet, London; Jeremiah Tower, San Francisco; J. M. Turnell & Co., London; Tina Walker, London; Caroline Wood, London; Stacy Zacharias, Alexandria, Virginia; A. P. Zendar, London.

Picture Credits

The sources for the pictures in this book are listed below. Credits for each of the photographers and illustrators are listed by page number in sequence with successive pages indicated by hyphens; where necessary, the locations of pictures within pages also are indicated —separated from page numbers by dashes.

Photographs by John Elliot: 9 — top, 18, 20 — top, 21 — top and bottom right, 22, 26-30, 33 — center and bottom, 34 — bottom, 35 — bottom left and bottom center, 37 — bottom right, 38-45, 46-47 — top, 48, 52-53, 58-59, 62, 63 — top left and top center, bottom left and bottom center, 64, 66 — bottom right, 77 — bottom, 78-81, 86-87 — top.

Photographs by Bob Komar: 20 — bottom, 21 — bottom left and bottom center, 23 — top right and bottom, 33-34 — top, 35 — top and bottom right, 36 — top, 37 — center middle and center right, bottom left and bottom center, 54-55, 70, 72-73, 82-85, 86-87 — bottom, 88-89 — top. Other photographs (alphabetically): Tom Belshaw, 32 — bottom, 36 — center and bottom, 56 — top and bottom right, 57, 88-89 — bottom. John Cook, 10-11, 47 — bottom right, 60-61, 63 — top right and bottom right, 65, 66 — except bottom right, 67, 68 — top right and bottom, 69, 76, 77 — top. Alan Duns, cover, 4, 8, 19, 23 — top left, 24-25, 32 — top, 35 — center right, 37 — top and center left, 46 — bottom, 47 — bottom left and bottom center. Louis Klein, 2. Aldo Tutino, 8-9 — bottom, 12-17, 50-51, 56 — bottom left, 68 — top left, 74-75, 90.

Illustrations: From the Mary Evans Picture Library and private sources and *Food & Drink: A Pictorial Archive from Nineteenth Century Sources* by Jim Harter, published by Dover Publications, Inc., 1979, 93-167.

Library of Congress Cataloguing in Publication Data
Time-Life Books.
  Eggs and cheese.
  (The Good cook, techniques & recipes)
  Includes index.
  1. Cookery (Eggs) 2. Cookery (Cheese) I. Time-Life Books
  II. Series: Good cook, techniques & recipes.
TX745.E43   641.6'75   80-14824
ISBN 0-8094-2893-8
ISBN 0-8094-2892-X (lib. bdg.)
ISBN 0-8094-2887-3

Printed in U.S.A.